PRAISE FOR

Immersion

"Marshall's latest book is a deeply personal and marvelously authentic narrative told with humor, suspense, humility, and authority. Linda depicts how language is woven into real life, how it instills insights and affections, and what it reveals about others—and oneself. I have spent over seven decades learning, using, describing, and advocating for language abilities, and I only wish I had written a book like this."

—Dr. Richard D. Brecht, University of Maryland Professor Emeritus, codirector of the American Councils Research Center, cofounder of Jeenie.com, and founding executive director of the University of Maryland Center for Advanced Study of Language (CASL)

"How does a woman transform herself from a bored, midwestern housewife to an international linguist warding off thugs in Tanzania, wading through bomb debris in Kenya, and deciphering code for the FBI in small African nations? Linda Murphy Marshall does it by giving herself over to her one true love: languages around the world, including Portuguese, Swahili, Amharic, and Xhosa. This stunning exploration of the sometimes painful, sometimes exhilarating process of learning to translate both words and her own changing identity is a remarkable tribute to Marshall's talent and the transformative power of languages."

—Barbara Hurd, author of *The Epilogues*

"*Immersion* is scattered with diamonds, attracting every reader to different, brilliant parts. Elegantly and eloquently, Marshall illuminates a linguist's experience. For non-interpreters, *Immersion* is a glimpse into the challenges and gratification of a life spent with foreign languages and policy-makers. For interpreters, this is an affectionate and invigorating dialogue with an exceptionally gifted and gracious colleague."

—Allison Hong Merrill, author of *Ninety-Nine Fire Hoops*

"Few people are familiar with the position of 'linguist' in intelligence work, but it is one of the most specialized and difficult jobs there is. *Immersion* draws back the veil on what it takes to fill this essential role: the deep love of language and culture, the determination to constantly challenge yourself, and the need for unfailing attention to detail. If you love languages or know someone who does (particularly a young person considering a career in language), this memoir is a must-read."

—Alma Katsu, former CIA officer, former government director of the Center for the Advanced Study of Language, and author of *Red London*

"A talented linguist delves into the ambitious project of translating her past. From small-town America to far-flung corners of the globe, *Immersion* illuminates one woman's journey away from the well-trodden expectations of womanhood in favor of forging another path. With every place she travels, every language she learns, and every experience she studies and interprets along the way, the narrator becomes more fully her truest self."

—Rachel Rueckert,
author of *East Winds: A Global Quest to Reckon with Marriage*

PRAISE FOR

Ivy Lodge

2023 Readers' Favorite Book Awards
Honorable Mention in Nonfiction: Memoir

2022 Best Book Awards Finalist in Nonfiction: Creative

"Thoughtfully conceived, this deeply personal, acutely observed recollection is a captivating voyage to the past. Readers who are mourning parents will particularly relate to the story. A moving, courageously frank, and sharply intuitive account about a manor filled with memories."

—*Kirkus Reviews,* starred review

"This book is a masterpiece of social observation and self-scrutiny."

—*Readers' Favorite*, 5-star review

"*Ivy Lodge* is a brave, beautiful book about the unspoken language of family. Linda Murphy Marshall is unafraid of looking in the dark corners of her childhood home in order to find meaning, peace, and ultimately, light."

—Dawn Raffel, author of *The Secret Life of Objects*

"Translation, at its essence, is the rendering of one into another. Murphy Marshall journeys deep into the labyrinth of memory, perception, and the shape-shifting forces of identity. A beautiful debut."

—Harrison Candelaria Fletcher,
author of *Presentimiento: A Life in Dreams*

IMMERSION

IMMERSION

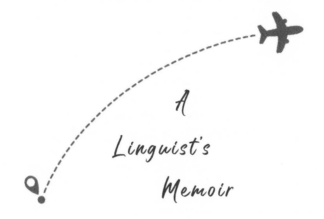

A
Linguist's
Memoir

LINDA MURPHY MARSHALL

SHE WRITES PRESS

Published 2024
Printed in the United States of America
Print ISBN: 978-1-64742-720-7
E-ISBN: 978-1-64742-721-4
Library of Congress Control Number: 2024909922

For information, address:
She Writes Press
1569 Solano Ave #546
Berkeley, CA 94707

Interior design by Stacey Aaronson

She Writes Press is a division of SparkPoint Studio, LLC.

To William P. Marshall

"She opened her curtains, and looked out towards the bit of road that lay in view. . . . She was a part of that involuntary, palpitating life, and could neither look out on it from her luxurious shelter as a mere spectator, nor hide her eyes in selfish complaining."

—GEORGE ELIOT, *Middlemarch*

"Your every new journey is your new window opening to new ideas."

—MEHMET MURAT ILDAN

TABLE OF CONTENTS

FORESHADOWING

Prologue:
Who Knew Where It All Would Lead

FORESHADOWING—*a literary device in which the writer gives the reader hints of what's to come later in the story.*

EXAMPLE: *When I went to Spain in 1970 on my first international trip, this foreshadowed not only a lifetime of trips but also a reenvisioning and restructuring of my life.*

I've traveled to many places through the years. After each trip, I returned home with hundreds of photos and souvenirs. Journals line my bookshelves, describing those places. These are the trips I tell friends about, often comparing notes as they share tales of their equally memorable trips.

I haven't written about those trips in this book. It covers a second set. No scrapbooks, journals, or souvenirs exist to commemorate them, except maybe a few mementos from my junior year in college in Spain. All I have are my memories for the rest.

Most people aren't aware I went on that second set of trips, don't know that my work as a linguist for the government put me in the midst of a war, a coup attempt, riots. They don't know I went to Kenya following a deadly terrorist bombing by al-Qaeda, that I accompanied a US president to Tanzania, or worked as an interpreter in Brazil's outback, as well as in its favelas. That I went to South Africa a few short months after apartheid ended.

Many people would probably be surprised to learn that I traveled to these places in sometimes dangerous circumstances. In many ways, it surprises me too, even now. It all sounds out of character for Linda Murphy-formerly-of-Kirkwood-Missouri. People who knew me back in Kirkwood, where I lived until the age of thirty-five, might have responded the following way if they had learned of my adventures.

"Linda Murphy? The girl who, at twenty-two, woke her little sister up in the middle of the night to remove a daddy longlegs spider from her bedroom? Boy-crazy Linda, who graduated from Kirkwood High School with barely a C+ average? Who wanted nothing more than to root for the football and basketball teams as a cheerleader? Whom classmates unofficially voted 'sweetest' in her graduating class? What you're telling me seems hard to believe, sounds like someone else."

Truthfully, that's exactly how I wanted people to think of me back when I lived in Kirkwood. That's who I was: cute, unthreatening, occasionally sweet. When I left Kirkwood to go to Denver for college, living away from home for the first time at the age of eighteen, my reputation followed me. A friend in my dorm, a fellow freshman, loved to mock me. He acted as though he saw before him a rare species only found in captivity. After finishing dinner, topped off with a long conversation one night in our dorm cafeteria, Steve leaned forward in his metallic chair, his long legs stretched out beneath him, elbows on the table, hands cupping each side of his face. Staring at me as though trying to decipher a puzzle, he shook his head. After a few seconds, he quipped:

"Murph, Murph, Murph. You're so funny. It's like you've lived in a box your entire life, and your parents just released you from that box to attend college."

I understood his point. Until I left for Spain two years later, my junior year, that description fit. My emotional and physical worlds remained circumscribed, maybe even stunted. The windows of my life remained largely shuttered. But then certain events occurred. I took new turns on my path: some sharp, some gentle; some gradual, some sudden. I made difficult choices while still other decisions occurred without my consent or control.

I didn't immediately find a way out of that box my friend referred to, but chinks started appearing in its walls, small at first, then gradually increasing in size, narrow openings that let in light, air, ideas, forcing me to look outside, to look beyond myself in order to find myself.

Those windows materialized as a result of studying various languages, along with subsequent work assignments to various parts of the world, places these languages led me. Each language in its own way introduced me to new ideas, new people, new ways of looking at myself, at my life. First Spanish, then Portuguese, French, German, Russian . . . eventually Xhosa, Amharic, Shona, Swahili, and others, till more than a dozen filled my coffer. These languages became my guides, blowing out holes in that original box in which I'd languished. They introduced me to new ways of thriving, to new ways of seeing myself, of seeing others.

Eventually, I altered my self-concept, looked beyond the environment in which I'd grown up, beyond ideas I'd clung to like lifeboats the first twenty years of my life. Languages and travel exposed me to disparate geographical regions, to the different values people cherish. They enabled me to become friends with all types of people, exposed me to different ways of living. In short, they expanded my once myopic vision. They took me by the hand and over the course of the next almost fifty years instructed me to look at this, and that, and this other thing. To reconsider this, and that, and other things. So I did. In the process I learned, grew, overcame challenges, discovered clues to finding the authentic me, to finding where I personally fit into this marvelous planet.

A paradox exists: in taking me away from English, my first language, these languages led me back home to myself . . . This book reveals those journeys.

THE PRESENT TENSE

Changing My Mind

THE PRESENT TENSE—*a grammatical term used to describe what's happening in the present, or a current state of mind; what exists in the present.*

EXAMPLE: *"In order to discover who I am, I am going far away."*

That first journey. Spain. So long ago. How do I remember events from fifty years ago when I barely remember last night's dinner? But markers I put in place prior to that journey were prescient. There's the year I dressed up as a Spanish señorita for Halloween in grade school, wearing a costume my mother made. A long red skirt with three rows of white lace at the bottom, a black felt vest. I wore a white blouse with puffy sleeves underneath. She fashioned a gauzy red mantilla, an elaborate Spanish headpiece, to go with it.

My best friend, Michele, who went trick-or-treating with me that year, tried to convince my neighbors that—at nine years old—

I'd arrived in the States as an exchange student from Spain. I mumbled some faux Spanish, imitating 1950s comedian Sid Caesar's stand-up routine I'd watched on TV. He knew a handful of words in a few foreign languages, French and Italian, for instance. Adding a credible accent, he tossed in made-up words that sounded like French, Italian, Spanish, etc. I did the same, though certainly not as well.

Michele began her monologue when neighbors opened the door: "Happy Halloween! As you can see, my friend here is Spanish, just arrived from Spain a few days ago on an exchange program, so I'm introducing her to our American holiday."

I would then respond, using the few Spanish words I knew, coupled with heavily accented English: "*Hola. Mucho gusto.* I'm here to study *inglés* in the *escuela*. Michele *es mi amiga*."

I went on to play the role of baby bear in my fourth grade's production of *The Three Bears*, a short play performed entirely in Spanish, requiring minimal speaking on my part, given my role. The inspirational teacher who introduced me to the language took attendance every day in Spanish; we answered *aquí* or *presente* when she called our names.

My first Spanish-related memory goes back even further, when friends and relatives told me at the age of four or five that my name meant something in another language—"pretty" in Spanish: *linda*. They told me this as though sharing a special secret, a code of sorts.

"Do you realize your name means 'pretty' in Spanish, Linda?"

This information thrilled me, made me feel special, while simultaneously creating dread about having to live up to such a name; everyone seemed to know its meaning. A few years later, when I reached adolescence, I imagined people looking at me—scrawny, flat-chested, my mouth full of metal braces, poker-straight brown hair and unibrow—perhaps feeling let down, certain my parents had made a mistake when naming me Linda, an exotic word for a not-so-exotic person.

Most of all I remember the year I spent in Spain. I don't remember every detail, each excursion to Toledo, Segovia, San Sebastian, Sevilla, El Escorial, and elsewhere. Nor do I remember each outing to Madrid's Retiro Park or every afternoon spent in El Rastro flea market. Evenings I strolled through the Plaza de España or had *té* in the Plaza Mayor fade into a pleasant blur. Afternoons spent at the Prado Museum studying Velazquez, Picasso, Murillo, El Greco, Zurbarán, and others meld together into a satisfying whole. I do remember the sum of these parts, though, how sights, smells, tastes, sounds, and the people of Spain enveloped and held me, how they continue to influence me, teach me, shape me, decades later.

Spain acted as a fallback, not part of my original plan for college. I'd grown tired of the atmosphere at my college. I enjoyed my down-to-earth friends who came from middle-class families like mine, friends who lived more "normal" lives, but my overall feeling consisted in being out of place, not "enough" among the many rich kids.

It seemed like everyone hailed from the East or West Coast, specifically from New York, Massachusetts, Pennsylvania, or California. Midwesterners often came from affluent Chicago suburbs, not St. Louis, the city closest to my tiny suburb of Kirkwood, Missouri. To most people, I must have seemed like an oddity. Classmates sometimes asked me—as though conversing with a curious foreigner—to explain life on a farm. It happened so often I stopped correcting them, developed a canned story about milking cows at dawn, taking care of chickens, pigs, riding on my father's tractor, when in reality he had a successful law practice in downtown St. Louis.

When I was walking to class one day, an affluent classmate from Southern California caught up with me to chat. "What's it like living on a farm, Murph? A lot of work, I imagine?"

"Yes," I replied. "I have to get up before dawn to milk the cows, feed the chickens, the pigs. You know, all the livestock have to be fed. My brothers and sister all pitch in. I'm not sure how they're managing without me."

The more I rambled on, the bigger his eyes became and the more amused I became, although I had no idea what I was talking about. I may have visited a farm once or twice in my life, but I had no idea how farms were run. Fortunately, neither did he.

Many of my classmates reflected the money and private school backgrounds they brought with them, with their Top-Sider shoes, their tales about extended stays in Europe each summer, their fancy homes, their designer clothes, and the girls with their Pappagallo shoes.

I'd never attended private school till college. My father didn't believe in them. Even if he had, he wasn't about to waste money on his daughters' education when his—and my mother's—goal consisted in marrying us off, not helping prepare us for a future career. He didn't see the point. The task of selecting where I attended college landed in my lap, with input from very few people.

My piano teacher had urged me to apply to Juilliard, planned to record me playing my Chopin and Beethoven pieces as part of the application process. I'd played on a local public radio station when I was eleven, won a number of awards; it was my small claim to fame. But my parents—mainly my father—said absolutely not. Why, I don't remember. They may have thought I didn't have the talent. Or they may have reasoned that the pool of eligible future husbands at Juilliard wasn't to their liking; I don't think they ever told me. Not a

stellar student, piano playing stood out as one area in which I excelled. By closing that door, my list of options narrowed appreciably.

I knew I didn't want to follow my high school classmates to the
University of Missouri (Mizzou) in Columbia, Missouri, or Kansas
University (KU) in Lawrence, Kansas. I didn't want to attend what I
feared would be an extension of high school, the same cliques and
jocks, the same popular kids and wannabe popular kids. I'd endured
enough of that in high school, forever circling the fringes of the popular group, never quite making the cut. I'd have given anything to
wear the red-and-white cheerleading skirt and top, though, to be voted
prom queen. I toyed with the idea of applying to Drake University in
Des Moines, but my father balked at the higher application fee.

After feeble attempts to find a college (my C+ grade point average
severely limited my choices), I applied to only three colleges: the
University of Denver, Southern Methodist University in Dallas, and
Colorado College in Colorado Springs. My first choice was Colorado
College, but I became so anxious during a timed writing sample test
at my high school that I froze when writing the blue book essay. They
rejected me.

Traveling to Denver as an incoming freshman marked my first
time in Colorado, so the geography came as a surprise. All of eastern
Colorado (up to and including Denver) spread out before me: flat,
extending to the horizon in front of our car. Driving there with my
parents, many of my worldly goods crammed into the back of our
station wagon, I envisioned mountains instantly springing up from
the plains once we crossed the border from Kansas into Colorado,
but eastern Colorado seemed like an extension of Kansas. At least I
could see mountains from afar once we arrived in Denver. I always
knew which direction was west.

By 1970, after two years at the University of Denver, I wanted out. Out of Colorado, out of the University of Denver, away from it all, at least temporarily. I wanted a geographic cure, naively thinking there was one. My father suggested going to Spain when I announced that I did not want to return to the University of Denver for my junior year. Surprisingly, a year in Spain—including travel to and from Madrid—cost my parents less than remaining in the States. I doubt I'd have thought of Spain on my own. If attending a college two states away, where everyone spoke English, where my parents remained a phone call away, overwhelmed me, what would happen to me in Spain, more than seven thousand miles away, cut off from everyone I knew? But somehow I found the courage to explore spending a year abroad.

Finding a program was relatively easy. More pressing became how to handle classes taught exclusively in Spanish, how to navigate life in Spanish when I could barely cope with my English-speaking college classmates stateside. How would I make new Spanish-speaking friends without repeating, "*¿Cómo estás?*" a hundred times a day? How would I find edible food? Someone told me they served whole shrimp in Spain, not the sterile (frozen), decapitated ones my mother served; they looked like specimens I dissected in my high school biology class. Even worse, people in the know shared that Spaniards ate octopus and squid, which they served "in its own ink" (*en su propia tinta*). I shuddered at the thought. Maybe I'd return home thinner.

Ultimately, I reasoned that continuing my studies in Spanish might serve as a way to survive my remaining two years in college. I'd tested into advanced Spanish at the University of Denver because of my high school coursework, and had taken a number of classes with two professors in college, handsome men, both originally from Spain. They looked like Spanish movie stars. I hadn't planned on taking Spanish as an incoming freshman, but during in-person registration they found me wandering through the maze of people, trying to decide which courses to take, brochures fanned out on tables manned by various professors. After introducing themselves, with very little effort these dashing Spanish professors persuaded me to enroll in their classes, based on my test scores from high school. Star struck, I signed up.

I did well in Spanish in college, but not so well in other coursework, barely passing required university science courses: geomorphology, physiography, climatology. Geomorphology had seemed like such a good choice initially. We passed interesting rocks around the classroom, carefully examined each one, even venturing out on enjoyable excursions to the foothills of the Rocky Mountains where we identified more rocks, saw other interesting landforms. By the end of class I could easily identify pyrite, "fool's gold," and quartz, but not much else. The names of other rocks began to blur, all looking similar, like everyday rocks at my feet. Added to that, I needed to master a sea of technical terms.

Fortunately, the University of Denver required no math if you fulfilled the science requirement, or my fate would have been sealed. I suspected my high school geometry tutor had probably developed a hair-pulling disorder—trichotillomania—while working with me, his already thinning hair becoming increasingly sparse during our weekly sessions at my parents' dining room table.

"Do you understand now what a line segment is, Linda? We've gone over it a number of times, and it's one of the most straightforward, basic terms in geometry."

"Yes, of course. I understand," I lied.

"Good. Well, let's move on to the homework problem containing polygons, all right?"

But, of course, I hadn't understood any of it, just said yes so he and his bad breath would leave my house, leave me alone.

Navigating a minefield of coursework became increasingly demanding, having to avoid science, math, anything remotely technical, so Spanish looked more and more appealing. Using the process of elimination, it seemed the most logical choice, going to Spain an extension of that choice.

Before arriving in Madrid in August of 1970, I had never ventured outside the United States, not even to Mexico or Canada. My travels had consisted of trips to a handful of states. I flew to San Francisco in ninth grade to visit my good friend Betsy, the daughter of my parents' friends. My family also drove cross-country to visit my grandparents in New York every summer, so my exposure was limited to a handful of states en route to New York. Nor did I have friends outside the US, even at the University of Denver. My high school hosted a Brazilian exchange student my senior year, but I let my chronic anxiety get the best of me and never spoke to her.

In my mind, Spain symbolized romance: castanets, mantillas, lace, flamenco dancing, elegant women strolling through cobblestone streets, cooling themselves with decorative fans. It meant toreadors with their bull-fighting capes, dapper men serenading beautiful señoritas with their guitars. I mistakenly believed that their version of Spanish would resemble my professors' style of speaking, would be identical to that of my high school teachers: slow, clear, with a vocabulary limited to a few hundred common words, always avoiding the tricky subjunctive mood, those annoying contrary-to-fact statements: "If I were rich, I would buy a castle."

When I arrived, my preconceived ideas fell apart. Evidence of Generalísimo Francisco Franco presented itself everywhere, a dictator who had ruled Spain with an iron fist since 1939, who supported Nazi Germany and Fascist Italy during World War II. His Guardia Civil soldiers stood on many street corners, armed with their semiautomatic pistols. They watched, on the lookout for possible trouble, wearing their distinctive berets and dark uniforms, somber stares clouding their faces. When I spotted them, I felt alternately safe, yet nervous, about their presence.

Army tanks stood out on the Universidad de Madrid campus (currently known as the Universidad Complutense de Madrid), their warlike, gigantic guns loaded with indelible dye should unruly students (Spanish or international) decide to riot. In case of trouble, the Guardia Civil would spray offending students with the indelible paint, making them easily identifiable, to be picked up later by Franco's henchmen. Elsewhere, not-so-innocent-looking men wandered around (*"hombres verdes"*) shouting their catcalls at me—at all young women—as I walked each day to the Ciudad Universitaria campus, to my destination: the Facultad de Filosofía y Letras, the Faculty of Philosophy and Letters.

This reality clashed with the image I'd carried with me for decades, from a postcard my well-traveled aunt and uncle had sent me in first grade. It featured an attractive Andalusian couple dancing the flamenco, dressed in ornate, lavish traditional costumes. But this Spain was not the Spain I read about in tourist brochures. Nor was it the Spain depicted in my grammar books, books with sample dialogues between "typical" Spaniards as they strolled arm in arm on their leisurely *paseos*. As my new Spanish friends repeatedly told me in heavily accented English when I shared my initial shock: "Spain is different."

On a positive note, I didn't see anyone using drugs, at least not openly. Our US-based program director made it clear that if the Spanish police arrested us, no one from the US embassy would rescue us. I hadn't needed persuading, but, if I had, that warning would have convinced me to stay out of trouble.

The Spanish I heard in Madrid didn't resemble my professors' version stateside. This was rapid-fire, with the distinctive Madrileño accent, the lisp-like "theta" sound, along with idioms specific to Madrid, words and phrases I hadn't learned stateside. I spent the first two weeks exhorting people to, "*Por favor, hable usted más despacio,*" "Please, speak more slowly." *Despacio* became the most important word in my lexicon, the most frequently used. If I could have magically created one of those bubbles to reflect word frequency from those first weeks, a giant font with *despacio* in the middle would have featured prominently, along with *por favor* and *gracias*, followed close behind by *lo siento* ("I'm sorry").

Until my listening skills adjusted, my exchanges with Spaniards sounded superficial at best. In addition to asking them to speak slower, saying please, thank you, and apologizing, I could tell them my name, assure them I felt "fine, thank you," communicate my age, my home-town. Not much more. The survey literature class I'd just taken that summer at Washington University in St. Louis, analyzing Chilean poet Pablo Neruda's work, though interesting, had not prepared me for this.

The transition presented a challenge. I was an astronaut trying to adjust to a new atmosphere, unable to breathe at first; a scuba diver entering the air lock chamber to equalize pressure. My first week in Madrid, I wrote in my journal, "I don't think I've ever felt as alone or independent before. I can't think about it or I get the most empty feeling inside."

I soon became familiar with the linguistic term "false cognate," where a word sounds like a similar word in another language but has a different meaning. I walked into a *farmacia* one day shortly after arriving to buy a bar of soap. Quizzical looks greeted me when I asked where I could find the *sopa*, meaning "the soup."

"*Quisiera comprar sopa, por favor,*" I began. "I'd like to buy soup, please."

"*Señorita, no vendemos comida aquí. Lo siento.*" "Miss, we don't sell food here. Sorry."

I had believed that, when absolutely necessary, if you didn't know a word you could just add an "a" to the end of the English word. Magic! But not so, since *sopa* means soup, not soap (which I should have known). I also learned not to use the word *embarazada* when embarrassed about something I'd done—often, as it happened—since it means pregnant in Spanish. I must have said, "*Estoy embarazada!*" "I'm pregnant!" half a dozen times before someone finally set me straight.

I needed to get up to speed quickly, because after a monthlong refresher class in Spanish, I would hear only Spanish from regular university faculty in all my courses at the Universidad de Madrid. Nowhere to hide. No one to translate or interpret or slow down for me. No subtitles. No time for mad dashes to a dictionary to look up words. No language app. No American professors doing sabbaticals in Madrid, teaching their courses in English.

I enrolled in what sounded like interesting courses: the Spanish philosophers Unamuno and Ortega y Gasset; art history, painting at the Prado (taught at the museum); poetry, the Spanish novel, history, social problems in contemporary Spanish society; theatre. Thankfully, I slowly learned to adjust, writing in my journal in September, "There's so much I want to learn. I feel like a sponge, grabbing at every bit of knowledge I can find, trying to achieve *lo imposible.*"

Many students in my program chose to live with Spanish families, but I knew that wasn't for me. Too intimate, too much pressure to socialize, to act "sociable," as my mother would have termed it. ("Come out of your room! Come talk to our guests, Linda!") My anxiety made that kind of arrangement painful. I wanted to remain anonymous, alone if I felt like it, not on display. Blending in became a plus now, worked to my advantage in Madrid, where, because of my dark hair and complexion, Spaniards sometimes confused me with Spanish women, even asked directions after I'd lived there several months.

My four-story dorm near campus housed international students, our only common denominator speaking Spanish. Young women from Switzerland, France, Chile, Cuba, England, China, Japan, Jamaica, Italy, Trinidad, the Philippines lived in the dorm Colegio Mayor Juan XXIII; nearly thirty countries were represented. Two sisters from Guatemala became close friends, Lily and Jannina. I would visit them at their home in Guatemala City a few years after our year together in Spain.

The year contained many firsts. The first time I viewed the US from afar, shocked to hear Spanish friends criticize my homeland. According to them, Nixon (the president my year in Spain) was corrupt ("*un cabrón*"—"a dumbass"); the CIA ran the US; the US meddled in other countries' business, behaved "imperialistically." I'd never heard such negative comments before, certainly not from my staunch Republican parents, nor from other friends back home.

Although these new Spanish friends spoke fondly of the late John F. Kennedy, they laughed when I initially referred to him as "Juan" Kennedy in our conversation, admonishing me for translating a proper name, one of many Spanish cultural—language—lessons I learned. Most of them—both sexes—regarded American women as "fast," with loose morals. I met with little success trying to persuade them otherwise. What they based their opinion on, I never knew: American movies? Books? Other American students they'd met?

It marked the first time I'd taken an art appreciation course, visiting the Prado Museum twice a week in addition to classroom time. I learned to look at paintings more closely. I'd probably visited the Saint Louis Art Museum only once or twice before my year in Spain—one of those visits occurring years before with my Girl Scout troop. Nor had I visited many other art museums.

The final for my Prado course proved difficult; professors required us to identify the artist as well as the name of the specific painting from slides featuring only part of an elongated hand in an El Greco painting, for example. The class instilled in me a lifetime love of art: art appreciation, theory. It planted the seed for me to eventually create my own sketches and paintings. Before Spain, *other* people engaged in these activities, not me. Never me.

It marked the first time I'd lived outside the US, the first time I'd made friends from other countries, those living in my dorm as well as those I met at the Universidad. The first time I attended plays by international playwrights—their plays all performed in Spanish—Bertolt Brecht's *The Caucasian Chalk Circle*, Seneca's *Medea*, Max Frisch's *The Chinese Wall*, in addition to numerous lectures, concerts, dance performances. Attending a concert by the visiting Vienna Boys Choir gave me an appreciation of that talented group.

Other firsts: late night serenades at my dorm by La Tuna, a well-known Spanish singing group dating back to the thirteenth century. Traveling throughout Spain, the tiny cafés in the plazas, taking mass transit, learning new customs, for instance, the way older, widowed women dressed all in black. The cathedrals, museums, the deep blue skies of Madrid, managing life on my own.

More firsts: new foods: paella, tortillas, empanadas, tapas—those little appetizers they served at bars—even the Marias were new to me, those animal-cracker-like breakfast biscuits they served for breakfast at the dorm, as well as flavored yogurt—all new. Living in a dictator-ship represented a dramatic first for me. Similarly, speaking Spanish all day, no longer just in a controlled classroom setting. Spanish no longer constituted an abstract concept for me but became a tool for survival, for learning as much as possible; it opened up this dramati-cally new context for me. Most of all, though, I found that I excelled at something other than piano playing, namely a foreign language.

I hitchhiked for the first (and last) time in Spain. Ignoring my father's pre-Spain warnings, I subscribed to the naive philosophy that, because I was young, I must therefore be immortal. And, because I was in a foreign country, I was immune to harm in certain circumstances, like hitchhiking. It was as though I'd been temporarily lifted from reality. It also represented a rebellious streak on my part; if my father hadn't mentioned it, in a rare moment of paternal outreach, it might not have occurred to me to do something so clearly out of my comfort zone. Regardless, many of my friends hitchhiked in Spain; why not me, I reasoned. I decided to give it a try with an American friend.

We planned to hitchhike from Madrid to Lisbon for spring break, a distance of nearly four hundred miles. We worked out a code in case someone dangerous looking/acting picked us up. I waited with my friend, a very attractive, buxom blonde, on a busy city corner in Madrid for our first ride, thumbs up, each of us carrying only a small travel bag and purse. A driver soon stopped, a middle-aged businessman, dressed in a suit for work. This somehow made him seem safer in our naivete.

He drove a fire-engine-red compact car, a four-door Spanish-made SEAT (Sociedad Española de Automóviles de Turismo), small and noisy. My friend sat in back with a pair of scissors in her bag, in case of danger. This was part of our plan. She promised me she'd have no problem using the scissors to defend us, whereas I knew I would never muster the courage. I sat in front next to the driver, scrutinizing him as he headed toward the *carretera*—the highway—traveling southwest to Lisbon. He assured us he planned to go that direction.

If the driver began to show signs of aggressive behavior, from my spot in front I would turn to ask her, "*¿Qué hora es?*" "What time is it?" Translation: We need to get out of the car at the next sign of civilization. If he became more hostile, I would ask her (ready in back with her scissors), "*¿Qué hora es ahora?*" "What time is it *now*?" meaning we would make him stop immediately, regardless of proximity to civilization. If he began behaving threateningly, I would shout, "*¡Salta!*" "Jump!" at which point we would (carefully) leap from the still-moving car, safe from harm.

One problem with our plan involved the car's noisiness; my friend couldn't hear the conversation in front. Already nervous, I wore a long—reaching my ankles—khaki-colored trench coat on a warm spring day in a car with no air-conditioning. Far too warm for a coat, I used it as my armor. I tightly belted it, hugged the door; a chastity belt would have completed the picture. But when the driver suggested taking a "detour," *un desvío*, up into the mountains, I grew alarmed, craning my neck to look back at my friend. "*¿Qué hora es?*" I asked her, per our plan. Glancing at his watch, the driver responded, "Three fifteen."

Still looking back at my friend, I realized she hadn't heard a word I'd said. She stared out the window, daydreaming or looking at passing scenery. We hadn't factored her possible inattentiveness into the plan, nor the potential noisiness of the car, nor the participation of the driver.

At this point he began to inch his hand toward my khaki-draped leg, even though that required reaching several feet to do so since I had wedged myself against the door. Genuinely worried now, I repeated my sentence with our additional word cue, louder this time, trying to get my friend's attention: "*¿Qué hora es ahora?*" "What time is it *now*?" I put the stress on the important word in our code: *ahora*. My friend still didn't hear my words. It occurred to me that her scissors were probably buried deep inside her overnight bag.

Becoming impatient, the driver looked over at me, chastising me in Spanish, "You just asked me what time it was, and I told you! Now it's three twenty! Five minutes later!" He then motioned to an exit up ahead that led up into the mountains, mentioning something about stopping at a rustic cabin he knew of along the way, so he could "show us the view." Panic rose up inside me. Why hadn't I listened to my father? This man would attack us because we'd acted foolishly. Practically screaming, I turned around in my seat to shout at my friend, using the final part of our code: "*¡Salta!*" "Jump!"

Finally, she heard me, but she froze, as though she'd forgotten the code's key. The startled driver, probably confused by my behavior, braked his car to a sudden stop. We jumped out, running away, shrieking as though a mass murderer had us in his sights.

Circling back a few minutes later, but barely slowing down, one by one he tossed both our overnight bags out through an open window (we'd forgotten to factor retrieving luggage into our escape plan), then sped off. Initially, we thought he was returning to kidnap us, so when we saw his car circling back, we began to scream again. He looked more frightened than we were. People living in the small village also looked alarmed, refusing to speak to us at first, even after the driver had sped off.

We ended up taking a train to Lisbon. Never again did I foolishly believe myself to be immortal, suspended in a safe bubble overseas, believe that nothing bad could happen to me—in Madrid, Spain, or Denver, Colorado, or Kirkwood, Missouri, or anywhere else. I knew better. I knew I'd been lucky. Foolish, but ultimately lucky.

My sense of self shifted that year in Spain. Before, I always put my parents on a pedestal; they knew best in all things, even though I fought them on many of their decisions. Smarter, with better judgment, they had my best interests at heart, I believed. But when they visited me in Spain that year, I realized they were experiencing a fraction of life in this Spanish-speaking country. Not speaking the language, they couldn't really understand the culture. It also marked the first time they depended on me, at least temporarily: depended on my language skills, my knowledge of navigating life in Spain. They relied on me to interpret for them, to act as their mouthpiece.

When they tried to go it alone—primarily my father—a humorous outcome often resulted since, at least back then in tightly controlled Spain, not many Spaniards spoke English. For example, when we were taking a cab together one day, my father, probably tired of his daughter being in charge, thought he'd try out his high school Spanish. Impatient, he asked our cab driver to turn around, to go another way to reach our destination. Instead of saying that, though, he announced, "*¡Huevos revueltos!*" meaning "scrambled eggs."

The cab driver lifted his hands off the wheel in frustration, shook his head, then looked back at me as if to say, "What?! Help me!" at which point I took over.

Another time, I took advantage of my parents' rudimentary language skills. On our way to San Sebastian in northern Spain, we stopped at a tiny restaurant for dinner. I counseled my father against ordering steak, a favorite meal, in such a remote area, but he insisted. Not surprisingly, his steak failed to meet his expectations. As we waited for the check he became increasingly agitated, his voice raised, even his body language telegraphing his anger. Other diners started to take notice of us in the small restaurant, apparently not a frequent tourist attraction. When our waiter appeared with the check, my father instructed me to convey his displeasure, to tell the waiter just how unsatisfactory he found his meal. "You tell him I'm outraged! I don't know where he got this beef, but it's not a good cut. Besides, the chef cooked it far too long. I asked for medium rare, not well-done!"

Normally, to make himself understood in Spanish he spoke English louder, slower, assuming this would break the language barrier, but not this time; he didn't want to risk not being understood. Our young waiter stood next to our table, looking from my father to me, then back again, eager to please, smiling at all of us. After pausing a minute, deciding how best to proceed, I told him in my best Spanish that we'd enjoyed the meal very much, thanking him profusely.

"*Muchísimas gracias, señor. ¡La comida fué deliciosa!*"

He nodded, pleased at hearing my comments, slightly bowing at my father, who squinted at the young man, then asked if I'd conveyed his displeasure, if I'd communicated his words exactly. "Yes," I lied, careful not to make eye contact with him as he interrogated me.

"Well, he's taking it awfully well," he replied, puzzled. Years later I confessed everything, which prompted his laughter. Too late to go back, though. He wouldn't have laughed that night. Back home, when we went out to dinner as a family, my father routinely voiced his dissatisfaction to restaurant staff about not having enough croutons in his soup, for example, or about the quality of the food, or service, embarrassing us all, so in Spain I anticipated he might not like his meal, might be vocal about it.

Sometimes my attempts backfired when I failed to accurately read my environment. The time friends came to visit, for example. We headed to a *mesón* one evening, a traditional Spanish bar. I wanted to impress them. When they ordered sangria, I avoided the wine but absentmindedly picked at fruit at the bottom of the pitcher all evening, nervous about impressing them. I didn't realize the fruit had soaked up alcohol from sitting at the bottom of the sangria pitcher. Even though I hadn't taken a single sip, by evening's end I could barely walk, much to their amusement. I zigzagged all over the street. Not an impression I wanted to leave them with.

My time in Spain became a time of discoveries. By the end of the academic year, I realized I wanted to continue doing this: studying languages, foreign cultures, meeting people from diverse countries, traveling. I didn't know how I planned to use Spanish, how I'd make a living, but I knew my future lay with Spanish, with foreign languages, that somehow I'd find a way.

The whole is greater than the sum of its parts, according to Aristotle. When isolated, some experiences that year in Spain don't stand out. I could have replicated many at home: sampling Spanish food, using mass transit, cultivating international friendships, attending multicultural events, etc. The year in its entirety, though, lifting me out of all I'd known the first twenty years of my life, ultimately set me on a new course. It set in motion a new way of seeing myself, of seeing others.

Before going to Spain, I considered myself a mediocre student, albeit someone with "potential." Piano playing proved an exception to my lackluster record, an optimistic counterpoint. Maybe like one of those people with a touch of the savant syndrome, I somehow channeled my existing abilities and emotions into those performances. But that lasted only until my parents' decision vetoing my desire to apply to Juilliard, thereby convincing me I didn't have enough talent, possessed no future in piano performance, at which point I abandoned that pipe dream.

My year in Spain, then, made me hopeful that I wasn't a lost cause, that I did have talent in something: Spanish. Languages became stepping stones to a universe of possibilities, the key to unlocking any potential I did have. I found my niche, gradually throwing off shackles from the previous unflattering self-concept I'd dragged around like an anchor.

After returning to the University of Denver my senior year, I began taking classes in French, then in graduate school branched out into Portuguese, German, Russian. In so doing I learned about other people, about art, literature, customs, cultures, in short, about life in far-flung places. Eventually, I would travel extensively, even to places off the grid, would witness firsthand what I'd only read about in books until then.

In 1956, at six years old, I wandered around our small yard in Kirkwood, Missouri, humming the theme song from a popular movie, *Around the World in Eighty Days*, wondering about such an expedition, traveling to so many places in a balloon, seeing the world. Little did I realize that, one day, knowing other languages would be my ticket into that life and out of my circumscribed existence. Like that balloon, languages would lift me out of my tiny world, carry me far beyond it, but not without getting past numerous challenges, many of them self-inflicted. Like branches of a beautiful tree, that original tree began with Spanish. The year I spent in Spain planted a tree. I began to go on the journey of a lifetime, a journey to myself, a journey home.

2

THE CONDITIONAL TENSE

Possible Paths Forward

THE CONDITIONAL TENSE—*a grammatical term used to indicate what might happen, could or would happen, or what might still happen.*

EXAMPLE: *"Following my assignment in Brazil, I knew I would never know what would happen unless I took this leap of faith."*

STATUS QUO

Mid-afternoon. Lying on top of the beige, queen-size bedspread in the master bedroom of my modest Kirkwood, Missouri, ranch home. The home—and my life—resembled a throwback to the Eisenhower years: one-dimensional, bland, predictable. I spent a few moments of downtime while my small children—one and three years old—took their naps in a room they shared one door down.

I engaged in a rare moment of reflection in my busy life, looked through a mental rearview mirror to 1971—fourteen years before—

when I'd just returned from spending my junior year abroad in Spain. Inspired. Transformed. Borderline confident. I ticked off benchmarks that separated that period from the present. Among them: returning to the University of Denver my senior year. Graduation. Going home to St. Louis that summer. Working full-time and living at home with my parents for two years. Earning a master's in Spanish, then a PhD in Hispanic languages and literature from a local university at the age of twenty-seven. Working full-time as a translator for a government agency in St. Louis for three years.

I hadn't found the work particularly challenging, but jobs using a foreign language represented a rarity in the Midwest in those days. For the most part, I translated NOTAMs, Notices to Air Missions, from Spanish to English. NOTAMs are short pieces of information put out by the Federal Aviation Administration (FAA) concerning flight operations, conditions, or changes at aeronautical facilities. They can also be used to notify relevant people of hazards or construction on runways or at facilities, or to provide information about airspace restrictions. My translations required minimal vocabulary, and the work rarely extended beyond boilerplate tasks, unlike the riveting material I longed to work with. It wasn't what I'd read about in spy novels, the kind of work that changes the course of history or of individuals' lives.

Easy to remember my last day at that government agency: the day my first child was born. I went into labor at work. I thought it might be Braxton-Hicks contractions—false labor—but headed home, just in case. Shortly after walking in the door of my home, my water broke. I hoisted myself into the car, headed to the hospital with my husband at the wheel. Then, little more than two years later, our daughter was born.

The unwritten and largely unspoken rule in my family of origin dictated that, once a woman gave birth to her first child, she quit her job to become a full-time wife and mother. This philosophy also prevailed in my conservative-minded suburb, population 27,000, even as late as the mid-1980s. When women became mothers, they channeled their energy into home-centered activities: child-rearing, cooking, housekeeping, laundry, supporting their husbands' careers on the home front, and through entertaining. Women's liberation hadn't permeated that part of the Midwest yet. Maybe bridge club, church activities, an occasional lunch out with friends, a smattering of civic or charity work managed to be squeezed in on the side, but only if time permitted. My mother, both my brothers' wives, and my sister all followed this rule; so did both my husband's sisters, as well as my paternal aunts. My mother's sister Jane stood out as a renegade, the only exception in my immediate circle. She lived outside New York City (Rye), taught middle school in the Scarsdale school system. I viewed her as this exotic bird I rarely got to interact with, a staunch liberal on top of everything else, so she bordered on being a persona non grata within my conservative family and community.

As I settled into motherhood, I felt increasingly housebound in this life I'd backed into. Unlike my husband, I didn't play golf, had no desire to learn. I attended more than my fair share of bank weddings, a ready supply of young couples tying the knot every week: female tellers, young male bank officers. I knew a handful of people he worked with. Even those relatively harmless events bored me. I'd sit at our assigned table during the reception as my husband hobnobbed with colleagues, leaving me to entertain myself. Sometimes I passed the time by playing mental language games: conjugating irregular verbs in a language I was working on, the past tense of the Portuguese verb *ser*, for instance: to be: *fui, foste, foi, fomos, fostes, foram.*

I was, you were, he/she was, we were, you (plural) were, they were . . . I didn't enjoy the revolving door of relative strangers' weddings, wasn't particularly adept at mingling with his associates and their families, and so my mental exercises gave me at least a partial reprieve from putting my mediocre social skills on display.

I loved being a mother to our two children, more than anything, but disliked—wasn't good at—what I thought of as "domesticities," Sisyphean tasks that women (primarily) repeated endlessly with no forward movement, and very little challenge to intellect or creativity. These jobs fell to me to complete for the most part. Everything requiring using my mind or my particular brand of creativity shifted away from me, or fell by the wayside, not deemed worthy of doing. Much of it seemed like pure drudgery. Laundry done? Check. Dishes washed? Check. Home cleaned? Check? Toys picked up? Check. More of the same the next day. If I'd been skilled at cooking or gardening or sewing, I might have enjoyed those activities, but I was abysmal, trying to pass Hamburger Helper off as homemade stew.

Seven years before, I'd been immersed in my graduate school language studies, a fascinating period: six years studying a new language (Portuguese), working with brilliant professors, fellow graduate students, teaching undergraduate language courses, doing research. My job as a translator for the government followed. That life had ended, though, both the school and the work. My life as a suburban housewife loomed before me in my mind's eye, more of the same, at least until the kids reached high school? College? I looked at the beige walls of my one-story home, sensed them closing in on me, aware that the longer I remained out of the workforce, the less chance I'd have to reenter it. In the eyes of potential employers, my skills were rapidly becoming outdated.

As I lay on the bed, staring up at the ceiling in my suburban home, my magical year in Spain faded like a story I'd made up, or read in a book a long time before, a story about someone else. Some days I questioned if it ever happened, but then I looked at my journals, my books, my scrapbooks. It did happen. To me. I was there.

A few days before, I'd written in my journal:

This world I find myself in isn't "me." I don't belong. I'm not sure where I do belong, but it's not in Kirkwood as a housewife, marking time. People here look at me strangely when I tell them who I am, what I want out of life . . . I want the ability to choose, the freedom to be who I'm supposed to be . . . I feel like I've been left behind, but in a prison, left to rot my life away.

Lonely, even though I rarely found myself alone, I coped the best I could, reading, working in my home, enjoying my children, bright spots in my life. The lives of most of my local female friends also revolved around their homes. They did what I did. Every day. Just like me. Not working (or with very part-time jobs) but at home full-time with young children. A few earned "pin money," a term my mother used, referring to a small amount of discretionary money, sometimes an allowance a woman's husband gave her.

Rarely did anyone broach the subject of being at home all day, discuss how our lives had slowly narrowed down to a sliver. When I ventured out on errands at a local shopping center, whenever I heard someone speaking Spanish—a rare occurrence in those days—I sometimes followed the person around, hungry to hear authentic bits of a language I loved, like trailing after an old friend.

At a barbecue my husband and I hosted, I remember that women swapped recipes, shared child-rearing practices, debated the best laundry detergents for stain removal, while the men drank too much beer, discussed their jobs, sports, yard work. When my parents invited all of us over for dinner, the same pecking order fell into place: women on one side of the room, men on the other, or in different rooms. I crossed the line at my own peril, inviting snubs or rude comments. Sometimes I'd do nothing more than stand next to my father and brothers, yet still receive the message, often without a word being spoken, just a well-placed look at me, as though to say, "What are you doing? Why aren't you in the kitchen doing the dishes, talking about child-related topics? We're having a grown-up conversation here."

Remembering these incidents, my thoughts turning to the generic bedspread beneath me, I caught myself. My creative juices were drying up; I'd become a bona fide housewife. With my hands folded on my stomach, my eyes closed, I waited. Waited for the sound of little voices stirring, little voices that kept me sane, tethered to life.

The linguist in me searched for the word to best describe my state of mind. It surfaced from inside like one of those inky fortune-telling balls: depression. But right behind it lay feelings of guilt, ready to smack the depression down, channeling my mother: "How dare you act depressed when you have two precious, healthy children, a beautiful home, a husband who works hard to support all of you! Shame on you! Count your blessings!" My mother's mantra played throughout my life: whenever sadness about anything overcame me, she'd repeat it. No wallowing or self-pity allowed.

More than a year before, I'd applied for a job in the Washington, DC, area as a linguist. An attempt to prop up my flagging self-confidence, it served as a theoretical foray into independence, a test balloon I launched. Let's say, hypothetically, I found the courage to change my life, I thought. Did I have the necessary skills to get a job? To support my children and me? Had my language skills remained marketable? I created a parallel universe in my mind, one where life took on a different shape. The conditional tense: If I passed the tests and they offered me a job, *would* I accept?

Part of the application process involved taking several language tests in Spanish and Portuguese, both written and aural. To my surprise, I did well on all four tests. A job offer had materialized like a gift from above, arriving in the mail a month before. I'd put it on the narrow childhood desk in my closet-sized study with the canary-yellow walls, a tiny room crammed with hundreds of language dictionaries and books, my sanctuary. Several times a day, I unfolded the letter to reread the words, "It is our pleasure to offer you employment . . ." I couldn't believe someone official had written those words to me, *me*, someone who couldn't even sew buttons on straight or cook a real stew or iron clothes without singeing them.

I was stuck, though. I hadn't mailed in the response form with the appropriate box checked: I will/will not accept the offer. And the letter contained a time limit. Speak now (soon) or forever hold your peace, to quote the question posed by ministers at weddings during vows. I'd already received a follow-up letter, "Previously, we sent you an offer of employment and, to date, have not received your response. This offer is good until XX-XX-XX." I needed to make up my mind. Fast. Of course I knew I'd ultimately check the box "will NOT accept." I lacked the courage, the life skills, the confidence to make such a bold move on my own, the wherewithal to set everything in motion, to make such a dramatic decision. For four years I'd been playing with and taking care of my children, watching snatches of soap operas, going through the motions of being a housewife, waiting for my husband to get home from work each day. Besides, he had made it clear he didn't want to move. He enjoyed the status quo. Who wouldn't? Meanwhile, I remained stuck between two lives: one in Kirkwood,

Missouri, where I played the role of mediocre housewife, albeit an enthusiastic mother, with another unknown life out of reach, one I'd caught a glimpse of that year in Spain, a place replete with foreign languages, with living an independent life, of being in control of my life.

What happened next only happens in movies, but reality truly is stranger than fiction. I was still lying on my bed, my mood steadily darkening, when the phone rang, interrupting my gloomy thoughts.

"Hello?" I whispered, not wanting to wake my still-sleeping children.

"Linda? Is that you? Do I have the right number? This is Bob Herron!"

I wouldn't have recognized his voice, so ensconced in my latest role of housewife and mother, if he hadn't identified himself, despite his having been someone so important from my graduate school past, seven years before. My former mentor, head of the language department, and the professor who taught me Portuguese, wanted to talk to me. He'd encouraged me endlessly while I attended graduate school, had even nominated me for Phi Beta Kappa. I'd lost touch with him, though. That life clashed with the one I was currently living, giving dinner party guests paper napkins with their steak Diane.

"Linda, it's Dr. Herron. How are you? I hope I haven't caught you at a bad time?"

I sat up like a shot, as though he could see his former protégée through the phone, a frumpy woman closing in on middle age, wearing sweatpants topped with a rumpled turtleneck, stained with bits of my children's lunches, taking a nap in the middle of the afternoon. Clearing my throat, I assured him it wasn't a bad time as I smoothed the wrinkles out of my turtleneck and pants. It occurred to me that he wouldn't recognize me if he saw me.

"Not at all! Great to hear from you!" I answered, sounding artificially perky.

"Fantastic! Well, I'll tell you why I called. I was asked to recommend someone who could act as both an interpreter and translator for a church group going to Brazil this summer for several weeks. The group is made up of college-aged kids accompanied by a few adults. They'll go to remote areas in northeastern Brazil, after a brief stay in Rio. It sounds fascinating; truthfully, I wish I could go."

"Yes. It does sound fascinating, but why are they going to northeastern Brazil?" I asked.

He explained that they'd be studying the causes of extreme hunger in that area. The Lutheran Church had agreed to sponsor the journey, to pay all expenses, including paying the translator.

"Do you think you'd be interested? Could you get away for a few weeks? I know you're busy with your family, but I can't think of anyone else I'd rather endorse."

This must be what it feels like if you win the lottery, I thought. Hard to believe that, only an hour before, I'd combed the house with my small son, looking for one of Mr. Potato Head's arms: under our multicolored, worn-out couch; under a beige corduroy easy chair; under his bed. Keeping my kids' toys in some semblance of order seemed the only way I exercised any control over my own life. This phone call catapulted me back to another time and place, one I missed. Working with languages, with interesting people, extracting meaning from words, from sounds, from different cultures—I missed it all.

In addition to working as interpreter for the group, I'd be expected to deliver a crash course in Portuguese in Florida and in Rio de Janeiro in advance of heading to the backlands of Brazil, the *sertão*. I'd also do ad hoc work as a translator, translating documents and conference proceedings, and anything else conference sponsors needed translated.

Translation refers to rendering written material from one language to another. Interpretation refers to doing this with spoken material. Simultaneous interpretation—one of my assignments in Brazil—presents numerous challenges. An interpreter interprets without a break in communication, communicants speaking nonstop as though the interpreter weren't present. In consecutive interpreting, in theory participants pause to allow an interpreter to catch up before proceeding. Communicants often neglect to do this, however, forgetting that an interpreter needs those gaps to do his or her job. I'd perform both simultaneous and consecutive interpreting for this assignment, as well as translating the group's findings into Portuguese.

I hesitated before answering my former mentor. My previous work for the government agency in St. Louis had been as a translator and, while employed there, I'd interpreted for Brazilian dignitaries visiting St. Louis one afternoon. I found it exhausting, challenging, exhilarating. A more important consideration existed, though: How could I leave my small children behind for three weeks, upend my life? Their lives? My husband's life? Would he agree?

"Let me talk to my husband tonight. I'll get back to you," I told him, as though my husband and I enjoyed an equal partnership and had grown-up conversations. "I'll call you back tomorrow after we talk."

After I hung up, my body now fortified with newfound energy, I hopped out of bed, my mind spinning with ideas. I felt hopeful for the first time in months. I needed to make this work. I needed to convince my husband to let me go. I had to go. He'd already given me his blessing to fly to Washington, DC, for two days to take the four language tests (the government paid for my flight and hotel room).

This would require more convincing. Both sets of parents lived in the area, plus my three siblings, so he'd have backup in taking care of our children, but he frowned on anything that took me away from my responsibilities at home. After I returned from taking the language tests, when I briefly broached the possibility of us moving to Washington, DC, together, before anyone had even made me a job offer, he balked.

"You said you wanted to take the tests. You never mentioned actually taking the job or our moving out of St. Louis," he pointed out, stretched out on our family room couch, not looking up from his newspaper to acknowledge my presence. "I let you do that. Supported you . . . Enough already. I can't keep taking the kids to my parents' to babysit. It's not good for them to live in this chaos; kids need stability. They need their mother. With them. At home."

"But we'd have two incomes, you know? As a banker, you could get a job anywhere. This would mean a chance to have an exciting new start on the East Coast," I replied, close to begging. "It would jump-start our marriage." But he just shook his head, returning to his newspaper.

Somehow, over the course of that same evening of my mentor's call, pleading like a child, I'd convinced him of the merits of accepting the assignment in Brazil, or maybe he just tolerated the idea. In hindsight, maybe he thought I'd fail, or that the trip would cure me of wanting to return to the workforce. He may even have thought I'd return to life in Kirkwood inspired to improve my cooking and housekeeping, to work on my social skills. I'd embarrassed him numerous times on neighborhood bridge nights where I performed miserably, interacted awkwardly, overpowered by anxiety. Or maybe he thought I'd return from Brazil deflated, work harder in my role as a housewife. Whatever his reasoning, he reluctantly agreed. I called my former graduate advisor with the news before my husband could change his mind. I glimpsed a new road unfolding before me, albeit miles and miles ahead.

For the next three weeks I read background material on the specific regions in Brazil where I'd be working; I did my homework. But I also lay awake at night, obsessing over what this all meant, this odyssey, this test, a trip that would no doubt be fraught with physical, linguistic, as well as emotional challenges along the way. My previous identity slowly began to recede, then inch forward, like waves on a beach. A part of me couldn't wait, while another part felt panic-stricken.

ON THE GO

Flying over Florida's coastline, I spotted boats, perfect little squares of land below, cotton ball puffs of clouds suspended by invisible threads from above. After we landed in Miami, I took a taxi to the hotel, lugging my two enormous suitcases, jammed with teaching materials: dictionaries, grammars, articles. I spotted college-aged kids in the lobby—possibly part of our group?—but decided not to approach them. I feared letting everyone get to know me too fast, before I even figured out what was what. I always did that: donned the mask of someone likable, even when it meant being untrue to myself, eager to be who people wanted me to be. I didn't want to repeat history. Besides, I'd been living in a bubble for nearly four years; so much could go wrong.

The North Americans gradually got to know each other, were given a crash course on Brazil by our group leader: politics, people, culture, terrain. One documentary we watched dealt with Alcoa Aluminum, its role in a small Brazilian town where people's homes had been leveled, their small subsistence farms destroyed, forcing inhabitants to move to the city to find other ways to support themselves. We examined photographs of areas we'd visit in upcoming days and weeks. Finally, we shared stories about ourselves to include our expectations for the trip. I admitted to having no expectations, only an eleven-year love affair with the Portuguese language. I confessed to actually disliking the word *expectation*. It connotes the idea of waiting, possibly in vain, for something. I knew too much about that. I wrote in my journal that night: "I'm learning to be by myself on this trip, though it's painful: without the artificial stimuli of radio, TV, without the false security of other people, without the demands of my precious little children . . ."

The six-hour flight from Florida to Rio had provided me with a mini-immersion in Brazil, people leaving their *poltronas*, their seats, milling around as soon as flight attendants turned off the seat belt sign. When Brazilians on our flight learned of the group's assignment, they made it their mission to teach the group new phrases, as well as reinforcing ones I'd taught the group in Miami.

During the flight, my first unofficial assignment consisted of translating words from an old spiritual song, "He's Got the Whole World in His Hands" for one of the American lay ministers in our group. He wanted to teach it to Brazilian children on the plane.

"Could you please tell us how to sing this traditional African American spiritual song? I think these Brazilian kids would love it," he said, enthusiastic about the prospect of Brazilians and North Americans sharing bits of their culture.

"Well, I don't know it off the top of my head, but I'll do my best," I responded, and proceeded to interpret the words for them as we sang along.

These types of interactions happened often in Brazil: ad hoc requests to translate documents, songs, prayers, schedules, conference proceedings, to help with phone calls, shopping, buying stamps, taxi negotiations, church services, even to translate matchmaking arrangements conducted via handwritten notes . . . anything and everything. The material ranged from words to silly songs to those of a scholar differentiating between the effects of hunger and malnutrition. I eventually became accustomed to it all, but secretly feared I wouldn't meet expectations of the people who had hired me, not to mention my professor who'd recommended me. I had met no one in the group prior to meeting up in Florida, so I represented an unknown entity in their eyes, credentials unimportant in the Brazilian backlands; I would need to prove myself hour after hour, day after day. No one cared—or knew—that I had a PhD. It was irrelevant to their purposes.

After we landed in Rio, the group separated into four cabs to travel to our hotel, Grande Hotel São Francisco, located in Rio's city center, near the water. With more than two hundred rooms, it looked like a throwback to an old movie set. I expected Humphrey Bogart to stroll into the lobby, his fedora hat cocked over one eye à la *Casablanca*. One chaperone speculated that the furniture was typical of the Queen Anne style, whereas phones looked like they'd come from the set of a 1940s gangster movie. Bathtubs looked child-sized, the bed too. At five foot four, I barely fit in either.

Our first night in Rio required an adjustment in my normal routine, in my thinking too. I could hear saxophone and clarinet music playing from a distance ("You'll Never Know Just How Much I Love You"). It sounded eerie, as though I'd been dropped into a different era, an alternate setting. Cars honked, even their horns sounding different. They revved their engines, the sound filling the night air. A lack of screens on hotel windows made it possible to lean out, look around. My sense of smell was assaulted by all sorts of—not all of them pleasant—scents when I stuck my head out into the night air: smoke, exhaust, cooking oil, spices, rotten fruit, open garbage, floral perfumes, wet animal fur, even sewage.

I spent the next few days continuing to teach my crash course in Portuguese to the group. Most days we met in a conference room three hours a day, a room the hotel reserved for us in their business center, a functional space with a long table holding enough chairs for all of us, twenty or so, plus a chalkboard where I could illustrate points, emphasize hard-to-understand language concepts, even though it was a beginner course. One day another group had reserved the business center so I held class in the mezzanine, the *sobreloja*. An area open to the public, where Brazilians talked, mingled, shopped, went about their business, occasionally looking up at us as I explained certain grammatical concepts. Feeling exposed, vulnerable, I feared one of these Brazilians might approach me to correct my Portuguese. No one ever did, though, thankfully.

I brought handouts from home with me, common expressions to give my new students, college kids, just enough to ensure they could interact a little with their future Brazilian friends, who apparently did not speak much English, especially ones we would encounter in remote areas. I wanted to bridge that gap as much as possible in advance.

My senses seemed to have been reprogrammed, stripped of their original input, as though my body held a library where someone had removed every book and replaced them with completely new books. I heard Portuguese around the clock, not English. To the untrained ear it sounded like Spanish, only spoken by someone with a cold; nasal. Then there was the sound of Brazilian music. Brazilian members of our group—whom we would meet in a few days, after leaving Rio— brought albums with them. They played them every free moment, especially at night after the official activities had ended. This music introduced me to Antonio Carlos Jobim, Gilberto Gil, Chico Buarque, Gonzagão, Gal Costa, and others. I loved the rhythms, the sounds of the *cuíca* (a type of drum), the *zabumba* (another type of drum), the triangle, the accordion. Until I went to Brazil, I'd only heard accordion music on *The Lawrence Welk Show*, or when someone accompanied polka dancing at a wedding. This music revealed a completely different beat, a set of unique sounds. I loved it, loved all of it, including the samba and the bossa nova. When I celebrated my birthday toward the end of the trip, the Brazilians in our group presented me with all the albums they'd brought with them so I could take a piece of Brazil home with me. Few gifts have ever rivaled this. This slice of Brazilian music was one of the best gifts I've ever received. Other music came in the form of songs the children sang, for example, "*Deus te ama e eu te amo*," "God loves you and I love you."

Smells greatly varied from ones back home: the smell of exhaust from the cars, from buses, much stronger than what I'd known, and occasionally mixed with sweat, urine; the smell of food cooked on the street; sea air. New tastes: *pão de queijo* (cheese bread), *bacalhau* (cod), as well as their most famous dish, *feijoada*, a stew made from beans and pork, a real stew, not like my Hamburger Helper version.

My sense of sight also underwent a dramatic change. What I saw every day didn't resemble Kirkwood, Missouri, in the least: the houses (from shanties to mansions), the people, the clothing they wore, even the vegetation. I saw red flowers that never bloomed—*bonecos de ciganos*—in Rio's Floresta da Tijuca, a rainforest in Rio—one of the largest in the world—went hiking, bird-watching, and saw magnificent waterfalls. The highlight was seeing the famous Christ Statue and Corcovado, a 2,300-foot mountain outside Rio.

I caught glimpses of unrecognizable animals I'd never heard of, for instance capybaras, little mammals that resembled miniature pigs, or rats, running wild around parks we visited. Colorful birds. Enormous frogs. Donkeys. Goats.

After less than a month in Brazil, differences in my sensory perceptions began to occur, gradually, but irrevocably. I didn't notice the effect until shortly after returning home to Kirkwood. I spent some time in a local shopping center outside St. Louis. The colors people wore seemed blindingly bright; even the whites of their shoes, their pants, their T-shirts blazed like spotlights. Nothing had seemed that white-white in Brazil. Colors had looked more washed out, more so than back in the States. It was as though someone had washed everything multiple times. In Brazil the palette didn't appear artificially bright anymore, didn't shout its existence at me.

As I sat on my bed that first night in Rio, anxiety set in; the absence of my children caused me so much anxiety I could barely breathe. I kept picturing a world map with Kirkwood on one side, Rio on the other, with so much land and water between us. The distance seemed to stretch forever. Too far away. Out of touch. The morning my daughter was born, I had left my son at home in my mother-in-law's care to go to the hospital before he woke up, crying as I kissed his sleeping face goodbye. This felt similar, yet its impact tenfold. Once our group left Rio, I knew I'd remain out of touch: no phones, no time for letters to reach home or to me, no Internet yet. No more than five miles had ever separated my children and me, yet now five thousand miles lay between us. Making matters worse, I knew sleep would be difficult with all these city sounds; I wasn't used to so much noise back in the suburbs. When I went to bed that first night, I stuffed cotton in my ears to muffle Rio's sounds: traffic, raucous parties, vendors, pedestrians, workers heading home after their shifts. No one seemed to sleep in Rio.

"I miss my family," I told my roommate, a nineteen-year-old

North American college student in our group, no longer able to keep my feelings locked inside, near tears. I still pictured that map with miles between us.

"We're your family while you're here," she reassured me. It helped, but not much. Did my children think I'd abandoned them? As they were still so young, I'd found it difficult explaining that we wouldn't see each other for three weeks. Three weeks in the life of two little ones might as well equal three years.

The next morning we visited the favelas, shanty towns perched in hills just outside Rio. I'd read about them in graduate school, but reading about them differed greatly from actually being within these sprawling communities, ragtag life unfurling before me like an enormous painting I'd studied at the Prado so long ago. They reminded me a little of Picasso's *Guernica* painting, so much movement, busyness, chaos. Even as the only North American who spoke Portuguese, no interpreting was necessary; anyone could see the inhabitants' struggle to survive against enormous odds.

Our little group of twenty North Americans shrank in comparison to the size of the local population. This wasn't some show I watched on TV. Years later, I read that Brazilian authorities had curtailed visitors entering the favelas, ultimately banned visits from outsiders in most places, deeming it too dangerous. Crime syndicates eventually took over some of the favelas. Yet we walked freely through several in 1985.

The contrast between life inside and outside the favelas shattered my equanimity. Tiny, multicolored structures seemed to have been piled willy-nilly on top of each other, or were jammed next to each other, perched in the mile-high shadows of row after row of high-rent high-rise apartments visible along Copacabana and Ipanema beaches that we'd passed on our way to the favelas. Here in the favelas, children ran through the streets with rudimentary kites (*pipas*) they'd made, filling the skies above with patches of faded colors, as though tattered pieces of the favelas had escaped to the heavens above, bits of the children's hopes rising to the heavens.

The first favela our group visited, Rocinha, ranked as the largest, with over 250,000 inhabitants. In some shacks, water dripped from a hose that ran from shanty to shanty. Gravity worked for or against inhabitants as the water wended its way down through small boxlike constructions. In other sections neighbors appeared to share a spigot at the bottom of a hill. Wires crisscrossed each other above makeshift homes, a massive tangle of phone or power lines that looked like a giant cat's ball of yarn, only it was wire, not yarn.

Sewage ran through a pipe to open receptacles, gradually running down into the sea. I'd never seen so many people crowded together, dust covered, playing in the streets or talking, living in tiny corrugated structures, one stacked on top of the other, squeezed between another one on either side.

Clothing hung from open-air balconies, flapping in the fickle wind. Occupants had strategically placed antennas on structures. Clothing worn by both adults and children looked like castoffs from other countries, sports team logos or names of American or European colleges or products prominently displayed. Stained, ripped versions of previously worn clothing. Kids ran around barefoot or wore flip-flops with holes worn through the soles.

A man in our group, an expert on poverty, boldly claimed that adults living in the favelas possessed no personalities. He argued that people's overriding need to survive had erased their personalities. I didn't believe him for a minute, but I knew better than to contradict his words since my time in-country amounted to only a week or so. I didn't think of myself as an expert, but all you needed to do was look around, see the cavernous gaps between rich and poor in Brazil, especially when the haves and have-nots lived in such close proximity, at least here in Rio. But underlying their hard-scrabble lives lay overwhelming evidence of parents' devotion to their children: checking on their whereabouts, tending to babies (the mothers carrying them everywhere in makeshift cloth sacks wrapped expertly around their chests as they did double duty, working while also caring for the babies). Adults didn't have the freedom of keeping older children by their side all day long, but I could see strong threads linking mothers or fathers to sons, to daughters; they instinctively seemed to know where to look if their children wandered off, the children also able to locate a parent if asked. I could hear the devotion in the parents' words when we spoke.

As we walked along unpaved, dusty streets, slowly making our way through the favelas, kids followed us everywhere, asking to take our pictures. I translated conversations from English to Portuguese (mainly questions from our group), from Portuguese to English (answers from favela residents, who had their own questions). Topics included: liberation theology, land reform, food for the hungry, survival, female pastors, government aid. Liberation theology became a popular topic during the 1960s, especially in Latin America, advocating care for the poor, as well as political liberation for oppressed people.

Forced to stop when too many people surrounded us, impeding my movement, I spoke at breakneck speed to keep up with everyone, Brazilians and North Americans, everyone constantly interrupting each other, speaking over each other, expecting the interpreter—me—to render it all in real time, in perfect Portuguese or English, pressing against me with urgency to ensure I could hear their words. It was as if Brazilians and North Americans feared they might never have another chance to communicate their thoughts.

I had broken new personal ground already. Back in Kirkwood, Missouri, I spent most of my time—when in the company of adults—waiting, asking for approval/acceptance/permission/information. A follower, not a leader, at least with adults in my orbit. I must have sounded like a child speaking to disapproving adults, much more powerful adults.

Here, though, group members pushed me out in front, made me a leader, if for no other reason than my language skills, that necessary link between everyone. Back and forth, English and Portuguese speakers had a lot to say, a lot to ask. They needed me to serve as a conduit between both groups, to bridge the gap between them, hopefully leading to understanding, at least at some level. Hanging back, asking permission, kowtowing: that tactic didn't have a place here.

In more formal situations—which I'd also take part in during upcoming days—as an interpreter I played an invisible yet pivotal role, in a booth or off to the side, softly speaking into a microphone for all to hear, often out of visual range. But it involved countless opportunities to walk among Brazilians, to spend time in their homes, in their civic centers, on the streets; I stood in the midst of it, the heart of it. With hundreds of spokes all converging on me, I became a hub of the wheel.

Many informal settings popped up, all requiring me to interpret both from Portuguese to English and from English to Portuguese. That presented another challenge. Normally, linguists refer to the "target" language of interpreters (translators too) as the language into which they interpret, usually an interpreter's language of origin, his logical comfort zone, his language since birth. Ideally, then, my job should have consisted in interpreting from Portuguese, a language I'd learned later in life, going toward my language of origin, my comfort zone, home base: English.

The source language, on the other hand, means the language from which an interpreter begins, the puzzle to decipher. Normally, someone else would have interpreted exchanges from English into Portuguese, namely a native Portuguese speaker. But we didn't have the manpower to follow normal translating/interpreting protocols, at least not in Rio, especially in hundreds of informal, impromptu settings, so I served in both roles. No one else knew both languages, so I alternated between English and Portuguese, went both directions. It occurred to me later that, in essence, I moved between who I was leaving behind and who I was on the verge of becoming, between a known path and another possible path forward, still unknown.

In addition to showing an interest in conventional topics such as housing, food, and education, the North Americans also wanted to know about more straightforward matters. "Ask that woman the ages of her children, and if they're in school." "Do they know how to read?" "Where are the churches?" "What's that gizmo hanging on the wall used for? Do they use it to dry clothing?" Whatever questions or curiosities bubbled up in their active minds, almost all was appropriate to ask Brazilians they met.

The Brazilians in the favelas posed their own questions to the group for me to interpret: "Do you have children?" "Where are your husbands?" "Do you live in a mansion?" "What's your job?" "How many pairs of shoes do you have?" "Would you like to see my home?" "Could I take your picture?" "Why are you here?" "How old are you?"

I didn't have the time or opportunity to sink into the background. No one relieved me, no one else could serve as a link between these two worlds, so I soldiered on, loving it while simultaneously nervous I might make mistakes.

The favelas represented a different type of society, changing the channel from my sheltered, privileged existence to one where scarcity reigned. The lack of water, the open sewage, trash heaped everywhere, the poverty, the filth, the smells. People spilled out of doorways as though part of a magic trick; how could so many fit into such small spaces? Overcome by so much noise, I practically had to shout to be heard, putting my face right next to the speaker in order to hear; I wanted to get it right. Surprisingly, the words flowed, though, Portuguese to English, then back again. Surprisingly, I functioned well in this challenging setting.

No formal rules existed for interpreting conversations. A North American college student asking a five-year-old if he owned a toothbrush counted just as much as a North American group leader asking for specifics about help the Brazilian government provided. The words and questions all formed part of language, led to an ultimate goal: meaning, understanding. I stood straddled between two worlds, with Portuguese words feeding into a new lexicon, a new way of existing, a new way of interpreting information my senses provided, along with my place in it.

Next up on our journey: from Rio and the favelas on to Salvador, to Itaparica, a small island—still in the state of Bahia—about fifty-six miles off the coast of Salvador. I'd left Kirkwood a week before, but it seemed like months had passed.

The convent where we stayed in Itaparica, built in the 1930s, reminded me of an ancient Spanish villa with its beautiful courtyards and gardens open to the elements. We met up with the other half of our group there: Brazilian students, along with a few Brazilian administrators, joining us on our journey. Little boys in town sold us seashells, gave us flowers. Fishing boats floated peacefully offshore. Fishermen fixed their nets.

We'd gone from a highly congested urban area to a rural area. The rooms featured wooden shutters with no ceiling, open air with just an elevated roof, along with a single light bulb. Mosquito netting was draped over my bed to help keep the enormous cockroaches from crawling over me at night. Frogs the size of baseball mitts camped out in our bathroom, luxuriating in leftover moisture.

Fifty-four of us traveled together now, including ten translators; I acted as the only North American translator, the only native English speaker. At meals, an interpreter sat at each table since very few Brazilian students spoke English. Nor did the North American students speak more than broken Portuguese. During official proceedings after dinner, I took turns with other interpreters, sitting at an outdoor booth to convey the words of each guest speaker. At one point, an enormous bat flew into my booth. It startled me, but I somehow kept my composure, didn't lose my place in proceedings. When you're working as an interpreter, it's important to concentrate every fiber of your being on what's being said. You're splitting your mind in two: half of you listens to what's coming, while the other half translates words you've just heard, speaking them aloud, of course. You're speaking and listening simultaneously, splitting your mind into three time zones: what was just spoken—past—and your interpretation of it—present—while readying yourself for words to come. If you make any missteps, it's hard to get back on track, to catch up. The danger is losing the context, the flow, the language, all in a matter of seconds.

I came to know the three North American female leaders in our group better once we left Rio de Janeiro with its frenetic pace. All three enjoyed fulfilling careers. Two were single, making their way in life without a husband or partner, extremely independent:

financially, physically, emotionally. Little by little I shared the broad parameters of my life back in Kirkwood. They listened attentively, careful not to interject their opinions unless asked. I didn't have many friends like them back home. They didn't care when I confessed at being a horrible housewife, cook, housekeeper, party hostess, seamstress, bridge player, etc. Nor did they seem to notice my twenty or so extra pounds. I'd lived in such isolation the past four years that this surprised me. The day after I was inducted into Phi Beta Kappa, a few weeks after I received my PhD at twenty-seven, my father had walked into our home, an errant fur ball from my husband's German shepherd catching his eye.

"You're not much of a housekeeper, are you?" he noted, shaking his head in disapproval.

When I shared my father's remarks with one of my new friends, she commented, "Who cares?" looking at me quizzically. "What decade do you live in, anyway, the 1950s?"

More and more, conference coordinators asked me to interpret for the entire group, particularly during official proceedings. At one session, I sat in the booth for more than an hour without a break, wearing headphones, using a microphone. I fantasized that maybe this resembled the life of a UN interpreter. They probably didn't have to contend with bats entering their workspace in the middle of a conference, though.

After one session, the Brazilian sound engineer approached me as I put away the new tools of my trade: microphone, dictionary, pens, headphone, pad of paper. He extended his hand.

"I've done this for years; you're the best interpreter I've ever worked with," he told me. "I've asked for you by name at the next session. You remain calm, keep your voice low, not to mention keeping up with the pace of the conference."

I thanked him but wrote in my journal that night, "My heart can't take it—but I love it," adding, "I seriously don't know how I can go home after (1) experiencing this, (2) using my skills to their capacity, and (3) living with three truly liberated women. This trip has really bombarded me on a lot of levels . . . and you can't 'go home' after that. You know, 'suburban housewife' with the station wagon was always a lie. But now it'll be a travesty."

I wished I could magically transport my two children to Brazil, have them experience a day in my life here, spend time with them, tuck them in at night. I wanted them to see me at work, interpreting. I wanted them to see me as a role model, show them I could do more than I did every day back in Kirkwood, Missouri, searching high and low for Mr. Potato Head's missing arm, trying not to burn dinner. I wanted them to see that more of me existed than fun mommy who played games with them, read books to them, made up stories, went on discovery walks. I contained many more facets.

Even in graduate school, studying languages, or when I worked as a translator for a government agency, I think I viewed my love of foreign languages as a sideline, a hobby I enjoyed; self-indulgent, my mother might have termed it. Something I did while waiting for my real life to start. A higher calling awaited me: marriage, children, taking care of my home, of my husband's needs. Languages came to mean something almost illicit, but they set me apart from my husband, my parents, my siblings, became a bubble in which I both found myself and hid. I imagined my mother warning me, "Get this out of your system now, Linda, because once you're married, or at least have children, this all goes away. No more fun and games. You'll join our ranks, follow our lead."

Although she never said those exact words, I knew she considered my work with foreign languages self-serving, even when I received a salary. Regardless, my trip to Brazil had made her doubly antagonistic. A few months before, shortly after I received my official job offer from the DC government agency, we spoke for a few minutes on the phone; she made her feelings obvious.

"Well, you said to call you when I got back in town; I'm home. What's going on?" she said, her tone flat, uninterested. I imagined her at the other end of the phone line, twiddling her thumbs or multitasking, signaling to my father that she'd join him in a minute, just as soon as she dispensed with me.

I told her about the job offer, and she practically shrieked into the phone, "Does that mean Joe [my husband] will have to move?!"

"I guess so," I answered, shrugging my shoulders.

"Well, what does he have to say about that?"

"I guess he's not thrilled," I replied. Then I heard her singsong voice speaking to my father, informing him that I'd gotten the job offer, feigning enthusiasm.

"Oh, Sam! Can you come here? Linda is on the phone and has news she wants to share with us!"

One day, still on the island of Itaparica, the Brazilians presented us all with a surprise culture lesson. I interpreted for Marcos Arruda, an activist who'd been imprisoned and then lived in exile for eleven years. After an hour or so, when proceedings broke for lunch, I headed to the communal area to enjoy a pleasant meal. The Brazilian members of our group had made other plans, though, had decided to conduct an experiment at lunch. As each person in the two groups entered the dining area, he or she was instructed to pick a number out of a hat. That number corresponded to the table where we were to sit, as well as what we would eat. Not being aware of this plan, I took my number, headed over to a table matching my slip of paper.

Four people sat at each table in the open-air pavilion. Sitting down, I saw a feast in front of me. Someone had gone to great lengths to make the table look beautiful: a cloth tablecloth, freshly cut multi-colored flowers, elegant china, silverware. Serving dishes, platters, bowls overflowed with food, including seafood, rice, beans, pasta, fruit. Guaraná (a Brazilian soft drink), Coca-Cola, Pepsi, and bottled water chilled inside a large aluminum drum overflowing with small cubes of ice.

Striking up a conversation with the Brazilian woman next to me, I commented on the abundance of food, assuming that every table shared an equal amount, although I hadn't bothered to look around to confirm this. I was the only North American at my table.

"Unbelievable, isn't it? A feast. More than enough for everyone here at our table," I commented in Portuguese, eager to try everything.

My Brazilian dining companion quickly set me straight, speaking sternly to me in Portuguese. "Do you not see the other tables? They have very little food, practically nothing. It's all dependent on the number you drew. You and I randomly chose the 'rich' table, while the 'proletariat' table and the 'poor' table have been assigned to others. It's totally random, just like the life into which you were born."

Looking around for the first time, I realized what was happening. Tables near us featured a few small bowls half full of beans, containing nothing else. Nor did they have beverages or flowers or tablecloths or fine china or silverware. I just assumed everyone shared the same items; I hadn't even looked around before sitting down, or I'd have noticed the disparity among our tables. Was that how I viewed my life, I wondered? My head in the sand? I hoped not.

Once I realized that many other tables had next to nothing to eat, I got up, carrying with me one of the overflowing platters. I approached other tables to share my food, but a Brazilian group leader stopped me. The situation quickly escalated, becoming tense. Those seated at the "proletariat" and "poor" tables were also instructed to stay put when they attempted to get food from those of us seated at "affluent" tables.

"Sit down," the Brazilian group leader reprimanded those of us who'd left our original tables, trying to share. "We designed this exercise to reveal the imbalance in the structure of our society, the injustices, so please just sit down at the table corresponding to the number you picked; stop changing things. You're going to destroy the lesson."

According to the organizers, the goal lay in displaying a slice of life, peeling back the dynamics of the twentieth century. Emotions ran high. In the midst of it, I translated for the Brazilians and North Americans. The conflict escalated, replicating a scene many Brazilians experienced, left feeling vulnerable, sad, humiliated.

The lesson resonated with me, namely to try not to take my blessings for granted, most of it due to an accident of birth. Who could say how different my life might have turned out if I'd grown up in a different country, in a different family, to richer or poorer parents? What if my parents had expected me to provide half the family income when I got married? What if no one had helped me take care of my financial responsibilities? Get an education? I was seeing firsthand the important role our unique heritage and environment play in creating the people we become, that role often due to the society into which we were born.

During the next several days, presentations became less generic, less filled with terms I'd studied in language courses. Speakers introduced me to new terms such as: food insecurity, malnourishment, primary commodity export revenues, subsistence farming, severe wasting. All this in advance of our upcoming field visits into the interior, the *sertão*. Because the vocabulary grew more technical in certain instances, some of the interpreters opted out, so I worked in the booth alone, without backup for extended periods. Located just behind the audience but close enough for the interpreter to see the speaker, the booth looked like a double version of an old phone booth. A small table (equipped with a microphone, a pencil, blank sheets of paper, earphones, electrical equipment) barely fit in the small booth. Unlike a phone booth, however, its fourth wall remained open since, ideally, an interpreter needs to also keep speakers within visual range, in case the audio fails, to look for other clues.

Occasionally, participants stood in a circle with their backs to me. When someone shifted I couldn't see the speaker, so I was forced to move around—microphone in hand—to ensure I didn't lose sight of the speaker. Interpreters often have to read lips if the audio isn't coming through or if the speaker is soft-spoken.

In most instances, the speakers forgot about me, not stopping to allow me to catch up. I wrote in my journal that night:

> There are only about four or five of us who carry the load [as interpreters]. But I love the work. I translate everything, from the highest level—the simultaneous translating—to the field work we'll be involved in, to a love note from a Brazilian girl to one of our guys (she wrote at the bottom, "ask Linda to translate"). From the sublime to the ridiculous. I love it, love it, love it.

Some of the people I worked with knew the pressure I would face when I returned home. One new friend told me point-blank, "If you don't go home, do something fast, get out of your Kirkwoodsuburbia-housewife situation, the anger inside you will explode somehow."

I told her truthfully that I didn't know how I could go back to that life.

"I want to live a life like these dynamic, motivated, fascinating women. I have a stronger sense of who I am here," I told her.

This same friend followed up with, "Is this the real you, here in Brazil?"

I didn't answer, but thought I knew the answer. When I'd started out, the only North American interpreter/translator, I remained mostly apart from the other interpreters. The Brazilians ran everything. But gradually, maybe witnessing my hard work, they made me an integral part of the team. One Brazilian, João, even asked if we could meet to work on specific vocabulary terms in advance of lectures about agrarian reform. With every passing day, the vocabulary became more specific. Improvising when a speaker talked about land rights, class structure, market liberalization, rural social welfare, it became more difficult. I—along with the Brazilian interpreters—needed to anticipate specialized vocabulary guest speakers might use.

After a few days, the group left Itaparica, headed back to the mainland, to Salvador, then we flew north to Recife, another port city, as well as the capital of the state of Pernambuco. Founded in 1537 by the Portuguese, it was the first slave port in the Americas.

Shortly after our arrival, I walked around Recife with members of the North American group. We walked down cobblestone streets, past white stucco homes with red tile roofs, past donkeys milling around. Shoe stores seemed to pop up on every corner, as well as men making some kind of juice out of sugar cane. Friends greeted one another by kissing one cheek, then the other. A few of us bought churros served with condensed milk. Others drank *graviola* (like pineapple juice) or herbal tea from a *cúia*, a special gourd. Vendors sold fried fish, fruit, tokens (*fichas*) for the phone.

With each successive leg of the trip to less populated, less modern locations, changes I was undergoing took hold. A bit more confident, more assertive, more independent. Less insecure, needy, seeking others' approval. Every day, every mile away from my home caused the most recent mental picture of myself to fade a little, as though produced by an overexposed photograph, exposed to light, to the elements. Rio signaled a completely new experience for me, but as a major international city, I still maintained a toehold in the known world. Traveling north to the state of Bahia—to Salvador, to the island of Itaparica—life became more remote, rustic. Everything seemed new. I needed to be ready to use my Portuguese around the clock, if necessary, like a doctor on call. Finally, for this last leg, we ventured into the *sertão*, the backlands referred to in Brazilian literature.

Cut off from everything I knew, from everything familiar—my children, my home, my family in Kirkwood, Missouri, even my language of origin—this became a real test. I floundered in an ocean of new experiences, new people, new food, a new reality. It amounted to sink or swim. I experienced a gradual turning away from my past; I'd been set adrift. It reminded me of science fiction shows in which the actors are virtually stripped of their essence. But in my case the subtractions included acting in a submissive fashion, living in an atmosphere where foreign languages didn't form an integral part of my life, tamping down my thoughts, my opinions. What remained now was the start of a core: threadbare but authentic.

From Recife to Natal, we headed further north, still on the coast, closer to the equator than I'd ever traveled. One of the Brazilians shared with me that technicians assigned to this remote part of Brazil sometimes died from the isolation, from living conditions. "*Naoda*," he called their emotional state, a term I couldn't find in any of my dictionaries.

Ten hours' drive by jeep from Natal to the *sertão*, we traveled due west, to no-man's-land, about two hundred miles from the equator, as though we tottered on the edge of the globe. Nothing to see but scrubland, an occasional windmill, some bushes, brush, mud homes, vultures, low-lying vegetation, a distant mountain every once in a while, dead animals, cacti, holes, ruts all over the road. No billboards or signposts or hotels along the way, which added to my sense of isolation. The bush/scrubland (*o mato*) gave off a sweet smell, almost like marijuana.

We visited a clinic on our way, where doctors and dentists saw patients once a week. A nursery with four child-sized dirty beds stood out. Clinic administrators told us that patients rarely wanted to have operations, that they preferred to die of a lethal disease than risk dying in the hospital.

We stopped in a small community with seventy families. One woman ran the entire enterprise, had built it from nothing. A well, a church, a cave-like back room where women cooked food for everyone, a meeting room, and a community center formed part of this small town. A monkey rocked itself in a hammock; a parrot sang to itself in a makeshift kitchen, speaking Portuguese, of course. A little girl, ten, whose mother had died in a lover's quarrel, leaving behind eleven children, showed me the club used to kill her mother.

The community prepared a special dish for us, bacon from a pig they'd slaughtered in our honor. Flies covered each strip of bacon like sprinkles on an ice cream cone, but not eating it would have been considered rude. I shooed the flies away as onlookers watched me, then took a few tiny bites, careful not to grimace, trying to remember the sacrifice they'd made in preparing this special dish for us.

People in the community stared at us, emotionless. Members of the local population asked questions, which I translated for the North Americans, as well as the North Americans' answers. "What do your homes look like?" "Do you have children?" "What do you eat for meals?" the Brazilians wanted to know.

I met women who looked fifty or sixty but were actually in their early thirties, gaunt, stooped over. Ten-year-olds looked six. At five foot four, I towered over most of the women and many of the men. The women's hair lay stringy, lifeless on their shoulders, the teeth of others missing or dark. They washed their clothes in reservoirs, the same place they drew their water. Someone in the village had built a well, but only recently. Children swarmed around us. One hammock fit two to ten people. I caught sight of beds with no mattresses, bedding, or pillows, stained in patches. No screens protected the open windows from outside elements. Goats remained penned up to avoid being shot if they wandered onto a landowner's property. The women cooked over open fires. Everyone wanted their pictures taken. Signs on some doors said in Portuguese, "God came so that you might have life." Portraits of the Pope and of Jesus hung side by side in almost every home. Many men had left to find work at a farming cooperative.

Locals constructed their homes using bricks, although some structures looked more like mud huts, with perimeter fences made out of sticks. A drought had hovered over their lives for five years, but lately severe floods had wiped out homes and crops in the path of the floodwaters, the ground too dry to absorb any of the moisture. Light came from lanterns. Mud covered their floors, with an open pit for cooking. A small engine the size of a tractor's served as a generator for everyone in the community. It spurted, wheezed, as though on its last legs. One mother went crazy, they told me, because of a lack of food. She lived in a special home somewhere; I wondered if she received adequate professional help.

We drove from community to community in the outback, stopped at the Centro Social Urbano, a place for children between the ages of three and eighteen. The kids wore little T-shirts, white with blue print. They sat bare bottomed on cold-looking concrete floors, singing. Some ate dried, salted, putrid-looking meat, or sticks of crude brown sugar. Their stomachs looked bloated, distended.

Translating on behalf of a North American woman, I asked leaders of a local community group why they didn't band together, demand their rights from big landowners. As the Brazilians called back their answers, the room grew even warmer, people pressing closer to me to listen and reply to various exchanges in Portuguese and English. I thought I might faint from the heat, from the closeness of people, from emotions pouring over me: sadness, helplessness, anxiety. How could they adapt to this environment? I wondered.

One community we visited seemed organized. A few people had electricity, broken down television sets. They showed us hammocks they'd made, asked me to read their books (translating them) to the North Americans. They looked at pictures of my children, of others' children, following us around as though trailing movie stars. They clung to me, hung on as though they'd won the prize at a fair, speaking a version of Portuguese quite different than what I'd learned in graduate school. Different slang expressions. Different accents, specific to the various regions we visited. Incorrect grammar was the norm. Vocabulary specific to topics that hadn't previously formed part of my lexicon. I kept plugging away, tried to acclimate my ear, make allowances for grammatical deviations, learn the most important idioms, listen much more attentively than I would have—did—in English. The Brazilian interpreters in our group, as well as the people in these remote areas, educated me, told me when I'd made mistakes, helped me till I became more comfortable.

After a few days of this, I found a phone in an office of one of the local leaders. I tried to call home, desperate to hear my children's voices. The phone rang endlessly. I wrote in my journal, "I feel incredibly isolated," but added, "No more Brazil as a buffer between your past and future. It's here."

One challenge with interpreting consists in not being allowed to insert your own words/opinions into the mix when you're interpreting for someone else; your job is to stay as close as possible to the words of the person for whom you're interpreting. That sometimes proved difficult because a few North American college students in our group asked questions I thought bordered on inappropriate. One time in the outback they asked me to teach the kids "The Chicken Song," a kids' song used to get children to move around like chickens, for exercise. I told them I thought that seemed like a bad idea since the kids seemed older than the song's target audience, even though appearance-wise they looked younger. I feared they might take the song as an insult. But the North American students insisted, so I did my job, while the Brazilian kids laughed, clapped at the song, enjoying the experience. I'd miscalculated the Brazilian kids' response.

Everywhere we went, roads barely allowed passage, filled with ruts, uneven and narrow. The jeeps we rode in navigated the roads with difficulty, swaying widely from side to side like a small ship in high seas, rocking us dangerously. The local government hadn't paved them, so drivers developed their own system, a mental map of how to compensate for hills and valleys.

As we traveled we saw people selling meat—rat and bird meat, we were told when we stopped to investigate. Some even ate cobra meat after removing the venom. Availability of beef and chicken remained scant, so inhabitants found other sources of protein: rats, wild birds, snakes. They possessed no money or stores to buy clothing, curtains, tablecloths, so they used hand-me-down items, scavenged material. They compensated for the minuses in their lives with very little complaining, at least that I heard.

I witnessed people doing what they could to survive. Sometimes at night, unable to sleep after a day packed with so many experiences, so many rapid-fire words I'd spoken, I wondered if that's what I needed to do to live a more vital life. Maybe I'd begun to learn from these resourceful, brave Brazilians that I needed to make my life count.

They wanted to know about our lives, our children, our families, wanted to know what crops and livestock we "raised" at home. The concept of welfare seemed unfamiliar to many of our hosts in the outback. It didn't even translate well: *bem-estar*, literally, "well-being" in English. Most of our new friends didn't know how to read, lived in conditions of extreme poverty where formal education was certainly not a given.

Everywhere we went, overpowering heat saturated makeshift homes we visited, the heat so dry I felt caked with dust most of the day. People crowded around me, trying to be part of exchanges, which only intensified my feelings. Multiple voices instructed me simultaneously: "Tell her this." "Tell him that." "Ask their opinion of such and such," or "What are they doing?" Vocabulary spanned every conceivable topic: from liberation theology to birth control. From cooking practices to money issues. From how they spent their free time to how they fed a family of six, seven, ten with only subsistence farming to bring in funds. What did these Americans think of Madonna? Of Mel Gibson?

They usually forgot that I constituted a single person, not a translation machine, that no one could clone me into three or four people to turn their Portuguese words into English, or English words into Portuguese. As though I knew every single word in the Portuguese language, every single idiom, localism, slang word . . . But still, I loved it. Being in that environment, playing an important role, stretched me in ways I didn't know I could be stretched. Taught me lessons I didn't know I needed to learn: about the human spirit, about the Portuguese language, about beating the odds, about courage.

Some lived in cave-like homes, usually with only one window, and my nostrils filled with smells of sweat, urine, cooking oil, all of it magnified by their close quarters. But they welcomed us with coffee or tea. Always, as though welcoming us into grand mansions. Their faces lit up with amusement, seeing a gringa—me—speaking their language, Portuguese. Maybe it flattered them, witnessing someone with such an interest in their language, someone who'd invested time, effort, using this language to bridge gaps between people from different countries, different cultures. Maybe I considered myself a small part of their community, at least in some transient way.

After a few days, we continued our travels on the rutted, ruined roads back to Natal, where North Americans and Brazilians discussed their findings: the cause of so much hunger in Northeastern Brazil. The group asserted that the problem didn't lie with the existing drought; it lay with fences, fences confining them to tiny, infertile spits of land due to the power of rich, oppressive landowners. Making it into a rhyme of sorts, they chanted: "*Não a seca, mas a cerca.*" "Not the drought, [but] the fence." But my job wasn't to find answers. My job as an interpreter consisted of ensuring that they heard everything, understood everything, that I'd left no words on the cutting-room floor. From translating verses of "The Chicken Song" to reporting on causes of hunger, my opinion didn't matter on any given subject, if I agreed or disagreed. That wasn't my job.

One of our final nights in Brazil, I wrote in my journal:

I love all the people and the noise and the music and the smells and the diversity of life you find. It is such a source of constant stimulation. And the Brazilians are great—as different from Americans as they can be, but fantastic . . . de tudo um pouco. A little of everything. For the first time in my life I don't want time to march on; I want it to stand still so I can stay here (but bring the kids). What can I do when I go home to change that reality, to live the Serenity Prayer, accepting what I can't change and changing what I can change?

Increasingly, I channeled the words of feminists, women I'd read about who overcame obstacles to find their true calling. I'd set off on this journey, cut off from my previous base of knowledge. I'd been tested to see how I operated in total isolation, able to draw on very little from my previous life for support. Like my year in Spain, something about speaking these languages—Spanish in Spain, Portuguese in Brazil—allowed me to shed my former skin, assume a different persona, at least temporarily. New language equaled new Linda somehow.

In the *sertão*, part of my isolation arose because of our small groups, ten or so to a group, with one Portuguese translator in each. Surely, a reason existed for this, a reason for being cut off from familiar sights, sounds, experiences? A reason for being introduced to people from a developing part of Brazil with so little, children wearing rags, with beautiful little faces, struggling to live full lives, eating dried-up, scabby meat. Often I became overwhelmed with emotion; it was too much. But then I told myself that if they could live like this and still smile, laugh, how dare I cry? I saw this special kind of strength that made them fighters, people who never gave up, despite overwhelming odds stacked against them. Maybe if I took a small portion of their courage, I thought, I could transfer it into my own life, at least in my own way.

BACK HOME

After twenty-five days away from home, twenty of them spent in Brazil, I returned to Kirkwood, Missouri, a changed person in many respects. Having participated in something transformative, the question now became—in keeping with the conditional tense—could I continue? Would I continue to forge a new path? Had I made enough headway in twenty-five days to create lasting change?

On the way home, I bought a flimsy, inexpensive coaster I found tucked out of the way in a Miami airport gift shop. I still have it. It reads: "If you don't do it, you'll never know what would have happened if you had done it." My new mantra. Conditional tense: What shape would your life take if you went home, made different choices? What could it become?

After marathon talks with my husband, he changed his mind, said he did want to accompany our children and me to the East Coast, that he'd get a job in the DC area in the banking sector. I checked the box on my job offer: "I WILL accept . . ." took it to the post office, and got busy with preparing for the move.

During the next month I made numerous arrangements, both in the DC area as well as in Kirkwood. Two weeks before our departure date, I wondered why I was the only one finalizing arrangements. I asked him about it.

Sitting with me in our beige family room after we'd put the kids to bed, he confessed that he preferred a more traditional lifestyle, explaining his attitude. "I want a hands-on wife at home with the children. I just think two-career families create chaos," he argued, repeating what he'd told me before, when I'd taken the language tests in DC. Pausing a few seconds, he continued. "I want to be happy. I'm going to stay in St. Louis." Meanwhile, I'd gone too far, emotionally and physically, to slide back into a life that no longer fit.

Two weeks later, the four of us drove away from our home in Kirkwood, Missouri, in our beat-up red-and-beige Chevy Vega to a condominium I'd rented in Columbia, Maryland. My husband accompanied us to Maryland, then flew back to Missouri alone. My children and I began our new lives.

In many ways life presented more difficulties in Maryland than what I'd left behind: physical, financial, emotional obstacles to overcome. I set out without a support system, handling everything by myself. My family of origin maintained their distance, not understanding my need to lead a different kind of life. People who knew something about my exodus from Kirkwood, who knew the work and sacrifices the move entailed, sometimes asked in the months and even years ahead, "Was it worth it?" I waited a few years before answering the question. Too early to know.

I knew that every person I met in Brazil—Brazilians and North Americans—helped me begin to discover—or maybe rediscover—the essence of Linda. Helped me remember my worth, that I could live a different life than women in my family, than many of the women in my community. That discovering my true identity became a calling, the act of charting a new course in my life, of exploring places and people previously beyond my reach. I marveled that these important messages reached me via another language. How many books by feminist authors had I read before going to Brazil? At least a dozen. Books by Simone de Beauvoir and Gloria Steinem. Colette Dowling's *The Cinderella Complex*, Betty Friedan's *The Feminine Mystique*, Marilyn French's *The Women's Room*, Susie Orbach's *Fat Is a Feminist Issue*, Alice Walker's *The Color Purple*, and others. The books nudged me, reminding me of other ways to make my way in the world. But not till I traveled to Brazil, heard these women's ideas spoken, not until I lived them, both in Portuguese and in English, did they became flesh-and-blood examples and not abstractions. Only then did I begin to internalize such previously radical-sounding ideas. The country and people of Brazil and the beautiful Portuguese language signaled the start of my journey. Accepting a job with a government agency in the Washington, DC, area also signaled the beginning steps of carving out a more authentic identity for myself, leaving behind a life that no longer fit.

Shortly before moving to Maryland with my children, one night I had a strange dream. In my dream I remained in Brazil but climbed up through a narrow tunnel, alone. When I got to the top, I found myself far above the earth. I found it exhilarating, yet frightening. Once I reached the pinnacle, lots of people stood ready to help me as I climbed over a trellis-type structure. I held onto many outstretched hands. At one point I swung over the earth, a globe—green, blue, brown. I saw the globe clearly as I swung back and forth. Somehow my Brazilian friends made an appearance . . . with me. The vision in my dream stayed with me, made me hopeful about my decision to leave behind family and friends. Made me feel less alone.

I often wonder about the fate of those amazing men, women, and children I met in Brazil, particularly those living in the backlands, the *sertão*, as well as those living in the favelas. Remembering my short time in the area, I'm filled with many emotions, above all, gratitude for lessons I learned in Brazil, for being inspired to take the next steps after returning home. I'd received lessons about life's randomness, about courage in the face of overwhelming obstacles.

Standing in my rented condo with my children in the fall of 1985, looking at their sad faces, at our new, sparsely furnished home, mixed feelings washed over me. No one could deny that I'd come a long way on my journey of self-discovery, a journey that began with a Spanish detour in 1970, picking up momentum again in 1985. But I still had a long way to go. The conditional tense played out in real time: Would I succeed in the next phase, in Maryland? Could I overcome the many obstacles, including numerous detractors who held me back? Could I make my children happy? Could I hang onto those tiny seeds of confidence I'd planted in Brazil, internalize all I'd learned? I honestly didn't know yet.

3

THE PAST PROGRESSIVE TENSE

One Step at a Time

THE PAST PROGRESSIVE TENSE—*signals something happening at some point in the past, an ongoing, continuing action.*

EXAMPLE: *"Zambia was pushing me farther afield, away from my previous reference points."*

JUNE 1990 — LUSAKA, ZAMBIA

Though I turned the volume up higher on the VCR, it wasn't loud enough to mask nearby gunfire. How to gauge how far away the booming sounds originated? For all I knew, a few houses away . . . or a mile. I had no experience with this. But noise blasted my eardrums. Judging from overlapping sounds, it might have come from several guns firing simultaneously. I looked out the bedroom window of the home where I was house-sitting to see if I spotted flashes from a gun. I vaguely remembered seeing that in the Westerns I halfway watched with my older brothers growing up.

No one considered that my pre-trip training should include measures for defending myself against rioters. I had no lessons from which to draw. No one had warned me that this might be a possibility: angry, desperate people with guns. On my first TDY (temporary duty travel) to Zambia I'd brought along a special metal gadget smaller than a pack of cigarettes. You inserted it into your hotel door lock to make the conventional lock more secure. I'd decided against bringing the bulletproof shield disguised as a briefcase. When a State Department official offered it before my first TDY to Zambia during the summer of 1988 I'd thought it a ridiculous plan. Using a briefcase as a shield? How absurd. I couldn't picture being able to react faster than a speeding bullet, having to whip the briefcase up to chest level from the side of my body in time to protect myself. I'd barely managed to catch a softball when I played with friends during my childhood; I doubted I'd improved much.

I declined the official's offer. "I don't really think I have quick enough reflexes for this to work," I confessed, wincing at the thought. "But thank you anyway."

"Suit yourself," he'd replied, shrugging his shoulders, probably hoping that better prospects than me would eventually appear in his office. In hindsight, I wish I'd asked why he thought I needed to protect myself in Lusaka. I believed Zambia to be a stable country, a place where former British colonists still lived. What made him think I might need to defend myself from gunfire? What *didn't* I know? But I didn't ask, not wanting to reveal my nervousness or naivete. That first TDY in 1988 had also marked the first time I traveled to the African continent; I hoped they wouldn't think I was a coward in addition to being a rookie. And I hadn't needed to protect myself on that first TDY, and a second one a year later had also passed without incident.

But the briefcase didn't seem so ridiculous on this third assignment to Zambia, as I continued to look out the window, as though I could use my sense of sight to see rounds of gunfire being exchanged. In reality, I was less than ill-equipped to respond to whatever was happening outside those four walls; I might as well have walked outside with a white flag.

Meanwhile, the movie I'd selected to muffle the gunfire—*The Blues Brothers*—lacked what I needed: a distraction, the ability to mask potential danger. I thought it was supposed to be a musical comedy? I'd played it twice, still wasn't laughing. John Belushi and Dan Aykroyd were comedians, right? I didn't have any interest in actually watching the movie, but the music, along with the actors' over-the-top behavior, partially muted the sporadic rat-a-tat-tat outside. But it sounded like it was coming closer.

I found no other movies in the homeowners' stash that didn't belong to the horror or shoot-'em-up category: *The Shining, Raging Bull, Alien, Apocalypse Now* . . . *The Blues Brothers* would have to do. Not my house, not my movie collection, but yes, my current problem to deal with. Alone.

The house looked high-tech. I managed to figure out how to turn on the TV, but a fixed announcement in English spread across the screen: programming canceled. The words were frozen: "Some disturbances have broken out in Lusaka, but everything is under control. Remain calm. Go about your normal lives. Those breaking the law will be arrested."

When the rioting ended, local publications maintained that the unrest was the worst in Zambian history, with 27 civilians killed, 2 policemen shot or stoned to death, another 153 people injured, and over 1,000 arrested. Dozens of stores were looted, vehicles set on fire, with mobs rampaging through the streets, trying to take over the TV and radio stations, and many of the roads, according to press reports.

Prior to coming to Lusaka, my third assignment to Zambia's capital, I'd agreed to house-sit for a State Department couple—the Hellmans—while they traveled back to DC for family leave. Why not? I didn't realize the house was located in the middle of nowhere, far from the center of Lusaka, from civilization. Didn't realize their alarm system would be out of commission or that the Hellmans would accidentally leave their walkie-talkie back at the embassy—my only link to the US Marines guarding the US embassy—leaving me incommunicado. Didn't realize there'd be no way for me to communicate with anyone, even by phone, since I didn't know anyone's phone numbers at the embassy. Most important, I didn't realize the country would be in the midst of turmoil during my stay at their home. Adding to my predicament: I knew no one. I'd just arrived. Friends from my 1988 and 1989 assignments to the country had left Lusaka for other postings in 1990.

I didn't know riots would break out the day I landed at the Lusaka airport. Didn't know looters and rioters were potentially targeting homes of embassy employees from the US and Europe since Westerners arrived with household goods containing three years of hard-to-find nonperishable goods for their tours. Didn't realize that no one would keep track of me, my whereabouts, my safety. Didn't know rioters would take over the road to the airport shortly after my arrival, making any possible departures by air an impossibility.

I walked away from the TV during a scene in *The Blues Brothers* featuring Dan Aykroyd with John Belushi singing "Everybody Loves Somebody" on stage. Distractions worked only to a point. I slowly pulled the bedroom curtains aside again to peek outside, careful to hide my face.

I spotted a short man walking around the grounds, shorter than me, under five foot four, maybe a hundred pounds or so, not wearing a uniform. He appeared to be unarmed, but that could be a good sign or a bad sign, right? I didn't know if he represented friend or foe. Could he be the Hellmans' guard? I couldn't exactly ask him without risking exposure, my safety. "Hello. Are you the Hellmans' guard, or does your plan consist of ransacking their home, stealing all their food, then killing the only witness/me?"

Why did he continue to stroll around the grounds, no sign of urgency in his gait? Didn't he hear the gunfire? He certainly didn't look official, casually strolling around, fussing with his walkie-talkie. Whom did he need to communicate with? Rioters or a security company? Meanwhile, the Hellmans' dog ("Greasy") didn't appear to recognize him. He—the dog—proved to be a major catalyst for concern during the night, yipping at every leaf or twig the wind skittered across the yard, at every rustling of tree branches. He had a low threshold for sounding his canine alarm. Whatever the identity of the man outside, his slightest movement sent the dog into a barking frenzy. Of no use to me, Greasy looked like he was part Chihuahua, small, high-strung; he wouldn't scare a squirrel. Regardless, his owners had put me in charge of his care while I remained in their house, part of the house-sitting arrangement. Besides, we only had each other.

When it came time to let him out to do his business, I opened the door a crack and gently nudged him outside, watching as he zigzagged across the yard, looking for the perfect patch of grass. I accompanied him a few times, first ensuring no one was in sight. The guard—or whatever his role—appeared unfazed by the small dog's barking, and eventually the dog tired of yipping, returning to the door to be let in.

An hour earlier, when I had first heard gunfire, I decided the safest place to sequester myself was the master bedroom. I remembered asking someone the summer before—casual chitchat, icebreaker conversation at an embassy cocktail party—what to do if danger seemed imminent. I struggled to reconstruct that conversation, the words that person—the regional security officer/RSO—had told me. Safe haven, I think he called it. Why hadn't I paid more attention?

A long, narrow hallway led from the main part of the house to the back, with doors every twenty feet or so and rooms jutting off to the side, partitioning the home into different living spaces. I carefully latched each bolt as I made my way back, sliding the bar to the side. Safe haven. Door by door. Lock by lock. Bolt-barrel slide locks, each with a horizontal bar I slid into a receptacle on the opposite side of the door with a satisfying click. I couldn't remain in the living room. Too exposed. Like being in a fishbowl, with glass everywhere, blinding me to goings-on outside, to unknown forces lurking. Not good. I needed to surveil my surroundings.

I locked my way back into the bedroom, door by door, lock by lock as gunfire seemed to grow closer. If someone gained entry to the home via the main entrance, in theory at least, residents could head to the master bedroom, closing, then padlocking each door along the way. It bought you some time. That would come in handy for me in coming days, as I repeated the ritual every night. I did wonder if the locks would hold if a man—men?—threw his weight against these doors. Could they shoot the locks off with their weapons? But if the looters' goal consisted in reaching the Hellmans' three years of food in the house's storage room, they'd find it before encountering the doors I'd locked. Maybe then they'd leave? Maybe I represented the means to an end, not an end in itself?

Most embassy homes I'd seen in Southern Africa resembled

fortresses, equipped with guards, locals who did or didn't take their jobs seriously. Solid concrete walls surrounded properties with broken glass cemented on top of perimeter walls to discourage would-be intruders, along with heavy-duty gates to keep people out. This house was less secure, more vulnerable. The requisite wall with jagged glass arrayed on top was present, but the property's front gate wouldn't thwart anyone's efforts, not even an active child. Easy to scale, the jagged top of the wall served as an unnecessary addition. Besides, when the embassy driver dropped me off, we discovered that no one preceding us had bothered to lock the gate. I had no idea who might be lurking outside the house, or inside, for that matter.

After several hours inside, assessing the situation, I contemplated my next move, considered my options. My thoughts turned to the man in charge of having me picked up at the airport, of transporting me to my home away from home for the next six weeks: Craig. I'd met him a few hours before news of the rioting circulated, shortly after my arrival. I'd been dropped off at his house by the driver, per Craig's instructions. After introductions, I got down to business with him. Had that really happened just a few hours ago?

"I need to get food, water," I reminded Craig. "Since I understand that the house is relatively far away, I'll have no way to buy anything at the embassy commissary and, as you know, you can't drink the local water, and I'll have no access to the Hellmans' supply. Plus, the driver told me on the way here that the family's alarm doesn't work. I'm not comfortable without one."

He assured me that a) he'd fix the alarm system when he dropped me off at the Hellmans' home and b) he'd take me to the embassy commissary on the way. None of that happened. Without consulting me, once news of the rioting reached him he instructed the embassy driver to transport me straight to the Hellmans' home.

"You're OK as long as you arrive before dark," he informed me when I protested this new arrangement, as though nighttime signaled the advent of unspeakable dangers?

The driver, Sandy, balked at Craig's instructions to drive me to the Hellmans' home, said he'd heard on his radio that rioting had turned more violent, with cars being stopped, roads being taken over by protesters, by mobs of people. He didn't want to travel on remote roads. But Craig—higher ranking than the driver—insisted on his plan. I subsequently learned from another embassy employee that Craig subscribed to the magazine *Soldier of Fortune*. That fact alone spoke volumes about his cavalier attitude. Mollycoddling a TDYer, me, held no interest for him. But Sandy, a local, acted nervous, making me all the more nervous; he could better assess the situation than anyone else.

When we arrived at what would be my home away from home for several weeks, the sun had already gone down; sunsets seemed to happen more quickly in Africa than in the States. One minute the sun shone like a huge ball of red fire on the horizon; the next minute it had dropped below the horizon, leaving you in darkness.

The house appeared to have no lights on, looked dark as a tomb. No sign of a guard patrolling the grounds. No one greeted me, asked for credentials. The driver stopped the car inside the unlocked gate long enough for me to grab my suitcase, as well as keys to the house Craig had passed on to me; then he sped off to avoid potential rioters and roadblocks. He had his own problems to deal with. I was on my own.

A one-story ranch, the modest home had a living room at the hub, with picture windows on several sides, a kitchen next to the living room, and a hallway leading back to the master bedroom. Side doors along the hallway opened up to other bedrooms. I found light switches as well as the storeroom.

I had no way to get food or water. For safekeeping, the Hellmans had padlocked most of their food in advance of their extended stay in the States, that is, except for a jar of peanut butter, a box of saltines, an opened box of Pop-Tarts, and a few jars of baby food, along with some dog food. I spread a swipe of peanut butter on a cracker, ate a cherry Pop-Tart for dessert, then grabbed a second Pop-Tart before locking my way back to the bedroom. I turned on every light in the house before I left the living room, not knowing if that made me safer or more vulnerable. I wanted to create the impression of an army of people standing at the ready to thwart potential trouble. On the other hand, I did wonder if maybe that signaled easy entry for would-be intruders, lighting their way. I didn't know but needed to think every step through. In a sense, I continued to work as a translator, translating nonverbal information, converting clues into actionable steps.

Ensconced in the bedroom, my living space reduced to an average-sized room with an adjoining bathroom, I half listened to *The Blues Brothers* movie, half listened to gunfire and unidentifiable loud rumbling I heard coming from nearby streets. Did I hear the sound of tanks? What did tanks even sound like? I couldn't even google anything since in 1990 most people didn't have access to the Internet. Why hadn't I watched more war movies? The sounds I heard sounded ominous.

One thing remained certain: except for a high-strung dog glued to my side, I had no one to call. Family, friends, even colleagues back in the States didn't realize my situation posed any danger since Zambia held little interest for mainstream Western media sources, due to its status as a remote African country rarely appearing in the news. Nor did anyone at the US embassy wonder about the status of one of a revolving door of regular TDYers who passed through Lusaka in more peaceful times; they were dealing with their own challenges during this unrest. The person in charge of me—Craig—seemed to have more important things on his mind. I also wondered, if the situation became dire enough to warrant evacuating US embassy personnel and American citizens, would a TDYer's name even appear on such a roster? If it did, surely it would appear at the bottom of that list. Not a comforting thought. I didn't have a name yet; I was just an anonymous TDYer, house-sitting out in the boonies.

I tried to settle in for the night, *The Blues Brothers* movie still playing in the background. Better to listen to that movie on repeat than to imagine the worst, listening for frightening sounds close by. At some point I located a long pole beneath the bed, its purpose unclear to me. I fell asleep still wearing my clothes, gripping the pole tightly in my hands. Before lying down, really just to calm myself down, I wrote a letter to a State Department friend I'd met two summers before in Lusaka, someone now posted to New Delhi.

"I think I would feel much more frightened if I *could*, but since I'm all alone and there's nothing I can do and no one to call, I'm storing up adrenaline, quietly . . . and writing you." Ending on a lighter note, I added, "When I said I didn't want to turn forty this summer, I didn't mean it literally."

Lying in bed that first night, I couldn't stop obsessing about my situation. I wondered if angry Zambians congregated outside, ready to storm the house. Wondered what I'd do if they did, how I'd protect myself. Rioting that had broken out shortly after my arrival in Lusaka had been in protest to an unpopular government decision to nearly triple the price of mealie meal, a corn-based grain used in porridge, *ugali*, a staple of Zambians' diet. The price soared from five cents a pound to twelve cents a pound, this in a country where most Zambians earned about twenty-one dollars a month. People had become understandably outraged, taking to the streets.

Since most Zambians were ill-equipped to feed their families, to pay the nearly triple prices of their staple food, it made sense that they might turn their attention to homes of more affluent Westerners living in their country, might contemplate raiding full pantries of people far more fortunate, guests in their country. I suspected I'd follow the same course of action if I had a family to feed and no way to provide them with food they needed to survive. Desperate times call for desperate measures, as they say. So, although I understood the origin of their rioting and looting, the mindset of those who had lost patience, I knew this constituted a particularly dangerous situation. I didn't want to become collateral damage, a statistic, in the wrong place at the wrong time. This was all too real. I wasn't an actor in some movie.

I tried to repeat positive thoughts to myself, congratulate myself for progress I'd made in recent years. I tried to concentrate on how far I'd come since those first days, weeks, months moving from Missouri to Maryland with my small children only five years before. I focused on all the changes I'd made in my life . . . so my mind wouldn't leap to a variety of worst-case scenarios at hand.

That first morning in Lusaka, I woke up after sleeping fitfully through the night. I made my bed, tucked in sheets, fluffed pillows— still half asleep—then suddenly heard a man's voice no more than three feet behind me, a chipper voice that sounded very real.

"Time to get up! Time to get up! Let's go! It's 7:00 a.m.! You don't want to be late!"

My initial fear was that someone had broken into the house while I slept and was taunting me. After that initial shock, I whipped around, realizing what I'd heard was an alarm clock, programmed using the recording of an American male voice. I had no idea such a clock existed, but it worked, shocked me awake. After deactivating the alarm clock, I showered, changed out of the stretched-out clothes I'd slept in, unbolted the locks leading back to the main part of the house from my safe haven, turned off dozens of interior and exterior lights I'd switched on the night before. Nothing appeared disturbed.

I fed Greasy, found a meager breakfast for myself (Greasy enjoyed better food than me), and waited outside for the embassy duty driver, who appeared at 8:00 a.m. to transport me to the US embassy. I'd never been so happy to see someone.

Moving from Missouri to Maryland five years before had presented me with far greater challenges than I'd anticipated, although I hadn't known what to expect in advance. That ignorance-is-bliss reality, beginning with the hundred boxes I packed in Kirkwood, Missouri, and unpacked in Columbia, Maryland, turned out to be a gift. If I'd known the difficulties that lay ahead, I probably wouldn't have been foolhardy enough to leave Kirkwood, to begin a new life.

That first year with my two small children passed by in a blur. No family. No friends at first. A single parent. Working full-time again after more than a four-year gap. Adding to my challenge: I'd never played the role of full-time employee and parent (single parent) simultaneously.

Until moving out of Kirkwood in 1985, I'd known little about practical matters. The house and car were in my husband's name, not mine. I held no credit cards. When I needed to buy a dryer (my condo rental in Maryland didn't have one), no banks would give me a credit card initially. I had no credit history, a distant work history. My financial footprint barely left an imprint.

I'd underestimated actual expenses, as well as how much of my paycheck would go to taxes, naively believing that my biweekly gross and net salaries would be identical. Before moving, I created a preliminary budget using my gross income, not my take-home pay, at least 30 percent less. I underestimated how many times my car would break down, requiring expensive repairs (four times that first year). I underestimated how much more expensive living on the East Coast would be than the Midwest (more than 85 percent more expensive). I underestimated the physical toll of single parenting: getting up at 5:00 a.m. each day, doing 100 percent of the parenting, housework, bill paying, home repairs, laundry, cooking, getting by on five hours of sleep a night before heading to work. I underestimated the backlash roaring at me from all quarters: from my family of origin, from my estranged husband's parents, his siblings, his aunt and uncle. Most important, I underestimated the strong emotions my four-year-old son and two-year-old daughter would exhibit, forced to leave behind their father, both sets of grandparents, three sets of aunts and uncles, five cousins, the only home they'd ever known, not to mention the introduction into their lives of full-time school and/or day care. Perhaps in an attempt to cast a positive light on my lack of preparedness, four months after moving to Maryland I wrote in my journal: "I imagine someday I'll be thankful I remained naive about how difficult it would be to move here."

That first year whizzed past. I moved from one crisis to the next, unwittingly barreling toward the next and the next and the next difficulty. The time I slipped on hardwood stairs, breaking my tailbone. The time three weeks after our arrival when my four-year-old son shot ahead of me (I was carrying my two-year-old daughter) at a local shopping mall, lost to me for fifteen nightmarish minutes. The uphill battles to find a qualified, affordable babysitter for my tiny daughter, and a highly rated preschool for my son. The time we went to a local carnival, dropping by a convenience store afterwards to pick up a box of Rice Krispies for breakfast the next morning. While I paid for the cereal, a fight broke out between armed, angry teenagers in the parking lot. Carrying my daughter and clutching my son's hand, I navigated our way out through the melee as both kids clamored for donuts they'd spotted in the display case. The time I came down with a bad case of poison ivy all over my face and body. The time both children came down with chicken pox—consecutively—when I had no vacation time accrued yet at work. The time I spent negotiating the terms of my divorce, those back-and-forth expensive conversations with lawyers, strained conversations with my estranged husband, the surfeit of emotions this all produced, my lack of support system through it all.

I put one foot in front of the other, though, kept moving ahead, trying to improve the situation. I spent every spare moment, every spare dime I had with and on my children: games, stories I invented, nature walks, movies, museum visits, art projects, duckpin bowling, ice-skating, swimming, playing catch, visits to playgrounds, listening to their stories, just being with them.

Finally, after more than a year, life started to settle down somewhat. Some normalcy. And after our second year in Maryland, I cobbled together enough money to move out of our rental unit, bought a condo at a reduced price in our same little cul-de-sac that the previous renter had all but destroyed. Cat pee had soaked into carpet and flooring; walls were scuffed as though he'd tried to decorate the wall with black marks. Appliances were caked in years of grime; leaves of dead plants had rotted into the warped hardwood floors. An overpowering stench hit me the minute I opened the door for the first time.

All I could afford was an adjustable-rate mortgage, so my payment varied from month to month, each month's bill an unwelcome surprise as it shot up. But it was home. Our home. I made the best of things. Little by little, my children and I made it our sanctuary, our oasis.

After nearly two years in Maryland, I met my future husband, a lifelong bachelor who fell in love with me and was dedicated to my small children. Nervous about remarrying, I made him wait two years before accepting his repeated proposals. We got married after my children and I had lived in Maryland for four years, in 1989. All four of us stood together at our church's altar to exchange vows, my children and I all "marrying" Bill, my husband, their stepfather. To cement that arrangement, the four of us spent "our" honeymoon together, at Disney World.

Through it all, language work I did for the government propelled me forward, gave me hope that I'd made the right decision in leaving my previous life behind, despite having a future that guaranteed nothing. Surrounded by like-minded language lovers, I knew I'd found my tribe, fellow translators who loved foreign languages as much as I did. I couldn't believe they paid me to do such interesting work, work involving translation, language, writing, work that made a difference, that shed light on world events, that enabled US decision-makers at all levels to be informed about international trouble spots, real and potential. I felt needed.

When my supervisors asked me to study an African "click" language—Xhosa (isiXhosa)—shortly after starting my second year in Maryland, I knew I'd made the right choice. Because of the variety of languages I knew, I supported multiple government agencies, but usually in a sterile office setting, unless a tutor guided my studies at a language school. My government office consisted of a desk in a row of desks. I sat there eight hours a day, invisible to most people, similar to my colleagues' workspaces. Dictionaries, headphones, a computer constituted my companions. I had to share a desk that first year. Space remained at a premium. Everyone shared, especially newcomers like me. In short, until I traveled overseas, my job didn't contain elements of espionage, excitement, spy movies.

For a year, 1987 to 1988, I worked one-on-one with two tutors, native speakers of Xhosa. After that year, having done well on compulsory language exams, my supervisors asked me to study Sotho, another "click" language, one-on-one as before, with a native-speaking tutor. And, once again, they paid me to sit in a classroom doing what I loved: studying languages, learning about other cultures, in this case, about sub-Saharan Africa.

Xhosa and Sotho form part of the Bantu language family, two of more than four hundred languages in this category. They're spoken by more than 350 million people in sub-Saharan Africa. Swahili also belongs to this family, and Zulu, a language similar to Xhosa, although considered a distinct language.

After years of studying Romance languages (Spanish, Portuguese, French), as well as a few years tackling German and Russian in graduate school, I ventured into totally foreign territory, not only studying these new languages but also familiarizing myself with their fascinating cultures.

Xhosa is well known as Nelson Mandela's tribal language, for its presence in songs of Miriam Makeba (especially her "click" song: "*Qongqothwane*"). Most recently, creators of Marvel Comics' movie *Black Panther* used Xhosa for the fictitious Wakandans' language.

Both Xhosa and Sotho have distinctive "clicks," features not associated with other languages in their linguistic family (Bantu). Cattle herders traditionally, the Xhosa and Sotho people migrated through Southern Africa, mingling, intermarrying with speakers of

Khoisan languages, which do have clicks. These clicks gradually became incorporated into Xhosa and Sotho.

The Xhosa and Sotho cultures revere traditional healers, including the initiation of young men, part of which involves applying white clay onto the young initiates' bodies. In addition, a betrothed woman's family must still provide a dowry, and the bride undergoes her own initiation rite. All of this stood out as new information for me. I became the proverbial kid in the candy store, learning so much about these people, along with their languages and customs. But I still needed to learn so much more.

Not many government linguists spoke or knew much about African languages in the late 1980s, at least languages in the Bantu family. The universe still rotated on an axis of Spanish, Russian, Arabic. Policymakers showed scant interest in Africa. But with the dissolution of the Soviet Union in the late 1980s, that began to change. US officials realized that a binary proposition—the United States and the Soviet Union—no longer functioned, knew they lacked an awareness of events occurring elsewhere. For the first time since African countries began to gain their independence in the 1960s from colonial powers (France, the Netherlands, Belgium, Portugal, Germany, Spain, Italy, England) this renewed interest manifested itself in work policies, trickled down to linguists, now tasked with mastering certain key African languages. It was pure coincidence that they hired me during this transition.

Unlike Spanish, Portuguese, and French, as well as other languages I'd studied, Bantu languages reaffirmed my personal theory that all languages were not created equal in terms of how easy or difficult they were to learn. The US State Department paved the way for translators in that regard. They developed a ranking system of language difficulty in terms of how long it took—on average—a native English speaker to achieve proficiency in various languages.

The State Department's system contains five categories. The premise of their scale: the further a language student's work takes him from English (if a student speaks English as his first language), the greater the difficulty. So, for example, Category I languages, including Afrikaans, Dutch, Spanish, Portuguese, and Italian, are considered easier to master because they're "closely related to English." On the other hand, Xhosa and Zulu, along with other Bantu languages, belong in Category IV—the second-most challenging—because experts determined that they constitute "languages with significant linguistic and/or cultural differences from English." In other words, the journey from English to these last languages is a longer one for native speakers of English.

English-speaking missionaries altered aspects of the Latin alphabet to accommodate unusual sounds when they first came in contact with African languages in the 1800s. In Xhosa and Sotho, they used English to transcribe these new-sounding languages, but used lower-frequency letters *c*, *x*, *q* to represent the various clicks (dental, lateral, palatal). These unusual clicks contrast with familiar sounds in English.

I didn't sound like myself when I spoke Xhosa or Sotho, nor did I feel quite like myself when I heard it spoken or when I read it; the languages introduced new elements of meaning into my life, similar to the case with Spanish, Portuguese, and other languages I'd studied.

Another reason State Department officials included Bantu languages in their second-most-difficult category dealt with its noun classification system. Nouns belong to different "classes," depending on the category a noun is in. For instance, there's a separate class for humans, another for plants, abstract nouns, diminutives, etc. The class a noun belongs to will determine the prefix it uses, may affect the entire sentence. So even a short sentence in Swahili may change: "I wrote (a) big book." "*Nilibhala kitabu kikubwa.*" But when you make it plural, it becomes: "*Nilibhala vitabu vikubwa,*" "I wrote big books." Book (*kitabu*) and books (*vitabu*) belong to different classes.

Using a dictionary can present difficulties because adding prefixes (or suffixes) to words can alter the spelling of the original word, making it a challenge to find a word's root. For instance, in Sotho, the word for house is "*ntlo,*" a word readily found in most dictionaries. But if I'm translating a sentence that reads: "*Ke ile ka feta ka tlung,*" "I walked through the house," I won't be able to find "*tlung*"—derived from "*ntlo*"—in my dictionary, thus making translation even more difficult, not to mention interpreting, when the language is spoken, a moving target.

Conversing in languages included in this language family poses difficulties for native English speakers. Clicks in Xhosa, Sotho, and Zulu sound unusual for English speakers, as do their consonant clusters, often found at the beginning of a word, making pronunciation (along with misapprehension) an issue. The dental click (written with a *c*) sounds like a "tsk-tsk" sound a parent might make to a child. The lateral click (written with an *x*) sounds like someone trying to get a horse to giddy up. The palatal click (written with a *q*) sounds like a cork popping off a bottle, ranking hardest for a nonnative speaker to make since it doesn't resemble sounds nonnative speakers make.

In order to pronounce words with clicks, you have to position your mouth correctly before speaking certain words. Needless to say, there's a lot of room for error, for misunderstanding when you're translating one of these languages.

For six weeks each summer in 1988, 1989, and 1990 I continued my forward trajectory, moving away from theoretical, classroom aspects of languages I'd studied, away from sitting in a row of government desks, on to those practical experiences of working in a country where people spoke Bantu languages.

My first assignment in Africa took place in 1988. I timed each TDY around my children's summer visits to St. Louis to spend time with their father. On that assignment the new smells hit me first: the ever-present smell of burning leaves, brush, sticks, a sweet new smell, despite having grown up in an era when everyone burned leaves each fall. I saw—smelled—my first charcoal heaters, used to heat up homes on chilly days. The smell of foods I'd never heard of nor tasted also stormed my senses: *nshima* (similar to cornmeal), *kapenta* (like sardines), *michopo* (meat cooked on the grill), *vitumbua* (almost like donuts, found at markets), not to mention a variety of fruits and vegetables.

Since my summer equaled their winter, during all three trips I enjoyed crisp, Indian summer–like weather. Sweater weather once the sun went down, but warm during the day. On my lunch breaks I'd wander around neighborhoods close to the US embassy, watching men play checkers on makeshift boards, using bottle caps as pieces, the small black and white spaces slightly misshapen. Or I'd make my way to local markets, rewarded with sights of colorful bolts of material women used to make their dresses, as well as fresh foods for sale. In addition, I walked through adjacent flea markets where people sold their wares. I saw no malls or shopping centers in Zambia, so markets served as popular places for locals to shop for everyday necessities.

That first summer, personnel at the US embassy in Lusaka initially acted standoffish with me. They probably viewed me as just another part-timer who'd arrived to put demands on them. Gradually, though, as we got to know each other, they shared their fascinating stories of relocating to different cities throughout the world every few years. These stories captivated me, their experiences and tips invaluable. I tagged along on trips to game parks, even to Victoria Falls, located between Zambia and Zimbabwe. I saw my first— outside a zoo—hippos, elephants, monkeys, warthogs, impalas. Even if no one had scheduled weekend trips, activities abounded for personnel from various embassies to enjoy. No one I knew sat at home binge-watching TV. Besides, TV-watching options were very limited: old reruns from the US or locally produced, low-budget programs.

Softball was popular with Americans, Canadians, French, South Americans, and Zambians, of course. Volleyball, with this same crew. I made a poor judgment call with volleyball, though, when one of the Marine guards approached me my first week in Lusaka to ask me to join the group the following weekend.

"Hey, a bunch of us get together at the Marine House on Saturdays to play volleyball. Any chance you know how to play?"

I knew how to play volleyball: you set up the ball underhanded, then thwacked it over the net, or just thwacked it over the net without the setup, if need be. "Yes. I know how to play volleyball; I played in high school," I declared, thinking what fun it would be to relive high school days.

My definition of "play" and the Marines' definition of "play" turned out to be quite different, though, a mistranslation on my part. When I approached the field behind the US Marine House that first Saturday, a game was already in progress. I watched as men and women who looked like they were Olympic caliber sent the ball whizzing from one side of the net to the other, slamming it into opposing players. I quickly reassessed my volleyball abilities and wisely bowed out, changing my role to that of spectator, but still enjoyed watching my new colleagues.

Something similar happened my first time in Lusaka when a State Department employee asked me to join a group hiking in the Zambian bush.

"I'm not much of a hiker," I replied, the volleyball experience and near-humiliation still fresh in my mind.

"Oh, these hikes aren't rigorous at all," he countered. "They're just really walks through the bush. I'm sure you'd have no trouble at all."

This time they were the ones who overestimated my athletic abilities, not me. I mumbled to myself, "I *told* you I wasn't a hiker," as I lagged behind everyone in the group, wearing my inappropriate-for-hiking clothes, fording streams, jumping from one rocky abutment to the next, plowing through the thick, prickly bush in the powerful African noonday sun, confident that snakes and spiders lurked around every corner.

Zambia is a former British colony located in a landlocked portion of central sub-Saharan Africa once known as Northern Rhodesia (Zimbabwe is the former Southern Rhodesia, pre-independence). Kenneth Kaunda came to power as president of Zambia after it won its independence from British rule in 1964, nearly a quarter of a century prior to my first trip to Zambia. He unified seventy-five distinct tribal groups, but Zambians became dissatisfied with KK's—Kaunda's nickname—single-party rule, demanding a multiparty state be instituted. KK claimed that a multiparty state would "lead to chaos." That situation worsened in the late 1980s when sales of one of Zambia's principal exports—copper—dropped off significantly on the world market, no longer a staple of the plumbing industry. Zambia went from being one of the richest African countries at independence in 1964, to one of the poorest.

The major demand made of me on these trips, from a language standpoint, consisted of putting together a puzzle, assembling pieces of these difficult Bantu languages to make sense of words, messages. What threats faced Zambia? How stable was their government, KK's leadership? What outside forces were making inroads into this part of Africa? Was regional instability imminent? Did the US need to pay more attention to the area?

Embassy employees took care of me during my trips. An embassy official picked me up at the airport, drove me to my hotel in 1988. State Department employees usually included me—along with other TDYers on work details—in extracurricular activities on weekends: the hiking, softball games, or volleyball matches with American or European embassy employees, shopping trips, out-of-area excursions, game nights, parties at different people's homes, movies at the Marine House. Once they got to know TDYers, Americans and Europeans posted to Lusaka for two to three years welcomed those of us there on short-term assignments, TDYs. There was a good system for tracking part-timers, ensuring we were welcomed as part of their community. In normal circumstances, that is.

The 1988 and 1989 trips turned out to be interesting, expanding my horizons enormously. Spain, Brazil, and Zambia represented in-creasing degrees of separation on a sliding scale from my experiences thus far. Degrees of separation from a known base of life experiences, language experiences, sensory experiences. Spain introduced me to Europe, to Spanish, specifically, to a culture I'd read about but never lived. Brazil took me farther afield, to remote areas, to a variety of Portuguese I'd never heard, to people I didn't know from previous work I'd done. Zambia propelled me further afield, into an African experience for which I had no previous reference points.

All my senses screamed, *This is new! I've never seen/tasted/ smelled/heard this before.* From witnessing fiery red sunsets, the sun an oversized orb, to bright colors in bougainvillea, jacaranda, cassia trees I walked past each day. I no longer formed part of a white majority; I represented a minority in a sea of Africans with their darker skin and hair, with their different background, culture. The perpetual sweet smell of burning leaves exposed some of these differences, as well as odors from foods people ate.

Using another analogy, while in Spain, I remained in somewhat familiar territory. In Brazil, I'd moved away from that known territory but still held it within visual range. In Zambia, that familiar landmass lay miles away; I needed to relearn almost everything. Increasingly, I sensed a lifting of the person I was back in Kirkwood, Missouri, moving to a more authentic, unfettered version of myself, almost like those out-of-body scenes you see in science fiction movies, where an almost transparent silhouette of the protagonist rises up alongside him.

I savored the sights, sounds, smells of Lusaka each day when I walked to the US embassy from the Intercontinental Hotel. I passed through a paradise of botanical colors, shapes. I saw, heard birds I'd never seen or heard before: bustards, cuckoos, kingfishers, bee-eaters, rollers. I watched employees of other embassies on my way to work, glimpsed hints of cultures they'd brought with them to Zambia from India, Norway, the Czech Republic, Egypt, the PRC, the Netherlands. In addition, I met and worked with dozens of FSNs, foreign service nationals, at the US embassy, in addition to State Department employees. FSNs are citizens of the country where a foreign embassy is located, a core of employees who provide various levels of support work and expertise crucial to running any foreign embassy.

I missed my children, despite knowing they were safe, having fun with their father and his new family back in St. Louis. My feelings sometimes echoed a sentiment from several years before in Brazil. I'd experienced such an abyss between myself and my children, I sensed the onset of a panic attack. Now ten thousand miles separated us, nearly double that distance in Brazil, not that an extra five thousand miles potentially impacted my ability to reach my children. In Zambia, though, letters reached me through the embassy's diplomatic mail pouch. Anyone back in the United States could put a regular US stamp on a letter and send it to any embassy in the world, regardless of how remote it was, and vice versa. It was before the Internet, so letters were godsends for embassy employees, long- and short-term. I wasn't moving around, so people could write me in care of the US embassy in Lusaka. That reduced my homesickness somewhat.

During my second summer stint in Lusaka, 1989, my routine remained much the same, but I'd made friends with an American couple the year before and they invited me to stay with them instead of at the local Intercontinental Hotel, where I'd spent my first visit. I enjoyed that: spending time with them in their home, with their Labrador retriever, Khan, eating homemade meals, having friends to go places with on the weekends. But my third time in Lusaka differed in nearly every respect from my two previous ones. In a way it became a culmination of factors building for years in-country.

On my first full day in Lusaka in 1990, I was driven through empty streets—some barricaded—pavement littered with loose stones, broken glass. We traveled past looted stores, shopkeepers boarding up storefronts, the occasional abandoned minibus, stranded vehicles, some scorched and ruined, still smoldering, past a few soldiers wielding bayonets, along with a scattering of vigilantes (mostly British expatriates) patrolling streets with automatic weapons in an attempt to restore order. By definition, expatriates are people living outside their native country. In this case, the native country was the United Kingdom, but many of Zambia's expats had lived in Africa their entire lives, or most of their lives, considered it home.

Riding in the embassy car, I pictured myself as an actor on a war movie set—observing my surroundings yet feeling somewhat removed—until my driver shouted, "Get down!" when it suddenly became real. I ducked. An angry protester charged our vehicle, ready to hurl a large stone at us. A few minutes later, the driver swerved to avoid someone else threatening looking who'd appeared out of nowhere to pursue our vehicle. As an FSN, the driver knew what to look for, what to avoid. I trusted him implicitly. After that initial warning, I ducked down in the car the entire way to and from work each day, as low as possible in my seat behind the driver, hoping to remain safe.

When I arrived at the embassy on my first official day, after a long, terrifying night, the rumor mill moved at a quick pace. Everyone had questions. Would rioters storm the US embassy? Then what? Embassy leadership remained in flux following the departure of the last ambassador three months before. A new one wouldn't be named for several more months, so the deputy chief of mission (DCM)—number two—acted as chargé d'affaires in the interim, referred to simply as the "chargé."

By 10:00 a.m., rioting had grown worse. Zambian authorities instituted a 6:00 p.m. to 6:00 a.m. curfew. In the early afternoon, the chargé instructed all employees to return home, to "guard their homes," in his words. I didn't relish returning to the Hellmans' home, didn't feel safe there, alone. I wanted people around me, not just my furry charge, Greasy. Someone did find a walkie-talkie I could take with me, but the home still had no alarm system, and miles separated it from the homes of other US citizens. Besides, I hadn't yet solved that ongoing mystery of the man who might/might not be my guard, a man wandering around the yard at all hours. On my way back to the Hellmans' home, I noticed deserted streets, but police dotted the area, creating required checkpoints.

The second night crawled by without incident, although I continued to hear not-so-distant gunfire. I'd hoped someone at the US embassy might suggest moving me closer to town, but that never happened. Nor did I ask. I knew people suspected my living situation made me nervous, but I didn't want to confirm that. State Department employees routinely traveled to or lived in far-flung, dangerous locations during their careers. Who was I to complain about a short-term situation? I also feared I wouldn't be asked back, to Zambia or other African countries, if I complained. I didn't want to risk that possibility, frightened as I was.

That second night I went through the same routine before going to bed, creating a safe haven back to the bedroom as I walked backwards through the narrow passageway from the main part of the house to the master bedroom, barricading myself to safety. I grew tired of watching *The Blues Brothers*, though, now watched other movies in the Hellmans' collection, including *Mr. Mom*, a favorite, although it didn't mute the gunfire as effectively.

Since I lacked human companionship, I often addressed Greasy.

"Do you really need to go outside? Really? You were out there not thirty minutes ago; I think you're just bored. If you do need to go, you'll have to go alone or at least do your business quickly, or both of us will be in trouble."

Once we got outside, I tried to stand in the shadows, remain inconspicuous, all the while loudly whispering at Greasy to hurry up so we could reenter the house.

I constantly told him to stop barking but was met with little success. A high-strung dog, the slightest noise from outside—the wind, a leaf, a branch rustling, the mysterious man patrolling the Hellmans' yard, a distant howl or bark of another dog, not to mention the sound of gunfire—continued to prompt him to bark. Even inside noises, creaking floorboards, squeaky appliances, elicited a growl or yip. I sensed no order I could use to interpret his level of anxiety. If only he'd act consistently: a high-pitched, frenzied bark for armed men surrounding the house versus a low-grade whine for someone's cat on the property. But all disturbances elicited the same panic. Truthfully, though, even though I couldn't expect him to scare off possible intruders, just having a living, breathing creature as my companion provided a calming effect, once his barking jags ended. Having to take care of him took my mind off my situation, at least temporarily.

The following day—my second full day—I intended to remain at the Hellmans' home. The chargé had ordered all embassy personnel—permanent staff and TDYers like me—to stay off the streets, to continue to "guard" their homes until further notice. Unfortunately, though, they made an exception for me. The chargé had discovered from an embassy employee that I worked with Bantu languages back in the States. He instructed the driver to transport me to the embassy, virtually vacant since the riots began. A brief, impromptu meeting took place with the chargé in his embassy office.

"Word has it that you're good with African languages," the chargé began.

"Hmm. I don't know. Maybe, but I don't speak any Zambian languages, and there are seventy-five," I explained, giving special emphasis to "seventy-five." I stood in his impressive office, a large US flag on a stand next to his oversized desk, with photographs of him alongside prominent politicians and celebrities, as well as family members, I guessed. I suddenly became self-conscious. Noticing a small spot from Greasy's dog food on my shirt, I wished I'd known that morning that I'd be meeting with the acting US ambassador. I'd have found something more appropriate to wear. I'd just been instructed to report to work. In fairness, on my two previous TDYs, no one high-ranking ever sought me out, so I'd packed casual clothing. No need to bring fancy clothes when I'd be holed up in a nondescript office all day, headphones glued to my ears.

"But you can figure these languages out, right?" he continued, undeterred, looking for answers that fit with his expectations, clearly eager for our conversation to end, for a solution to be reached. "These people mobbing, looting, breaking into homes aren't speaking English, even though, as you know, it's the official language of Zambia. We need to know where their grievances lie, their plans, if any. Most important, though, we need to ensure the safety of Americans in-country, of other Westerners too. You can help us with that, track what's going on," the chargé stressed, adding, "English may be spoken by the educated and in government circles, but look outside; nobody's speaking it now. We need you to get to work, to make sense of this." Waving his arm in a dramatic gesture, he added, "As you can see, no one at the embassy speaks any of these African dialects, nor at other Western embassies. You're as good as we've got."

Not exactly high praise, but he clearly had no interest in a linguistic explanation of why I deemed myself completely unqualified for his assignment. To him, I was just some TDYer who coincidentally knew "all those African dialects." Only they were languages, not dialects, complicated languages. People—even educated people—often erroneously believe that African languages resemble dialogue from some B-rated Tarzan movie, with a few dozen words and a matching grammar. Nothing could be further from the truth.

My parents nicknamed me "Last Word Linda." In keeping with my reputation, I longed to inform him before leaving his office, "But, sir, there are over two thousand African languages—*languages*, not dialects. Give me a tutor, a few months, and I'll do whatever you want." I wasn't naive, though; in the hierarchy of personnel at the US embassy in Zambia, he stood at the pinnacle, whereas I was at the very bottom, or close. I kept my mouth shut, made it my goal to spend every waking hour trying to tackle Zambian languages, at least the two most important ones: Bemba and Nyanja.

In one day I'd gone from feeling anonymous, invisible, on a temporary duty assignment, an ignored summer part-timer trying to stay safe in a country rife with rioting, mob scenes, chaos, to the only American permitted on the streets, the only one forced to come to work, except the chargé d'affaires, of course. I'd become indispensable overnight. Unfortunately, however, when I'd confessed that I didn't speak any Zambian languages, it wasn't false modesty. I didn't. Not a word. I just knew how Bantu languages "worked," the puzzle underlying their structure. That gave me an ever-so-tiny advantage. But I'd compare it to knowing how to put together a complicated model airplane, then having to construct and pilot an actual 747. Not much help.

The chargé handed me two ancient, dog-eared dictionaries, missing strategic pages, xeroxed so many times and so carelessly that the print often slanted off the page. In places the print looked illegible or smudged, as though the copier had tried to distance itself from its task. He also gave me an out-of-date, dusty, torn grammar book someone found buried in a storage room, dated from the days when missionaries proselytized throughout Africa. Handing the books to me, he patted me on the back and sent me on my way.

His departing words stayed with me: "We're counting on you."

Before I left the chargé's office, his secretary handed me a letter. She insisted I keep it with me at all times, show it to anyone stopping me, to prove I served in an "official" capacity. As though a letter held the key to ensuring my safety, to stopping angry mobs from stoning me.

"Oh, wait! Let's see what this 'official' letter says before we string up this troublemaker."

I couldn't imagine anyone saying that.

The letter did little to reduce my fears. I doubted its ability to impress angry Zambians, despite claiming I was on vacant streets on official business. I also doubted they'd take the time to read the letter. People didn't have enough money to buy basic food for their families now; why would they care about my letter, any letter? Should they? It read:

June 27, 1990

To Zambian government authorities: This is to certify that the bearer of this letter, Linda Marshall, is an employee of the United States embassy and is on official embassy business. Please allow the bearer of this letter to proceed freely on the responsibility of this embassy. Sincerely, US Chargé D'Affaires. Lusaka, Zambia.

While flattered that someone finally remembered I existed, especially in such a time of unrest, I feared venturing out on the streets. I'd read that mobs waged "guerrilla-type battles" in various places in Lusaka, one journalist reporting that "gunshots rent the skies from all directions." Reports also revealed that Zambian authorities were detaining children as young as ten, labeling them "suspected rioters," while authorities broke the bones of others during episodes of rioting. One man reportedly barely escaped a lynching; a thousand people had been arrested for breaking curfew.

My nights remained basically the same at the Hellmans' home, but now I had access to State Department employees' phone numbers and a walkie-talkie, and could communicate with US Marines, who conducted roll call each morning to make sure we'd survived the night. During one such roll call I listened as a woman screamed that "they" were climbing over a wall at the back of her home. This only increased my fears.

At night I pored over dictionaries and grammars the chargé had given me, trying to make sense of not just one Bantu language but two. All day every day I monitored open police channels, listening to bulletins and reports, hoping to glean information about what was—or was not—happening on the streets, hoping to get insight about the situation "on the ground."

The unrest in Zambia became more complicated and came to a head on June 30 when, after three nonstop days of rioting, the military switched sides. No longer supporting the Zambian government of Kenneth Kaunda, members attempted a coup. Troops summoned to restore order turned the tables to side with rioters. Initially, the press called the coup a success. Zambians congregated in Lusaka to celebrate the ousting of Kenneth Kaunda, one of Africa's most long-standing—twenty-six years—and most corrupt leaders. But then Kaunda's security forces quashed the coup, regaining power. KK declared that the riots had been caused by "power hungry" Zambians.

A supposedly religious man, he quoted the Bible in subsequent speeches to Zambians: "Those who live by the sword will die by the sword." Gradually, life returned to normal, whatever that meant in a one-party government with an authoritarian leader. But the curfew remained in effect for a month, till July 25.

I continued to work at the embassy each day, and house-sat for the Hellmans until July 16, when they returned from the US. Following the unrest, I was finally able to visit the commissary to pick up items I needed: cereal, powdered milk, eggs, even Diet Cokes.

State Department officials in charge of housing moved me to a house closer to town, another home to house-sit. During that time my mindset still ranged from pure terror—originating on that first night—to cautious relaxation. I embodied the saying: hoping for the best but expecting the worst. Who knew how long this precarious détente between Kenneth Kaunda and Zambians would last, especially after the coup attempt, especially now that university students had joined in the anti-Kaunda rhetoric? Who knew how that would impact me, others? Regardless, I started to adjust to the situation.

I learned a lot about myself that summer: first of all, that my language skills continued to expand, deepen. That I could teach myself the basics of two difficult new languages when an emergency demanded it, rise above the constant drumbeat of long-held insecurities telling me I would fail. Equally important, though, I learned that, when necessary, I could take care of myself physically in a dangerous situation. I could think on my feet, protect myself when no help appeared, when I remained completely on my own. I could improvise when necessary, devise a plan.

Facing physical danger like this was new, having little access to anyone or anything to rescue me. This represented a first for me; I'd passed a test. I could have asked to go home after that first night (though the airport was closed), or to be moved to a safer location. I could have behaved in a foolhardy way that first week when angry citizens rampaged, could have done something to jeopardize my safety or that of others. I also could have refused to help the chargé, told him I wasn't up to the task when he said he needed my help. But I hadn't. I could have merely coped with the challenges I faced, but I'd done more—I'd somehow excelled.

Following my six-week TDY for the State Department, supervisors wrote an evaluation filled with glowing praise, stating that my work that summer would "go down in the annals of history." Few people would ever read that positive feedback or know the extent of my accomplishments, given its classification level, but I knew I had achieved important milestones: personal and professional. That would have to suffice.

4

THE FUTURE TENSE

The Way Forward

THE FUTURE TENSE—*a grammatical term used to denote an action or condition that has not yet happened or does not yet exist.*

EXAMPLE: *"My life will change, but my friends and family will feel uncomfortable with many of these changes. I will experience powerful growing pains."*

I stood outside the door of Nelson Mandela's former jail cell at Robben Island, off the west coast of South Africa, staring at the small, barred window, his only link to the outside. Prisoners received letters every six months, visitors once a year. What was that like, I wondered, sitting or standing alone in that gray, damp cell with a sisal mat, a bucket, a dish, a small chair, and nothing more? What did he see beyond those bars? What thoughts occupied his time? Why hadn't he become a bitter man when he finally won his freedom? I marveled at yet another case of fate entering my life, taking me on its twisty, turning path, leading me to a stronger notion of self, of my personal role in my own life. I contemplated forces at play twenty years before, when supervisors had asked me to study a language I'd never heard of—Xhosa—a language that caused me to double back, reevaluate choices I'd made. I thought about the disparate paths I'd taken since moving to Maryland in 1985.

Before I traveled to Africa for the first time—Zambia, July of 1988—Africa made its way to me. Not by my design. Beginning in February of 1987. Through words, stories, images, photographs from my instructors, through outdated, racist, seventy-five-year-old textbooks, dictionaries. It coiled itself around me. I epitomized the saying: "You may leave Africa, but Africa never leaves you."

I sat in a small classroom of a private language school in Arlington, Virginia, each day for nine months. Two South Africans shared a wealth of knowledge with me about their first language, Xhosa, about their country of origin, South Africa. Every day they filled in spaces of that otherwise sterile classroom with Xhosa's clicks, with stories of growing up in apartheid South Africa, with Miriam Makeba, Hugh Masekela, Joseph Shabalala, Ladysmith Black Mambazo's music, with colorful photographs, maps. Using one of South Africa's languages—Xhosa—as a backdrop, they introduced me to their country's customs, its history, its personality.

In October of 1985, I'd left my home of thirty-five years in Kirkwood, Missouri, with my two small children after having accepted a job with a US government agency to work as a Spanish and Portuguese linguist. My credentials lay with those languages. My career course had been set, or so I thought. My sense of security on arriving in Maryland consisted of my knowledge of those specific languages, but little else. I navigated childcare, living on my own, supporting the three of us financially, taking care of our condo, driving in the DC area with its crazy traffic, despite my woeful sense of direction.

On January 27, 1986, my new career officially began. Some people in my first office welcomed me, others acted standoffish, while still others were even unfriendly at times. I later learned that there were those who resented me because I'd been hired at a higher level (because of my PhD, coupled with three years working at a government agency in St. Louis). Maybe I hadn't paid my dues in their eyes.

Complicating matters, at thirty-five I was at least ten years older than most other new hires, my peers. While they dated, socialized, or enjoyed married life, raised their families, I scurried home every day after work to take care of and spend time with my small children, free time a luxury I didn't have. Weekends meant catching up with my small charges. No one really knew where to slot me; I didn't "fit" anywhere. Colleagues my age had achieved positions several notches above me, usually as supervisors or senior linguists. They'd moved on from my level years before, so we had little in common. While I'd attended graduate school back in St. Louis, done freelance translating, been a mediocre housewife, and enjoyed raising my two small children, my new colleagues had climbed the work ladder.

The atmosphere in my first office resembled that of a bustling newsroom. Light gray metal desks stood side by side, row after row of these desks with their sides touching each other, metal rectangles with no space between; some people had to share desks. Chairs were sometimes flimsy, unreliable. Linguists' tools consisted of inexpensive government-issue ballpoint pens, shared, dog-eared Spanish dictionaries, other working aids, IBM Selectric typewriters. Smoking was still permitted indoors, so a few employees had ashtrays on their desks, smoking at will. Since the windows didn't open, air quality remained poor, a smoky, odiferous film covering everything and everyone.

One phone to the outside world—serving at least fifty people— hung on a pillar next to an aisle of back-to-back desks. Anyone making a call pulled down a chain from the ceiling that turned on a flashing red light, much like the siren on a police car but without the noise. Its purpose: to ensure that everyone within a two-hundred-foot radius knew not to talk about classified material while the phone was "up." Employees also loudly announced prior to dialing, "Phone's up!" in case employees seated in the vicinity failed to see the flashing light. That ensured that all eyes potentially focused on the person making a call or, worse, allowed fellow employees to eavesdrop on phone conversations, intentionally or not.

Working as a linguist in this atmosphere, I no longer enjoyed extra time to ponder which word exactly reflected the meaning of the Spanish I translated. Now my task entailed figuring out what it all meant, but doing it quickly; time was of the essence. Making matters more problematic, the Spanish I translated sometimes contained grammatical errors, or cryptic references, so it required work in making sense of it all. Added to that was what I thought of as a midstream situation: I sometimes felt like I was coming into the room when two people had already been conversing for several minutes, trying to make sense of their words without context. I hadn't experienced any of these factors in my undergraduate or graduate work. It added another layer of difficulty to being able to decipher words.

Linguists and checkers—people who reviewed the work of linguists—along with various levels of supervisors, worked in close quarters. A few checkers took pride in bleeding their red ink pens over the work of newbies like me, especially when that newbie possessed a PhD, maybe needed to be taken down a notch. Often I worked on a translation, information in support of government officials, then proudly placed it in the checker's bin, only to have it returned to me, unrecognizable, looking like ink from her red pen had leaked all over my once-pristine translation. Another bin served as a place to pick up work to be translated. Linguists were discouraged from sifting through the bin to find work to their liking. Eagle eyes watched to ensure you picked up the translation on top. No exceptions.

I sometimes thought of myself as a cog in a wheel, a factory worker on a conveyor belt. I had worked hard to stand out back home, not to blend in with the masses. The goal here stood in sharp contrast to that, especially since I sometimes detected an undertone of resentment with key people.

Despite lackluster working conditions, these linguists and analysts proved to be the most talented, hardworking, dedicated professionals with whom I'd ever worked, people whose contributions the public rarely saw, contributions that helped ensure the safety of the United States and its allies. These professionals stood out as unsung heroes in many cases, monitoring potentially volatile situations, contributing to the safety of troops and civilians posted overseas, US citizens working in all matter of capacities. I'd pick up a piece of "traffic," as they referred to it, usually communication between diplomats in other countries, and make sense of it, thus giving a heads-up to US decision-makers. Usually, a communiqué I published in and of itself wouldn't yield earth-shattering information, but it was a piece of the puzzle, contributing to a more complete picture.

After I'd worked in the same office for almost a year, a colleague told me about a position in another office of the same agency where I could translate documents coming from Portuguese-speaking African countries like Angola or Mozambique. I loved Portuguese, needed a change of pace from the Spanish work I'd been doing for almost a year. More important, I longed to escape my current situation, but agency rules dictated I stay for a year until I was eligible to transfer.

Circumstances in my office came to a head one afternoon. My immediate supervisor, Sherry, informed me that a supervisor two levels up in the hierarchical structure, Tom, her supervisor's supervisor, wanted to meet with me. I'd never said more than a cursory hello to him (managers frowned on employees jumping the supervisory chain).

The supervisors stood alongside me: my supervisor, Sherry; her supervisor, Karen; Tom, division chief. Nervous, I hoped he just wanted to congratulate me for having recently passed another battery of agency language tests.

Tom's office looked like a normal office, unlike the spaces in which the rest of us toiled. It had four walls, a door, even a window— a rarity. I looked around as though contemplating the palace of a king.

After casual chitchat between the three supervisors, Tom got to the point.

"I understand you just passed the next round of language tests, Linda, but I'm afraid that's not enough for this office. It's great you have a PhD; on paper you look impressive. Passing the agency tests is also a start . . . but, again, not enough."

Then he hesitated. It wasn't the kind of hesitation where you're swallowing, or catching your breath. It was one of those pauses used to create dramatic effect. Confused, I stood in front of him (he'd never asked me—or the other two women—to take a seat). I wondered what could be wrong. Hadn't I done everything they wanted? Sure, I'd taken annual—vacation—leave from time to time when my children became sick (you couldn't use sick leave for sick children back then; technically, you took care of them on your vacation time). They had come down with chicken pox back-to-back a few months before, which wiped my vacation time off the books. In addition, I hated missing teachers' conferences or field trips, adding to my absences. It also proved difficult to arrive at work by 8:00, and most people clocked in by 7:00 or 7:30, leaving few parking places for those of us forced to come in later.

In less than a minute, I'd flipped through my mental Rolodex to determine my fate, to second-guess Tom's words. I'd never liked surprises.

"I'm afraid we're going to have to let you go, Linda, as much as we dislike having to do so. You're aware that you're on automatic probation your first two years, right?" He sighed at this point again, granting me a purse-lipped half smile with cocked head, as though to convey how very deeply he regretted his words.

The room became blurry, voices a cacophony of sounds. I vaguely heard the clattering of chairs, pens, cups from outside the office, but they were muffled, as though far away. Karen and Sherry no longer flanked me. Lifted from the room mentally, a wall sprang up between us. Nor could I hear their voices anymore. I stood there, staring out Tom's office window, as though that's where either new freedom or a now grim future lay. My eyes wandered to papers on Tom's desk, but nothing really registered. I turned slightly to look at the door behind me, planning my exit. I had to get out of there.

My first clear thought: *How will I support my children?* I risked losing custody of them if I couldn't support them financially, of course. I'd never worked as a waitress, claimed no other skills besides secretarial, but had never shown much skill there. My parents would be disinclined to help me; they already looked down on people who worked for the federal government. Besides, they'd made their disapproval known when I moved away from the Midwest. So what would I do? Then I thought: *I can work at McDonald's; maybe they don't require you to provide proof of a waitressing background.* I knew that wouldn't bring in enough income, though.

Laughter snapped me back into the room, brought it all into sharp focus again. Why did I hear laughter? What had happened? Gradually, I returned to the scene, to Sherry, Karen, Tom. All three supervisors could barely stand, doubled over with laughter.

I must have looked confused, in shock, because Tom walked over to me—I instinctively backed away as he approached me—patted me on the back, laughing, then blurted out, "Just kidding, Linda! It's just a joke! You're doing a great job. We just wanted to have a little fun with you! You're always so intense, so frazzled. No worries! You look like you saw a ghost. You didn't really believe me, did you?!" Then he shook my hand. I wanted to slap the smirk off his face but forced a slight smile, removing my hand from his grasp, backing out of the room without a word. Karen—my supervisor's supervisor—followed me in hot pursuit.

"He wasn't supposed to go on so long!" she whispered conspiratorially, walking in tandem with me, though she couldn't stop chuckling. "I told him to say a *few* words, not recite the Declaration of Independence—we just wanted to have a little fun—but he wouldn't stop! You didn't believe him, did you?" Nearly double her elfin size, I could easily have knocked her to the ground with a well-placed shove, but my overriding feeling of gratitude—that I still had a job—rose to the top, like cream rising to the top of a rancid cup of milk. I have no recollection of the rest of the day.

Several days after I was "fired," Karen presented me with a gift, an attempt to make amends for Tom's overzealousness with their joke, a joke she initiated. The gift was a pair of bright turquoise tights. Amazingly small—her size—I couldn't have fit one of my arms into one leg, but I forced a smile, thanked her, and took them home, shoving them into the back of my dresser drawer, a reminder of that awful day. Years later, I realized their "joke" could have resulted in serious repercussions for all three supervisors, but I fell into survival mode; I had no interest in seeking justice. The moment had served its purpose, though; once I recovered, my resolve was even stronger, my goal to get out of that office. I'd done it once, escaped from a toxic environment back in St. Louis; I could do it again, would do it again.

The government agency where I worked consisted of hundreds of offices, branches of various sizes shooting off from numerous main government trunks, so after working my compulsory time in that first office I managed to get an interview for the job my colleague had told me about. I thought the new job would involve translating Portuguese, but the woman who interviewed me explained that no Portuguese billets remained. With its military-oriented structure— having a certain number of jobs in various career fields—they didn't need any additional Portuguese linguists, regardless of credentials.

"But we'd love to have you work with us, Linda; your record is fantastic. Dave [my colleague] speaks highly of you."

Crestfallen, I pondered my next move. I didn't want to continue working in my old office anymore. I'd have to think of something else.

The supervisor continued. "But we do need someone to learn a South African 'click' language: Xhosa. Do you have any interest in doing that?"

She had reviewed my scores from a battery of aptitude tests I took before I was hired. On this particular test, developers created a made-up language, introduced it on a single page of the test pamphlet, along with a brief explanation of its grammatical rules, as well as sample sentences and their accompanying translations. Like other test takers, I absorbed these rules, then, based on the grammar of this new, fictitious language, answered questions, translated passages, all within an allotted time period. Fortunately, I did well on this artificial language test. I loved the exercise. I had also performed well on the actual Spanish and Portuguese language tests.

"You'd train at a private school in Arlington, Virginia, for nine months, full-time, a class of one. Can you manage that? Dave said you have small children? You'll take a bus from here every morning, along with other students, but you'll be the only one studying Xhosa, working with tutors. What do you think?"

I'd never heard of Xhosa before that day, couldn't even pronounce the word (the *X* denoted one of the clicks), but I loved languages and wanted to make a change. I agreed, even though it made my life—and my children's—that much harder. The bus transporting those of us studying various languages at the school in Arlington left from work promptly at 7:30 each morning, so I left my children at their respective schools—two separate locations—by 7:00, when they opened, then drove ten miles to work, literally running to catch the 7:30 bus. If I missed it, I had to take the DC metro, adding a minimum of forty-five minutes each way to my day. Commuting to the language school in Arlington every day added nearly eighty miles to my daily round trip.

"Yes," I said. "I'd like to do it." What an adventure, I thought. To think that an hour before I'd never heard of this language, yet now I planned to immerse myself in it, the first nonnative person in the area—that I knew of—to study it. No more having to blend in, lost in the sometimes hostile masses, surely a path I would never have chosen on my own. But events arranged themselves in such a way that I believed no other choice existed. That choice altered my life, though I remained unaware of the extent of that change at the time. Like many other forks in the road, I hadn't set out to get a PhD, or to have a certain career. I hadn't initially planned to move to the East Coast or study African languages. I followed a path, made choices at certain decision points, with one thing leading to the next, then the next . . . and here I was.

After my first day of Xhosa training in February of 1987, I wrote in my journal that it took me most of the day just to learn how to master the name of this new language. The *X* at the beginning of *Xhosa*, a lateral click, sounds like you're riding a horse, urging it to go faster. Harder than it sounds, when you add other letters to the click— like the *h* after *Xhosa*'s initial *X*—it's a challenge. As I soon learned, *Xhosa*'s *X* proved to be the least of my pronunciation problems. In some words, multiple consonants follow that initial *X*, for example, the word *Xhwitha*, meaning "to pluck out feathers." I'd have found it easier to pluck out actual feathers than to say a word designating that activity. During those early weeks, my children followed me around our rented condo and elsewhere, practicing the clicks along with me. We must have looked like an odd trio on local playgrounds, the sound of clicking, popping corks, tsk-tsking, urging our invisible horses to giddy up.

They also invented their own non-Xhosa "clicks," for instance, a clucking noise not found in Xhosa. As with everything, though, we formed a constant threesome. My life consisted of going to work, spending time with my small children. Nothing else fit, at least in those early years: no dating, no nights out with friends, no weekend outings except with them. I didn't want to add anything to my life. I felt guilty enough for time spent away from them on workdays; anything else felt like abandonment. Even when they went to St. Louis to visit their father, I stayed close to home, never comfortable with being a single woman.

Mastering Xhosa's tones also proved challenging. In tonal languages a speaker raises or lowers the pitch of his voice, thus changing the meaning of words, even though the spelling may remain identical. Xhosa contains two tones: high and low. Chinese is also a tonal language but has four basic tones and a fifth neutral one; a layman can hear the singsong sound of Chinese, clear evidence of its tones. In Xhosa it's less obvious.

My language school hired a Xhosa tutor, Themba—(the Xhosa word for "hope")—a Black South African male in his mid-twenties, not for his pedagogical skills, nor for his résumé or for his teaching experience. The director hired him because of his fluency in Xhosa. Sometimes applicants for jobs teaching less commonly taught languages (LCTLs) claimed to "know" a language when they merely possessed a passing knowledge of it, or maybe knew another similar language, or had heard it on the streets, perhaps even understood it. Language school administrators met with challenges trying to verify credentials. Fortunately, Themba and my other tutor, Nenzi, both spoke Xhosa fluently.

This would be unlike the other, mainstream languages I'd studied; my days of having instructors spoon-feed me a language quickly faded into the past, those days of using glossy grammar books, ready-made lessons plans, dictionaries, literature. Instead, my tutors and I shared a partnership. I actively participated in my language learning. I needed to figure out the inner workings of Xhosa, extracting information, interviewing my instructors for critical data. I needed to unravel the puzzle with their help.

On that first day, the school director led me to a small, sterile classroom where Themba awaited me, standing unsmiling, his hands in his pockets. The room was equipped only with several whiteboards, a few chairs, pens, markers, and a long table with three large xeroxed books: a dictionary updated by a British missionary in 1918 from the original 1899 edition and two grammar books, one from 1966, the other from 1969. Pre-computers, we operated exclusively in a pencil-and-paper environment. I spent five days a week in that room for nine months, except for three field trips to the Library of Congress to look for much-needed material.

The school director made his introductions. "Themba, I'd like you to meet your new student, Linda. She comes highly recommended, has studied Spanish, Portuguese, French, along with other languages, so you should work well together. If there's anything you or Linda need, please let my staff or me know. We've provided you with a dictionary and a few grammar books."

Except for testing days when the director reappeared to evaluate my progress, I worked alone with Themba, alternating with my other Xhosa tutor, Nenzi.

After the director left, closing the door behind him, Themba came to life, looking almost angry. He picked up the 1918 Xhosa dictionary, *Kaffir-English Dictionary* printed on its cover. Holding it up, he waved it at me as though he'd found contraband in the classroom, then tossed it dismissively back onto the table. The thud when it hit the table startled me.

"We will *not* use this word to talk about Xhosa," he proclaimed. "That word ["Kaffir"] is an abominable word I will not tolerate in this classroom; do you understand?"

I had no idea what he meant, was unfamiliar with the word "Kaffir." Nor did I understand why the dictionary said "Kaffir" and not Xhosa. I quickly learned that it meant the equivalent of the N-word in English, literally meaning "infidel," but with blatant racist connotations. Early British missionaries had used it when referring to Xhosa. The preface to this same Xhosa dictionary referred to "Kaffir scholars," to "Kaffir grammar," and to "Kaffraria," where it claimed Xhosa people lived.

Themba's powerful words—his very first to me—seemed like an indictment not only of long-dead racist South African missionaries but also of all white people. After all, apartheid still flourished in South Africa in 1987.

After hearing Themba's harsh words, I rummaged through the markers on our table, locating a thick black one. I crossed out "Kaffir" in bold, broad strokes, writing "Xhosa" above the blackened-out word.

"Is this okay?" I asked him, hoping to counter the initial negative atmosphere. It seemed to pacify Themba somewhat, but switching the dictionary's title became the first of many tasks.

I was accustomed to grammar books with model dialogues in which two—or more—people exchanged pleasantries, benign comments bordering on the superficial. "How are you today, Mrs. Smith?" "I am well." "How is your family?" "We are fine, thank you." "The weather is nice today, isn't it? Would you like to join us on our walk?" "Yes, please."

In my Xhosa grammar book, however, vocabulary and accompanying sample conversations had quite different contents than in my Spanish—and other languages'—textbooks. Xhosa vocabulary emphasized words such as: to hit, to beat, to die, evil, workers, poison, knife, servant. Beginning on the very first pages, sample sentences for language learners consisted of: "The ugly servant is lazy." "The long hand is hitting." "You must not act greedy." "The police are chasing the man." "You are fighting." "He appeared dead to me." "Take the axe and chop firewood." "Drive my car and do not drink." "Call the servant."

"No, I am not a coward." "Repeat [after me]: Servant, bring me water," and "No, I am not a lazy fellow."

Where would I ever need to use such sentences? I wondered. Why would I want to? We scrapped these grammar books, created our own working aids, our own system, our own sentences.

For these and other reasons, Xhosa posed more of a challenge than any other language I'd studied thus far. It contained tones, strange-sounding (to English speakers) clicks, and an elaborate noun class system, similar to other Bantu languages. Samples below illustrate this, but they're straightforward examples in a sea of complex orthographic and sound changes that often occur:

Bonke abantu bafuna uxolo. All people want peace.

Lonke ilizwe lifuna uxolo. The whole country wants peace.

Sonke isizwe sifuna uxolo. The whole nation wants peace.

Zonke izizwe zifuna uxolo. All nations want peace.

No wonder no one else in the US government had signed up to study this language, I thought; it's impossible. I recalled fragments of supposedly "African" movies I'd watched growing up, ones in which Europeans or Americans treated African Indigenous people like children with a limited vocabulary. *Tarzan*, for instance. "Me Tarzan, you Jane." Moviemakers hadn't known—or cared about—the accuracy of their depictions. None of it reflected the complexity of the language I'd signed up for. Even how Xhosas tell people goodbye varied, depending on whether you were the one staying or leaving. If I was leaving, I would announce, "*Sala kakuhle,*" "Stay well," to those people remaining. On the other hand, if I was the one staying, I said, "*Hamba kakuhle.*" "Go well." One of a hundred idiosyncrasies of a complex language, an agglutinative language, meaning that prefixes, infixes, and suffixes were routinely tacked on to the beginning, middle, or end of words, to add to or change their meaning.

A popular movie helped me somewhat—the 1980 popular film *The Gods Must Be Crazy*. It featured an actor who spoke the San language. Xhosas came in contact with San speakers in the early 1800s, appropriating some of their clicks. The movie proved useful in making sense of the hard-to-pronounce clicks, although San contains many more clicks than Xhosa.

I enjoyed working closely with one or both instructors in my small classroom six hours a day, five days a week, but it was also exhausting. Themba and Nenzi knew Xhosa well, but the three of us brought our own idiosyncrasies to the teaching and learning experience. I watched what I said, didn't broach certain topics. For instance, early on, Themba had announced that no one in South Africa suffered from AIDS, his reasoning being that no homosexuals lived in South Africa. I avoided that topic, even though AIDS appeared in the news constantly in the mid to late 1980s.

Nenzi reminded me of someone with a split personality, some days dressed in traditional African garb with her hair piled on top of her head and wearing a long colorful print dress wrapped around her body, layer after layer of elaborate beads topping off her outfit. Other days she wore a business suit befitting a Wall Street trader. Her personality shifted accordingly. But the split sometimes reflected her behavior toward me. Often she lavished me with praise, exclaiming one day that I'd achieved the equivalent of three years' training after less than three weeks, comparing me to a "tree" she'd planted. Other days she stormed out of our classroom, angry at a trivial mistake I'd made, or she accused me of spying on her, demanding that the manager destroy her employment records. Once, though I didn't witness it, fellow language students reported that she had gotten into a physical fight with an Ethiopian woman teaching Amharic at our school. I never knew which of her moods awaited me. But with scant resources, instructors who possessed the requisite skills and agreed to teaching a student for a minimal salary were in short demand, so I did my best to get along with both of them. In turn, they tolerated my weak points, my idiosyncrasies. For instance, since the school employed two Xhosa instructors (Themba and Nenzi), they took turns teaching me. One expounded on something and then asked if I understood. During the day, they stated something, then looked up at me from their papers and repeatedly asked, "*Uyiqondile?*" "Did you understand?" Needless to say, I had to pay attention.

Stories Themba and Nenzi shared of life back in South Africa filled in bits of my knowledge gaps about their country, their culture, more than compensating for their pedagogical shortcomings. Each day we were immersed in each other's lives, insofar as possible for a privileged white woman living ten thousand miles away in a democratic country. As my Xhosa skills improved, they relayed this information in Xhosa, so I benefited from a double learning experience.

Themba and Nenzi educated me about South Africa's ten so-called "homelands" or Bantustans, substandard areas where Blacks were forced to live during apartheid, the particular homeland dependent on their ethnicity. Under that illegitimate system, Xhosas lived in the Transkei and Ciskei homelands. Themba and Nenzi also explained South Africa's townships to me, sprawling shantytowns built on the outskirts of urban areas. They told me stories about Blacks being forced to learn Afrikaans in school in order to better communicate with their white employers. They told me about arbitrary distinctions used to classify people into one of four official "races:" white, Black, colored (mixed), or Indian, distinctions based primarily on wildly unscientific tests. For example, the pencil test: if a pencil stayed in place in a person's hair when he shook his head, he belonged with non-whites. Different members in the same family sometimes belonged to different races, according to apartheid's illogical, racist system. But they also told me stories about Nelson Mandela (a Xhosa), as well as about the Xhosa people's sacred initiation rites, along with other customs. They opened a window into their lives for me, let me peek in, at least for nine months.

I knew their stories originated from what they'd personally experienced, but I felt like I was sitting around a campfire listening to dark tales conjured up by writers with overactive imaginations. How could this happen in the twentieth century? My eyes began to open to certain realities, realities that previously had existed as abstractions, or information I knew nothing about. Traveling to South Africa would force me to look even closer, the lens zooming in on life there.

When my full-time Xhosa training ended after nine months, I took a five-hour test in Xhosa. First, I transcribed a two-minute tape, writing down the Xhosa, then translating it into idiomatic English. Then I translated four newspaper articles from Xhosa to English. A week later, I took an oral interview test; I sat across from Nenzi while she broached a number of topics with me. I was expected to fully participate in these conversations.

Seven years passed before I traveled to South Africa. Seven years of translating, transcribing, analyzing Xhosa and other languages, of providing information on apartheid's twilight years and its effect on that country and on southern Africa. Equipped with headphones and a computer now, I sat at my gray metal desk, slotted in a row of desks, still sharing a single external telephone with dozens of other analysts and linguists. When a woman sitting in the row of desks directly behind me became pregnant, with each passing month the space between my desk and chair diminished. Work trips to Zambia in

1988, 1989, and 1990 provided a respite from those cramped spaces, but South Africa had to wait.

In February of 1990, the South African government released Nelson Mandela from prison. In April of 1994, the first free, general elections took place; Mandela became South Africa's president. In early October of 1994, six months after the abolition of apartheid, I made the long trek to Pretoria, South Africa, putting all my training and analysis to use. I finally had the opportunity to speak Xhosa, to hear Xhosa, to travel to a country where people who spoke Xhosa lived. I'd worked so hard tackling this challenging language, a language that symbolized my first glimpse of Africa.

My initial impressions of Pretoria, the city where I worked for six weeks, evoked a potpourri of images. Early settlers in South Africa, the Dutch, had left their mark. A few buildings near the US embassy reflected that influence. Cape Dutch architecture has rounded, rising gables with whitewashed walls. My hotel looked like a replica of something I'd seen in Amsterdam.

Every day I walked down residential streets to the US embassy. A solid sea of purple trumpet-shaped jacaranda petals carpeted wide streets, while overhanging branches drooped, heavy with more of their purple petals. I wandered through a child's phantasmagorical coloring book, one in which the child could only use a few crayons. On my way to work each morning the purple reflected sunlight, making the blossoms appear lilac. On my return home they took on a more velvet cast. I imagined lying down in the middle of those streets on a plush bed of petals.

On my walk to the US embassy each day, I filled my lungs with crisp spring air (October, South Africa's spring), walked past a proliferation of blossoming, deep scarlet-colored bougainvillea. When I arrived at the US embassy grounds, a sizable group of large grayish-black birds with iridescent-patched wings greeted me—hadada ibis, I later learned—the "loudest bird in Africa." Their cries sounded like laughter. They exhibited no fear of me as I approached. Each day I stood there, fascinated, listening to them for a few minutes, wishing I understood what they were communicating. They reminded me of the old Heckle and Jeckle cartoons I watched as a child, except that Heckle and Jeckle were magpies.

My love of the natural beauty surrounding me may have resulted from my Midwestern roots, with its shorter planting and blooming seasons. Such visual spectacles seemed less common, at least outside of botanical gardens I'd visited. Or maybe it originated from my eight-hour workday back in Maryland, crowded into a windowless, airless (often smoke-filled) office with fellow linguists and analysts. Or perhaps my enthusiasm was the result of having waited seven years for a chance to witness an authentic Xhosa experience.

It reminded me of the musical *The Music Man*, where Harold Hill teaches local children how to play their musical instruments without actually hitting the notes. Instead of playing the flute, clarinet, or trumpet, they hummed the notes. Instead of beating their drums, they hummed the tune. Nenzi and Themba had acted as my Harold Hill; I'd hummed the right tunes back then, but now, at last, I could actually play the music, at least a little.

Contrary to the situation in Spain or Brazil, though, I didn't come in daily contact with Xhosa speakers. Even though the Black South African population greatly outnumbered whites in 1994—and still does—Blacks worked on the fringes, in the shadows back then. Foreign service nationals—Black South Africans for the most part—worked at the US embassy as they had in Zambia, but in 1994, with an obvious exception of Nelson Mandela and some high-ranking officials, most Blacks didn't hold positions of authority, at least people I came in contact with. For the first time, though, I worked among Xhosa speakers, in their context, as I thought of it, in a setting where I occasionally heard snatches of Xhosa spoken. I could pick up a glossy *Bona* magazine, read news articles in Xhosa, articles about cooking, hobbies, celebrities, as well as Dear Abby–type columns, a far cry from the scant, rudimentary, racist, out-of-date materials my tutors had been forced to use in the late 1980s.

Apartheid had recently been abolished—1994—and Nelson Mandela stood as the newly elected president of South Africa. Plastered over street signs, at bus stops, people had taped makeshift signs printed in large script with the title of a popular Bob Dylan song: "The Times They Are a-Changin'," written by Dylan in 1964, thirty years before. Even though I stood at the periphery of this sea change, I tried to take everything in, absorb even the smallest details, history in the making.

Unlike my 1988, 1989, and 1990 work trips to Zambia when I hadn't studied Zambian languages in advance, except my slapdash efforts when called on during the 1990 coup, I had spent the past seven years either in a classroom studying Xhosa or actively translating or transcribing information in my office. This made my experience there seem different, more rewarding.

Traveling to South Africa seemed like a long-distance love affair cultivated over seven years' time. Finally, finally, I'd been given the chance to meet this "pen pal," or friend, or whatever I chose to refer to South Africa. Nenzi and Themba had supplied me with a steady diet of Xhosa, of information about South Africa, but now I had a seat at the table.

I never admitted it, or spoke it aloud, or even consciously considered it, but I identified with these marginalized people whose only sin consisted in being born the "wrong" color. What was my sin? I wondered. Being a woman in a male-dominated family? Rejecting a path other women in my family had taken? Leaving St. Louis? Getting a divorce? Starting a career? Whatever my sins, I believed them to be as arbitrary as allowing the color of the Xhosa people's—and other Blacks'—skin determine their fate.

The word *apartheid* means apartness, separateness, literally "apart-hood" in Afrikaans. That's how I'd thought of myself most of my life—apart. Apart from both parents, from my sister, both my brothers, my sisters-in-law . . . apart. Different. Like Xhosas, Sothos, Vendas, Zulus, etc. My family had cast me out—if not literally, then emotionally—for seemingly arbitrary reasons. My plight in no way compared to that of Blacks during—or after—apartheid, but a small kernel inside me thought, *Yes. I think I understand a bit of your plight, what it feels like to stand out, to have people consider you inferior, a pariah, a troublemaker for wanting your voice to be counted.*

Following the success of my Xhosa studies, a supervisor approached me about studying Afrikaans. I pushed back. Walking into her cubicle, anticipating the conversation, switching weight from one foot to the other, I waited for her to speak.

"Linda, since you have a background studying German, have studied and have worked with one South African language—Xhosa—for a number of years, it makes sense for you to begin Afrikaans so that, when needed, you could translate it. With your skills, it shouldn't take long at all. What do you think?"

Hesitating a minute, trying to formulate the right words, I replied, "I appreciate your offer, but I really don't have any interest in studying Afrikaans. I'd rather stick with other Indigenous African languages, if that's okay . . . Thanks, though!"

She never broached the topic again. How could I study a language Themba and Nenzi vilified, had indoctrinated me to dislike, a language I'd heard too many bad stories about? Besides, an unofficial, unscientific theory circulated within language analyst circles that linguists tended to take on the traits of those people who spoke the language or languages they worked. I'd already witnessed it in my office, where a handful of linguists working with Afrikaans seemed to hold themselves above everyone else, above linguists working in languages spoken by people questioning the authority of apartheid, for example. Agency linguists represented a microcosm of the world outside with its hierarchy and prejudices. I didn't want to risk becoming like Afrikaans speakers I'd read about, shortsighted as I knew that sounded.

I celebrated when a post-apartheid law ruled that, instead of only two official languages—English and Afrikaans—now eleven counted, Xhosa among them, as well as English and Afrikaans. Court systems in South Africa now required interpreters and translators in all eleven of these languages to be present for proceedings, if needed. Nine of them were Indigenous, Bantu languages. In a very real sense, millions of disenfranchised South Africans now had voices.

I wondered about this change in status of languages accompanying the end of apartheid. Would these languages now become vehicles for forging new identities among those who previously spoke them— Xhosa, Sotho, Zulu, and others—in the shadows, perhaps fearful of repercussions from white oppressors who didn't speak them? The Soweto riots in 1976 resulted from the Afrikaans Medium Decree forcing Black students and teachers to use Afrikaans in their classrooms. Black South Africans protested; they associated Afrikaans with apartheid. More than 176 people died during these riots, and over a thousand were wounded. Language mattered, continues to matter.

Even names of cities underwent changes in post-apartheid South Africa: from Afrikaans or English to Indigenous names. For instance, Cape Town also became known as eKapa, Joburg became eGoli ("place of gold"), Durban became eThekwini ("in the bay"), Pretoria was now iPitoli, and East London was iMonti. In this way the identities of Black South Africans experienced shifts, reflected even in the names of places where they lived. Their country was changing, just like in the words of the Dylan song.

More than a decade later, in 2007 and 2008, I took a closer look at this ever-evolving country, rocketing toward its unique future. If my training in 1987 had acted as a telescopic long-shot view of the Xhosa language, of South Africa, 1994 enabled me to come closer, to stay in-country, to witness changes arising post-apartheid, to meet some extraordinary people, along with a handful of Xhosas. But my 2007 and 2008 trips to Cape Town were designed exclusively to immerse me in the language, its culture, its people. If not a close-up, certainly this constituted exposure I'd never had. Most important, I saw most of it through the eyes of my in-country tutor, Mandla (meaning "power" in Xhosa). He served as my guide for both my 2007 and 2008 trips, helped me make sense of—translate—what I saw and heard. He took me places where I would never have ventured on my own. And the sole purpose of both trips lay in improving my Xhosa skills.

Every morning Mandla and I met at the language school where he worked. A modest three-story building, it featured open, sunlit classrooms, as well as a communal library of books spanning dozens of languages. A park across the street doubled as a market, filling up with people selling their wares at lunchtime.

Twenty years after beginning my Xhosa studies, textbooks and dictionaries were now easier to find. The Internet helped. Spending time in-country also helped. I learned so much during these 2007 and 2008 trips. I sat in a second-floor classroom, armed with an array of up-to-date books, dictionaries, pamphlets, printouts, all at my disposal for our morning lesson. No more vocabulary about beating people if they didn't obey. No more "Kaffir" dictionaries written in the 1800s. They'd gone by the wayside, like apartheid.

After spending the morning inside a classroom, engaged in structured lessons, I ventured outside with Mandla after lunch; we were in the heart of Cape Town. We spoke Xhosa exclusively, visiting various markets, townships, museums, friends' homes, other points of interest. January in South Africa meant summertime, gardens in bloom, people strolling throughout the city arm in arm, vendors hawking their wares.

Mandla exposed me to different sides of Cape Town, areas I couldn't have easily visited on my own as a solitary white woman. One day after class he drove me in his late model car to several townships outside Cape Town: Langa (meaning "sun" in Xhosa), Gugulethu, and Khayelitsha. Khayelitsha was the second-largest township in South Africa, after Soweto. I'd visited Soweto during my 1994 assignment in Pretoria. *Gugulethu* is a contraction for the Xhosa words *igugu lethu* ("our pride").

The townships reminded me somewhat of Rio de Janeiro's favelas: masses of people crammed together, forced out of more desirable cities into squalor, away from the white population, living in tight quarters in substandard conditions. One afternoon I followed Mandla's lead, entering a *shebeen*—a small, no frills bar—on a street of the Gugulethu township. Scant light reached inside, but I smelled beer, along with other unidentifiable odors. When my eyes adjusted, those initial shadows I'd seen morphed into various men—Black, middle-aged—standing around, talking, joking, leaning on the bar, sipping their beers. A few tables dotted the bar's small spaces. Mandla introduced me to many of the patrons, whom he seemed to know. The bar counter looked scuffed, the floors sticky. They definitely couldn't serve me a virgin piña colada here, my nonalcoholic drink of choice. I saw no women, either as customers or waitresses.

At Mandla's urging, and with trepidation at first, I greeted the bar's customers. "*Mholweni! Unjani? Igama lam ndingu Linda. Ndifunda isiXhosa,*" I sputtered, trying to speak politely. "Hello! How are you? My name is Linda. I'm studying Xhosa."

Initially, they stared at me, shell-shocked, wide-eyed, then chuckled. "Who is this *umfazi omhlophe*, this white woman? Is she really speaking our language?" their laughter telegraphed. Mandla loved witnessing their initial shock, their confused expressions folding into amused ones.

One of the older men extended a hand and, stifling another round of laughter, made small talk to me in Xhosa.

"We're fine, *Nkosazana* Linda. You are most welcome in our modest establishment."

He bowed slightly as he addressed me, keeping his handshake light, as though afraid gripping my hand might squeeze all the Xhosa words out of me.

"It's my pleasure, *mhlekazi*," I responded, hoping my shaky nerves didn't cause my hard work in Xhosa to disappear in a puff of smoke, as though I were a tape cassette someone had erased. Honestly, though, I think if I'd recited the alphabet they'd have acted impressed. My teacher confirmed my suspicions, namely that I surely represented the first *umfazi omhlophe* to enter their bar speaking Xhosa, the first white woman.

I knew not to rush our conversation. I knew many Black South Africans considered it rude to get right to the point, the way many English speakers do. In the Xhosa culture, it's customary to ask about someone's family, his health, his life before getting to the topic at hand. Anything else is abrupt, bad manners.

After talking with the men a while, we thanked them and left the *shebeen*. I continued to walk alongside Mandla. He led me to a modest storefront where a handwritten sign outside advertised its products. There he introduced me to another friend, a natural healer, an *igqirha*. She toted a baby in a multicolored cloth she wore wrapped around her chest, invited us into her tiny cubicle, an "office" the size of three bathroom stalls, where she kept various-sized bottles with remedies: plants, potions, strands of herbs. Mandla explained that township people could find anything they needed there. He made use of our time to buy something for himself but didn't reveal its contents to me or what it treated.

Our walks through these three townships focused primarily on the highlights of each township, on places where Mandla's friends congregated, because each location was too large to cover in a few hours. Then Mandla took me to his home for lunch. I met his wife, his mother-in-law, his nine-year-old daughter. Although extremely modest by American standards, Mandla displayed great pride in showing off his brick and mortar home. He insisted on giving me a room-to-room tour, including outside areas. I saw the carefully appointed living room with doilies gracing the couch's armrests and a coffee table with family photographs, including school pictures of his daughter, a refrigerator and a stove in his tiled kitchen, a master bedroom with its hand-crocheted comforter, even a fully stocked pantry. A member of a small Black South African middle class, Mandla wanted to share his success with me. His lifestyle did not resemble the poorer conditions of his friends in neighboring townships.

His wife and mother-in-law worked hard to prepare a sumptuous meal of chicken feet, greens, *umqa* (maize meal), cabbage, and homemade bread (*isonka*). Before eating they presented me with a cup of water to lightly wash my hands.

My day with Mandla served as a great education, providing me with insights I couldn't gain in a classroom, although he provided me with an excellent education in the classroom and on our walks. These special insights included stories elaborating on men's initiation ceremonies (*abakweta*), performed when boys came of age, as well as the age-old custom of *lobela* (dowry) made by a man to the family of the woman he wanted to marry. He also told stories about the Xhosas' cattle-raising history; the still-practiced tradition of polygamy; the importance of their *iintsomi* (folktales), their proverbs (*amaqhalo*), face painting in white ocher (*umchokozo*), and more.

One afternoon he also took me to his parents' home, where they greeted me with open arms, preparing another delicious feast. Everyone dressed in Western-style clothing, speaking both English and Xhosa fluently.

Another day Mandla and I visited the District Six Museum. It honors the sixty thousand inhabitants of an area where people were forced to live, corralled out of Cape Town under apartheid into the slums of District Six. I walked around the museum, looking at letters residents had written, studying memorabilia, photographs, maps. It all seemed like part of a science fiction movie.

We traveled to the museum by subway. Sitting on a long wooden bench next to my diminutive teacher, I became nervous. If someone chose to attack or rob the only white woman on the subway, fifty-year-old Mandla would be ill-equipped to defend me. Zimbabweans were pouring into South Africa at the time, eager to escape worsening conditions under Robert Mugabe's dictatorship. That day several Zimbabweans made their way through our subway car, looking around, then approaching us—and other passengers—to ask for handouts. Mandla whispered to me to ignore them, but my nerves remained on edge.

Toward the end of my time in Cape Town, on my own I visited Robben Island, a former leper colony where Nelson Mandela had been imprisoned, where he did hard labor during many of his twenty-seven years in prison. The experience had a lasting impact on me. I traveled nine kilometers by ferry to witness where "Madiba" (Mandela's Xhosa name) used a pickax to break up quarry limestone for thirteen of his twenty-seven years there. "Home" for the six-foot-one man consisted of a six-by-six-foot concrete cell, not much larger than a closet, with a barred window and a windowsill beginning probably at Mandela's chest. Tour guides were former political prisoners in the 1970s. My guide explained how even the meals prisoners ate came down to race: Blacks received corn with soft porridge, occasionally minced fish heads. Coloreds and Asians fared better, even enjoyed an occasional bit of meat and bread. In prison segregation still ruled; incarceration did not equalize the lives of prisoners, regardless of crimes committed.

The day I visited Robben Island and Nelson Mandela's jail cell was one of my last days in South Africa. When I left Robben Island behind, its drab, stark, bleached-out landscape, its blood- and sweat-drenched soil, its stories of resilience, of bravery, all ran through my mind. A lone ostrich galloped across rocky terrain, close to our vehicle as my fellow visitors and I headed back to the ferry. Watching the agitated ostrich, I thought of my life thus far, of these languages I'd studied. Maybe they all served as stepping stones to lead me home, back to my true identity, after numerous false starts. Did they represent conduits to achieving a greater understanding of myself, of my path? Maybe I mirrored some of what the Xhosa people did to survive. Maybe I, too, had survived. Perhaps I represented a buck private in an army of generals like Nelson Mandela. If not for Xhosa, I might never have received this increased insight.

5

THE IMPERATIVE MOOD

Duty Calls

THE IMPERATIVE MOOD—*a grammatical term referring to verbs that contain direct commands—negative or positive—or requests.*

EXAMPLE: *"You must do the thing you think you cannot do." —Eleanor Roosevelt*

We buried my father on June 27, 1998. Six weeks later, al-Qaeda-linked groups blew up the US embassies in Nairobi, Kenya, and Dar es Salaam, Tanzania, using truck bombs. The two dates remain forever linked in my mind.

In the immediate aftermath of the bombings, my work mentor phoned me, strongly recommending that I go to Nairobi to assist with post-bombing investigations. At least 224 people had died in both attacks, among them, 12 Americans. Blasts wounded more than 4,500 people.

The period immediately following a terrorist attack is one of heightened risk, of increased danger, a fact not commonly known. Law enforcement officials, investigators, intelligence analysts, medical personnel, anti-terrorism experts, communications personnel, and other "helpers" all converge at the site of a crisis in the aftermath of an incident, making it an ideal time for follow-up attacks, for terrorists to strike again with more impact.

Known officially as "double-tap strikes," a targeted strike site is sometimes hit multiple times in quick succession, meaning that the second attack often hits first responders, helpers, medics who rushed to the site to offer their assistance. Consequently, it's often more deadly than the initial terrorist strike. For this and other reasons, I did not want to go to Kenya, not under any circumstances. I explained this to my mentor, Warren, speaking with uncharacteristic boldness.

"This isn't a good time for me to go to Africa, Warren. My father just died. My family is in a state of shock. I'm in no shape emotionally to go on this TDY."

He countered with, "You outlined this *exact* scenario in your program proposal, Linda. You referenced having to prepare for pop-up attacks in unforeseen locations, crises that necessitated a quick response by the US government. With a great deal of effort you managed to convince high-level leadership to have you trained in Swahili for this specific type of event." Continuing, he added, "You may remember that, initially, most people thought that training you—anyone—in Swahili—represented a foolhardy idea, not worth the funds it would cost. But you prevailed, citing the very situation we're in now. You can't suddenly say it's not convenient."

It's true that I'd used my best powers of persuasion to convince a panel of leaders of a prestigious agency program that Swahili represented a linchpin in anticipating future language needs. At the time, to my knowledge only one other Swahili linguist with the necessary security clearances worked for the government.

Viewing the geopolitical situation through a historic lens in which the former Soviet Union was the focus, traditional government leaders logically asserted that a language—Swahili—spoken by our friends in Tanzania, Kenya, Uganda, parts of the Democratic Republic of the Congo, and elsewhere in Africa did not warrant attention. To them, it made no sense to focus on these countries, to train someone in Swahili. It made as much sense as training someone, say, in Dutch or Welsh, maybe even Esperanto, an artificial, constructed language; in other words, none at all.

My principal counterargument to this panel consisted in pointing out that more than fifty million people spoke Swahili as a first language, with many millions more speaking it as a lingua franca, a common language used to link people not speaking the same primary language. The mere number of people who spoke it in Africa made it enormously important, I argued. But now I'd abandoned that previous line of reasoning.

"I realize what I said, what my arguments were, but my father just died. I'm barely getting over the year leading up to his death. I need to heal, to remain in the States. I can't do this. I can't go to the site of a terrorist attack just when my emotions are running so high."

"I know, Linda. It's just awful to lose a parent. This is an incredibly bad time to have to travel to Africa under these circumstances, but you're the only one who can help with Swahili during this investigation. You did all the training for this purpose. The government invested tens of thousands of dollars in you, in your training. You're one of a handful of people with a security clearance who knows Swahili, who has trained for this specific type of event. Your skill set perfectly aligns with the program you presented. You correctly anticipated events."

It had all looked so good on paper three years before. I'd wanted to participate in a prestigious agency program made up primarily of scientists or employees with technical expertise. Many people still viewed mastering foreign languages as an elementary exercise, skills anyone could pick up. "Oh, you work with Spanish; I studied it in high school," I'd hear when I first moved East and explained what I did for a living.

For years I'd thought about studying Swahili. About ten years before, in 1988, I'd started my adventure with African languages, had studied Xhosa, then Sotho, another South African "click" language. I struggled to find appropriate material in a pre-Internet era, one in which apartheid still held South Africa in its grip. But the Internet reigned now, and a wealth of information existed about and in Swahili, a much better known language in the same "family" of languages (Bantu) as Xhosa and Sotho.

Under optimal circumstances, I should have begun my work in African languages with Swahili, a prototypical Bantu language. It doesn't have clicks or a sea of tongue-twisting consonant clusters or tones to master. Still a difficult language, it's less daunting than Xhosa, Sotho, or other African languages I eventually studied: Shona (another Bantu language spoken in Zimbabwe), Amharic (a Semitic language spoken in Ethiopia and Eritrea), Somali. Adding to its allure for me: up-to-date dictionaries, phrase books, grammars, glossy magazines, newspapers, the availability of contemporary literature—an embarrassment of riches at my feet. It was like being the high school nerd awash in textbooks. I was always devoted to and loved my original, hard-won friends (Xhosa and Sotho), both of them standing in the wings, difficult, elusive. But Swahili represented those popular kids in my metaphor, easier to know, not as complicated or difficult, loved by scores of people. That's what had drawn me to it.

The fact that I'd proposed a plan that married my eagerness to immerse myself in Swahili with a bona fide security concern made it a win-win situation. But I never imagined that fate would transpire to create an actual need to implement my ingenious plan.

The day I appeared before an eminent panel for the program, I chose my most convincing words about how long it takes to get linguists up to speed in any language, a fact requiring management to act proactively, not reactively. Back then, in the mid-1990s, all too often government leaders erroneously believed that if a crisis occurred in region X, someone could be trained in that language overnight, become virtually fluent in no time, with a little brushing up, much like my situation in Zambia during the coup attempt when the chargé found a dog-eared, out-of-date grammar for me to learn a language I knew little about.

"Surely you can see, from the lessons history has provided, that being reactive, from the vantage point of being language-ready, is foolhardy. The government needs to plan in advance, be proactive, not reactive. Languages aren't coats you can put on in the event of disaster. The skills have to be masterfully developed in advance," I argued.

I pointed out that fallout from the government's shortsightedness had occurred several times when trouble popped up in unforeseen locations. Managers frantically rounded up linguists who hadn't come in contact with the required language in years, decades, in some instances people ill-equipped to tackle challenges. Sometimes situations necessitated drafting linguists who'd studied another language deemed similar. "Oh, you studied Russian, so you can switch to Ukrainian; they both use the Cyrillic alphabet." Or, "You've studied Spanish, so Portuguese should come second nature."

Whatever the language scenario, certain steps had to be taken well in advance: qualified instructors located and cleared, suitable materials vetted, calendars scrubbed for both instructor and student or students. Most important, such a project required countless hours of diligent study to reach desired levels in reading and listening comprehension. After all, bad guys didn't go around speaking publicly in most cases. They didn't speak slowly, careful to enunciate every word, tempering their voices, announcing their identities. "Hello, my name is bad guy John Doe. I want to commit this terrorist act next Friday at such-and-such o'clock by doing such and such. I will need these materials to carry it out." Instead, their communications utilized cryptic passages filled with gaps, double entendres, one-sided conversations, special codes, and often a substandard version of the language. A linguist needed to know a language inside and out to keep up, and even more important, had to be able to fill in gaps.

During my interview for the program, I'd explained that, if a crisis occurred in any country that affected the United States or its citizens, linguists needed to be ready to lend a hand. A beautiful proposal, delivered with eloquence, with maps, charts, statistics, diagrams, one that accomplished my goal: selection to this premier program, a chance to study Swahili for a year with a tutor, similar to how I'd studied Xhosa and Sotho.

My lofty goal had come true; I'd spent a year studying Swahili in Washington, DC, with a brilliant tutor, a native speaker of Swahili. Then I'd gone to Tanzania and Kenya for back-to-back language immersions in those countries, working with other instructors one-on-one to improve my Swahili. After three years of hard work, I had just graduated from the prestigious program. On paper at least, I looked ready to make good on my pledge . . . But not now, not right now . . . please, not right now.

Warren had a valid argument, but I also knew that he did not, in fact, "know" what had transpired the year before, the year I lost my father. No one did. I'd spent a lifetime acting like a "normal" person, someone who'd lived a typical Midwestern childhood, whatever that meant: Girl Scouts, summer camp, sleepovers, with a stay-at-home mother married to a professional father and three siblings. I acted that part well, even told stories about my father's model railroading obsession, my mother's metal-detecting hobby. But, as my father revealingly liked to tell people, "We Murphys aren't crazy; we're just mean." Half right, I think. But I desperately wanted to fit in, have people like me, respect me. Sharing stories about my mother's sometimes cruel antics, about my father's volatile moods, his disrespect for women, would not have endeared me to potential friends and colleagues. In a very real sense, foreign languages had served as my ticket out of that environment.

The crisis surrounding my father and his eventual death had begun the year before, in Barcelona, Spain. He, my mother, and I traveled by ambulance from a family cruise to a small clinic outside Barcelona after my father suffered a series of strokes onboard. Despite his once-brilliant legal mind, during our vacation he showed difficulty stringing together sentences, as though his words lay jammed up inside him. He couldn't release them, a condition known as aphasia, I later learned. He also began having difficulty walking and showed signs of confusion, most notably on our last night when he wandered off after dinner. Family members searched the large cruise ship for him; we found him confused and irritated in the ship's auditorium.

"Where were you?" he asked, visibly irritated, seeing us race toward him just as the show was about to start.

"Looking for you," we replied, breathless from our searching, but he'd turned his attention to the stage.

On the final day of the cruise, when I joined my parents at breakfast, I knew my father had suffered a stroke: disheveled, his normally slicked-back hair stuck out in tufts from his head, buttons of his red plaid shirt revealed gaps where he couldn't button it. He didn't resemble my father. Seeing him this way made me profoundly sad.

"I think I had a stroke, Lin," he announced unnecessarily, as my mother dabbed her napkin at a corner of her mouth, sitting across from him, her perfectly groomed and coiffed figure belying the existence of a crisis. I rushed to get medical help; then the three of us went by ambulance to a small clinic outside Barcelona.

My mother and I remained with my father for nearly a week in Barcelona until we could medically evacuate him back to the States, back to St. Louis where he received superior medical care. During that week, I acted as official interpreter and translator ten to twelve hours a day, translating bills, insurance documents, invoices; interpreting nonstop for my father, my mother, for doctors, nurses, other medical staff, anyone whose path crossed with my father's.

I returned to Maryland just in time to continue my Swahili training as part of my competitive program. One of the perks of being a participant was being able to create my own program, with access to a generous budget. That enabled me to build a one-on-one language tutorial into it, along with a chance to go to Tanzania and Kenya to work with tutors, in addition to taking pertinent linguistic courses at nearby Georgetown University.

My real challenge during the next ten months—my father's final—lay in navigating my often strained relations with my siblings, their spouses, and my mother. During those months, my father underwent brain surgery, suffered additional strokes, then went through rehabilitation, followed by more strokes. He epitomized the Myth of Sisyphus, rolling that ball up a steep hill, only to have it roll back down on him, crushing his body and spirit. It made for a nightmarish ten months. By the time he died on June 23, 1998, I'd become persona non grata, for reasons I never fully grasped. My only goal, beyond seeing my father's health improve, consisted in surviving the backlash from my family, continuing with my work program.

Within that context of mourning my father's death, coupled with shifting, vanishing family loyalties, terrorists blew up the US embassies nearly simultaneously, using truck bombs. At the time, I represented one of a handful of Swahili linguists with a top secret security clearance working for the US government; no one else— cleared—could go to Africa to help out. I had to go, though, as I wrote in my journal, "I don't want to go to Africa and I'm not proud of that," adding, "I do not want to go, but I guess language keeps leading me where I don't want to go but need to." Prophetic words. I wanted more than anything to remain in Maryland, climb in bed, pull the covers over my head till life settled down: both within my biological family and in Africa. I wanted to be left alone. Take the phone off the hook. Sleep. Heal.

My negative attitude toward this assignment contrasted with my approach to previous ones when I looked forward to visiting Africa. My father's death and my family situation contributed to that, but something else occurred to me. I'd found myself in dangerous situations before in Africa, but never by design, never by choice. This differed from my 1990 trip to Zambia when I found myself in the midst of rioting and a coup attempt, thrown into it by circumstances beyond my control. I hadn't known in advance what faced me following my flight from the States to Lusaka. I envisioned a journey topping off two previous, similar work trips to Zambia, routine trips, with outings to markets, museums, dinners with new State Department friends thrown in after hours for good measure, enlivening my time in Lusaka. I hadn't known what awaited me in Zambia in 1990, my third assignment. Truthfully, if I had, I wouldn't have gone. "I can't do this," I'd have reasoned. "I'm not qualified for this work," I would have insisted, much as I found myself doing now, except that I did know Swahili.

I wouldn't have chosen to put myself in harm's way by going to Nairobi. To join forces with others in the aftermath of death and de-struction, to risk falling victim to follow-up attacks by sophisticated terrorists, by professionals who'd planned these bombings to occur just minutes apart? These were not amateurs; they had links to the Egyptian Islamic Jihad, to Osama bin Laden, to al-Qaeda, increasing my sense of powerlessness to do anything constructive to counter the disasters. This didn't represent false modesty on my part; this stemmed from my core belief that I couldn't offer anything useful to anyone. I jumped at my own shadow, could barely get out of bed. How could I participate in any effort to track down professional terrorists who had killed or injured thousands of innocent people?

As fate would have it, I received a short reprieve from traveling to Nairobi when FBI officials asked me to help out at their head-quarters in Washington, DC, to participate in their investigation, sorting through evidence in Swahili, lengthy phone conversations between possible perpetrators of the attacks. Embassies and citizens abroad fall under the jurisdiction of their home country, so the bombings were considered domestic terrorism in that regard, but also international terrorism because, in addition to Kenyans and Tanzanians, US citizens and the US embassy itself had been targeted.

I welcomed helping out at the FBI, hoped it would be enough, that my contributions would be sufficient in the eyes of my managers. It served as a stopgap measure, though, merely delaying my departure to Africa a few weeks.

On September 28, I traveled alone to Nairobi, flying via Frankfurt. I had no one to listen to my whining, my complaining: about how inconvenient timing of the assignment was, about how ill-equipped I considered myself, how terrified I was.

Landing at Nairobi's airport, I thought back to the previous summer when—as part of my language program—I'd come here under different circumstances. I'd spent six weeks in Tanzania and Kenya enhancing my Swahili skills by working one-on-one with a tutor in Tanzania and by myself in Kenya. Prior to that, I'd studied with my tutor in the States. Living and studying in Kenya and Tanzania offered me a chance to practice my Swahili in earnest in both countries, to increase my fluency. Following lessons at my hotel in the morning in Tanzania, my tutor and I had visited markets, museums, women's cooperatives, private homes. I met traditional healers, fishermen, people in all walks of life. The experience in both countries taught me so much, greatly enhanced my Swahili skills, but represented a wholly different situation than this one.

On my first day in Nairobi following the tandem terrorist attacks I met with a few survivors of the deadly explosions, accompanied by members of a team I would work with. One embassy employee told me about a woman, a twin, who awakened back home in the States at 3:30 Eastern Daylight Time, sure that something had happened to her twin in Nairobi, that danger surrounded her, without knowing why. She tried to reach her sister. I heard similar hair-raising stories, among them how the US ambassador herself suffered minor cuts on her hands and lips when flying glass struck her.

These stories were unsettling, and a file they gave me added to my distress. It contained multiple photographs of blood-spattered walls, mangled, charred bodies, rubble, blown-out windows, over-turned chairs and tables, computers with electrical wires strewn all over the floor as though they'd weighed next to nothing, light as toys. Mountains of printer paper covered floors like a giant's confetti; offices looked like a tornado had ripped through them. Reviewing these photographs as I sat in a US official's home, I felt an inexplicable kinship with all these affected people, people I'd never met. That sense of kinship only grew when I visited what was left of the US embassy the next day, though nothing in that file or in stories I heard would prepare me sufficiently.

The first thing the next morning, I joined a team at the bombed-out embassy, a five-story structure US officials would ultimately tear down, deemed too unstable to repair. The US ambassador, Prudence Bushnell, had warned of security threats, had reported that the location of the embassy wasn't sufficiently protected, but no one had taken heed, apparently. Nonetheless, a small silver lining occurred when the truck the terrorists used to transport their explosive devices in Nairobi couldn't reach its final destination: the ramp leading to a garage beneath the embassy. Because of the terrorists' missteps the truck exploded outside the building, instead of under it, the resulting damage not nearly as devastating. If the truck had made its way beneath the embassy as planned, the destruction and loss of life would have been far greater, but the vehicle was too tall to fit underneath. The terrorists' goal had been to level the embassy, to kill all the Americans inside; thankfully, that did not happen.

Wearing a compulsory hard hat, like everyone else, I followed three or four team members up several flights of now dark embassy stairwells. Elevator shafts had been blown out, as well as the building's electricity. No one else was inside now. Our footsteps were the only sound I heard.

Victims' bodies had been removed from inside the building, from adjacent buildings, as well as from the area surrounding the buildings. Survivors had been rescued from the rubble, classified documents and computers removed. What remained looked like the office I worked in back home, but one that malevolent forces had turned upside down, had shaken like a giant snow globe, doused with kerosene, then ignited. I twisted my head to take everything in, the skewed angles of objects, the upside-down book titles. I recognized pads of sticky notes, reference books such as Jane's Encyclopedias, used by the State Department, Defense Department, and intelligence analysts alike. I spotted disembodied knobs of equipment, government-issued bright red English Webster's dictionaries everyone used, pencil sharpeners, cords, ripped-apart bookshelves, office chairs, reel-to-reel tape players with their knobs blown off. Once again, similar to the Zambian riots of 1990, it was almost like walking onto the set of a movie, not real life.

Like a statue on a revolving pedestal, I stood in one place, slowly rotating 360 degrees to take it all in, speechless, afraid to move. Time stood still. I'd arrived the day before, yet I felt like I was going into shock. At my feet, I picked up a familiar document: a Letter of Appreciation. Blank. It read: "The Department of State – Embassy of the United States of America – Certificate of Appreciation Awarded to ……. for ……. Nairobi, Kenya." No name was visible, no reason given for honoring the phantom person. I wondered if he or she had survived the blasts. I hoped so. Of course, no one could use such a certificate now. I could still make out the dark blue seal of the Department of State at the top center, with its ornate black printing (Gothic?) throughout, but smudges of dark brown dirt and dust covered it. A layer of silt or dirt covered everything. I knew they'd already done major cleaning out, clearing out rubble and victims by now, but I waded through thick silt and dust, the origins of which I didn't want to think about.

Attempting to unfreeze myself, I walked around the office, watching where I stepped. Staring at the wide expanse of walls in front of me, I realized that human blood had created the giant swaths of red visible on the walls, not paint. Huge smudges smeared the once-white walls, giant strokes of red, as though Jackson Pollock had run through the building with a giant brush, carrying a bucket of bright red paint, leaving his mark haphazardly, hurriedly, indelibly.

At some point, I separated myself from the scene before me, looking around for my colleagues, but they'd vanished. I remained alone. I didn't hear a sound. The all-male team had left me, gone elsewhere in search of salvageable equipment, no doubt thinking I'd be able to find them, or maybe not thinking about me at all. They didn't know me, though, had just met me the day before, so they didn't know how anxious I could become. I'd learned on my previous trips to Africa that no one would mollycoddle me. State Department, Defense Department, Intelligence Agency personnel assumed that, within reason, I could deal with whatever life handed me without complaining, could navigate my surroundings, be resourceful, productive, handle things myself. I'd received that message again on this assignment.

Trying not to panic, I walked over to a large picture window, now a vacuous square hole with pieces of glass poking around its perimeter. I waded through debris to reach it. Something drew me to the window, light from the outside flooding into this otherwise darkened office. I also thought maybe I'd be able to spot my colleagues if they'd left the building and were waiting for me.

The explosion's force had caused glass to blow inward like jet propulsion while window frames blew outward, an embassy official told me. His stories reminded me of loading machine guns with varying-sized shards of glass, thousands of deadly spears, then shooting them out too fast for victims to avoid the onslaught. Someone on our team explained when we first stepped onto this floor that a woman had died standing next to the very window where I now stood. She heard loud noises outside, grenades aimed at embassy guards, got up from her desk to investigate, walked over to the window, then received the brunt of the blast, losing her life in a split second. That seemed particularly tragic, unnecessary. Her curiosity or vigilance cost her—I longed to know her name—her life. I knew I would have done the same thing upon hearing loud, disturbing sounds emanating from outside; I would have walked over to the closest window to investigate. I would also have died.

I needed to get out of this bombed-out building or I'd collapse in a pile of tears; they'd have to carry me out. I needed to stop looking at orphaned shoes, singed working aids, beat-up dictionaries identical to ones I used back in Maryland, the same drab gray metal desks and chairs, the same metal coat racks, lamps, the same government-issue wall clocks, file cabinets, the same equipment, the same type of indestructible plants we all brought from home to add a touch of color to our otherwise drab offices. Except that here everything lay in pieces or had been twisted, uprooted, bent out of shape or stood at an odd angle, even unrecognizable in some cases. The sun peeked through open chinks in the wall as though intent on offering some measure of optimism in an otherwise depressing building.

What had that solitary knob turned? To whom did that orphaned shoe belong? Where had its mate landed, or had it disintegrated in the blast? For some reason I ducked down, looking behind overturned chairs, desks, racks, trying to locate it. Crazy. Whose family photo was light reflecting off of in that cracked frame? Did the owner survive?

I needed to find the team. Silence carried a sound and weight of its own, deafening, wrapping me in a thick cover of sadness. The smell of death, of evil forces mingled with these lost souls. Why had I even come here? I wasn't using my Swahili yet. Why did I need to see this? This wasn't like Zambia, where men, women, children rioted, tried to overthrow a corrupt government because their very existence depended on it, because life had become unmanageable after the government raised food prices far beyond their modest means. In anger they took to the streets to protest their plight. This carnage had been painstakingly planned, calculated, executed by veteran terrorists who didn't live here, who conspired to kill Americans, by men who opposed US involvement in Muslim countries. These acts of revenge targeted civilians, not a corrupt government withholding food from the mouths of their children.

I wanted to cry, but I had no right to cry. I hadn't been here, didn't personally know anyone who died, hadn't been called on to do the unspeakably grim work of sifting through rubble for survivors, searching through charred remains. I hadn't been asked to administer medical treatment to wounded survivors. I had no right, yet tears were close to the surface. I wanted to sit down on the floor next to one of these twisted desks and cry: for the Kenyans and Americans who'd died here but also for my father, whom I'd never see again. My emotions were all mixed together in a heaping pot of self-pity and hopelessness.

Of all the people in my immediate family, in his own way my father showed the most interest in my language career, though the bar stood low. Whenever I did something language related that seemed noteworthy, my language skills in demand or used at high levels, I frequently wondered if it would make him proud of me, elicit his praise. Both before and after his death, my mind always wandered to those thoughts. When I visited him in the hospital in St. Louis after one of his many strokes following our Mediterranean cruise, physical therapists were working with him in another room when I arrived. I introduced myself to his roommate, who paused a moment, then asked, "Say! Are you the daughter who speaks all those languages?" When I answered yes, the man replied, "Well, he talks about you constantly." My eyes filled with tears at such a seemingly innocuous remark. This translated into high praise from my father, albeit secondhand. I didn't realize my father ever spoke to anyone about my career or my love of languages, much less to a relative stranger.

When my father lay in a coma several months later, shortly before his death, I returned to St. Louis again, visiting him in his hospital room. After telling him I loved him, how sad I was that he'd suffered so much the past year, I told him goodbye by using the phrase I'd learned in Xhosa. "*Hamba kakuhle,*" I whispered in his ear as I gave him a kiss on the cheek. "Go well." He would travel to another realm while I stayed behind, with all that entailed. If he'd been the one staying, with me leaving, I'd have whispered, "*Sala kakuhle.*" "Stay well." My last words to him, words I hadn't planned to say, but suddenly they'd seemed appropriate. I knew he somehow understood them. I knew I would not have spoken them to anyone else. I knew he was proud of me, in spite of himself, in spite of his views about what women should or shouldn't do, how they should or shouldn't relate to men, what part of the country they should or shouldn't live in, or if they should have careers. I think he secretly admired my life, a life for which I'd fought and sacrificed, despite his explicit wishes, despite a lifetime of pushback from him.

After remaining frozen in place for several minutes, I made my way back over to the hollowed-out stairwell, looking straight ahead, not at what lay all around me. I called down into the shaft of the wide, dark stairwell, stained with gashes of blood, hoping the team had remained somewhere in the building. "Hello? Hello? Where are you? I'm still up here! Where are you?" Did they even remember I'd come with them? What if they didn't, what if they'd left without me? My voice echoed throughout the embassy's crumbling skeleton. I tried to remove traces of panic from my voice, to sound nonchalant, reminding myself that I probably wasn't in any danger. But I knew that, regardless, they wouldn't appreciate my fragile emotional state. I found myself close to tears, overwhelmed by what I'd seen, by images swirling around in my mind.

Eventually, I heard faint voices rising up from several floors below. "We're down here on the main floor! Come on, we're ready to leave." I followed those sounds into the darkened embassy, trying to avert my eyes from the blood-stained walls, remainders and re-minders of human life—and death—left behind when terrorists detonated four to five hundred can-sized cylinders of TNT from their truck. I carefully made my way downstairs, holding onto a bright orange railing, still intact. Without electricity I relied on spots where explosions had torn through concrete, letting the bright Kenyan sun peek in, eventually locating the four men on the team. Shortly after, we left. I never wanted to go back.

Eventually, the US embassy—as well as other nearby buildings destroyed in the blasts—was razed, and a memorial garden was constructed in memory of those who lost their lives that day. What none of us yet knew, though, was that these sophisticated, nearly simultaneous African bombings—aimed at killing Americans, not Kenyans or Tanzanians—served as a prelude by these same al-Qaeda-affiliated terrorists for the deadly September 11, 2001, US bombings a little more than three years later.

Subsequent to my somber visit to the US embassy, I put my Swahili skills to good use. I helped the State Department, the FBI, and other US officials in their investigation of the deadly blast. Initially, investigators believed the terrorists to be of Middle Eastern origin, but the FBI discovered they'd worked in-country for quite a while in preparation for these attacks. Consequently, terrorists presumably had made contact with Swahili speakers who could shed light on the attacks. My task was to assist investigators by listening to open voice channels (in which Swahili was used) to determine who'd been behind the deadly bombings, who'd helped the perpetrators, where they'd built the bombs, and similar unanswered questions.

On my six previous work trips to Africa—to South Africa, Zambia, Tanzania, Kenya—locals welcomed me, encouraged my language studies. Flattered that a foreigner showed enthusiasm for their language of origin, they often sat down with me, explained nuances in their language: idioms, vocabulary distinctions, grammatical issues, and, most important, cultural considerations. For example, I learned never to beckon anyone using my index finger (or any finger), bending it toward me to signal I wanted the person in question to approach. Colonial powers—British in the case of Tanzania and Kenya—customarily did this to the people they dominated, with disastrous results. The gesture communicated condescension, even derision. My grammar books, even those abundantly available Swahili ones, did not contain this type of valuable information, though it should have been intuitive.

This post-bombing visit differed significantly. More than two hundred Kenyans had lost their lives because of the explosion, many more wounded, far more than Americans. Adding to their disenchantment, Kenyans believed that post-bombing work focused primarily on those twelve Americans who had died. Investigators concluded early on that Kenyans had not been the intended victims but were collateral damage. This added to Kenyans' resentment. In fact, follow-up reports stated that terrorists had explicitly—albeit unsuccessfully—attempted to avoid killing Kenyans. Their goal consisted in the wholesale massacre of Americans.

Historically, Kenya and the United States had enjoyed a close relationship, perhaps the closest alliance in Africa. Their relationship extended back to 1964, shortly after Kenya declared its independence, when the US established an embassy there. This horrific incident, however, strained that relationship, at least temporarily. The deluge of Americans arriving post-bombing did nothing to lessen those feelings of resentment, as more than a thousand US personnel from various agencies descended into Nairobi, determined to track down the per-petrators, overrunning a once-peaceful country.

I personally witnessed this change of attitude that summer in Nairobi, despite my limited contacts. Locals now met my fluency in Swahili with suspicion, even hostility in some cases. One afternoon after work, when I went to a local café, preferable to spending the remainder of my day alone in my hotel room, an employee ques-tioned me after I asked him the meaning of a Swahili idiom I couldn't find in any of my dictionaries.

"What are you doing? Why are you speaking our language? What are those papers you're reading? You need to leave."

"I'm just studying your language. I love Swahili, came here to improve it. I just wanted to ask you a question about something, but I didn't mean to disturb you. I'm sorry. I'll go."

He looked at me sternly, his eyes cold. I'd lost a potential friend, even though I'd never met him before that day. But to me he represented all the Kenyans who'd previously welcomed my studies so graciously, who had repeatedly helped me. More fallout from the terrorists, I guessed.

Nothing prepared me for what happened a few nights later. I sat in my hotel room reviewing my Swahili notebooks, grammars, newspapers, dictionaries. I liked to write down new phrases, words I'd heard or read that day, use them in practice sentences. I'd research their meanings, often not found in any dictionary. Sitting on my bed with books, newspapers, loose pieces of papers strewn out around me like a deck of oversized cards, a laptop by my side, I lost myself in my beloved Swahili, reading, translating, taking notes. Suddenly, all the lights went out; my computer screen went blank. Darkness enveloped my hotel room, everything in it; I had limited vision until my eyes adjusted. Unlike back home, no emergency lights clicked on in response to the outage.

I tiptoed over to the window, careful not to trip over cords or bump into furniture. I remembered the US embassy employee who lost her life doing something similar. Could this loss of electricity presage a follow-up attack in light of the various government personnel overrunning Kenya? Was I in danger? I carefully opened my curtains. Nairobi appeared before me in shadows, a mass of dark buildings etched in profile in front of me, not a single light visible. What had happened? From what I could see, everyone else had lost their electricity too. Should I call someone? Did the phones even work? But who would I call? I didn't know anyone's mobile phone number, just like in Zambia. There was no US embassy front desk to call because there was no longer an embassy. I stood there, completely alone.

This seemed worse than when I'd been trapped in Zambia, an unidentified man lurking outside, the sound of gunfire peppering the night's silence. At least then I could construct a safe haven by locking myself back room by room, creating barriers. I also had a dog to distract me. Despite his diminutive size, his bark was surprisingly strong. I'd read that a dog of any size acted as a deterrent to criminals. Besides, Zambians hadn't specifically targeted Americans, although they surely coveted the surpluses of food in their homes. Whoever planned these bombings, however, had their sights trained on Americans. People like me. I couldn't even depend on my hotel door lock to shield me from possible intruders. Any number of hotel employees surely had access to a master key; I might as well have left it open.

Nor did I have *The Blues Brothers*—or other movies—to distract me from possible danger outside my room. And no electricity meant no TV. I stood in silence, listening in the dark for sounds. At home I'd been in the dark before, of course, briefly gone without electricity, but there were always candles, flashlights, a functioning phone, my family, neighbors, a car. This exposed me to something new. I hadn't even gotten any training. I guessed that State Department officers or intelligence officials would know what to do. Why hadn't I asked them when our paths crossed? Because I hadn't anticipated this. No one trained me in advance for this or for anything similar. There'd been no time.

More silence. I stood like a statue, trying to hear something, anything. I could feel my heart beating, so fast, so loudly I was confident I could hear individual beats.

Without warning, the lights went back on after a few minutes; my computer whirred as it began powering up again. The brightness temporarily blinded me.

Shortly after the lights returned, someone pounded on the door. First, the lights had gone off. Second, after fifteen or twenty minutes, they'd come back on. Third, there was pounding on the door. One, two, three. Strong, masculine knocks. Bold knocks by someone in authority, someone on a mission, not tentative do-you-need-more-towels knocks. Then came a voice.

"Hello!" A deep, masculine voice, laced with a touch of impatience, not really asking a question.

I waited a beat, then answered. "Yes?" I replied, trying to sound older, brawnier, masculine.

"Are you the right person?" he asked.

What a strange, cryptic phrase, I thought. What did he mean? I hesitated, then replied, "No." It seemed like my only possible response.

My room, newly filled with light, somehow made my situation seem starker, more ominous, as though I played an unwitting role in some theatrical production, a play for which I didn't yet know my part. The stage needed lighting for this next scene in my imaginary production.

"Open the door," he commanded next, using that same authoritative voice. This, despite the fact that I'd told him I was the wrong person. "I need to talk to you," he added, as though that explained everything.

I slowly made my way to the door, banging my knee on a corner of the bed in the process, despite the lights having returned. My senses went on high alert as various scenarios flashed through my mind: US soldiers coming to my rescue? State Department officials? Hotel employees? Implausible, each scenario. What to do, though? Nothing came to mind.

Once, less than a year before, I'd successfully talked my way out of a tricky situation — in Swahili. On my last day in Dar es Salaam,

Tanzania, for part of my language training, I strolled past my hotel grounds, something I often did. I wanted to take pictures of the Indian Ocean. The sun shone, the sky radiated a deep cerulean blue, and the water reflected a turquoise blue while several majestic palm trees swayed in the East African breeze. It looked like something on a travel brochure. I took a few shots.

I knew not to take photos of people without first asking their permission (some East Africans believe the act of taking their photograph steals one's spirit). I knew not to take photos of government installations, buildings, or bridges, anything official looking. Photos I took that day contained nothing illegal, nothing man-made, just palm trees, the ocean, blue sky. Nothing more. But soon after I took a few shots, two Tanzanian officials ("constables," according to their badges, pinned to their beige cotton shirts) appeared at my side, riding dilapidated bicycles. The men's uniforms hung on their thin limbs, light brown khaki pants with a matching beige shirt, along with the badges.

The pair's spokesman, straddling his bike, still holding onto the handlebars, stopped in front of me.

"You have broken our law," he accused me somberly, in that elegant way East Africans spoke, enunciating each syllable. "No one is allowed to take photographs of official government facilities," he continued, admonishing me in English, giving special emphasis to "no one."

Even though I saw no trace of anything remotely official looking anywhere near me, I knew better than to antagonize these men further by questioning their authority. Last Word Linda was forced to stifle herself. I did muster the courage to ask to see credentials, though. One took a license-sized scruffy piece of paper out of his pocket that I barely had time to read. Written in Swahili, it looked legitimate, but I didn't know. Anyone could purchase papers or a badge in the shape of a star and pin it to his chest. He didn't look that official to me with his rumpled clothes, riding a beat-up bicycle.

Thinking fast, I decided to speak in Swahili, hoping to flatter both men, maybe avoid being mistaken for a tourist, or someone they imagined being up to no good. Smiling all the while, I explained that I was actually an "*mgeni*" (guest) in their beautiful city, leaving the next day, merely creating a souvenir of my too-short time in Dar es Salaam by taking a few pictures of the ocean, the trees. All true. Speaking Swahili caught them off guard, perhaps even mollified them somewhat, but the duo's spokesman persisted.

"I'll have to take you into custody; we'll need to look at the film inside your camera. We'll examine your photos there," he replied, switching to Swahili, presumably to remain in tandem with me.

Becoming increasingly nervous, I managed to remain calm, at least to appear calm. I didn't want to go to a police station. I didn't want anyone opening up my brand new camera, exposing pictures I'd recently taken in Zanzibar, an exotic island off Tanzania's coast, a place I knew I'd never visit again. But, more important, I didn't want to be thrown in jail in Dar es Salaam, Tanzania, carrying only a tourist passport.

We spoke for five minutes or so in Swahili, a conversation consisting mainly of me expressing my defense. This got me nowhere. He kept insisting I accompany him. Finally, he mentioned that he and his companion might stop and get a drink first, before transporting me to the police station. Then he stared at me, motionless, so I chose another tack. I took a chance that would either ensure being arrested for bribery or allow me to extricate myself from the situation.

"I'm so sorry, sir. I can't go with you. I have to go back to my hotel right now for a meeting; they're expecting me, but I'd like to offer you a little something for a soda or coffee . . . for your trouble," I added, still speaking Swahili, still smiling. Slowly reaching into a canvas bag I carried, I pulled out a wad of paper Tanzanian shillings (equaling less than two dollars), carefully handing it to him. Then I began to back up, slowly walking backwards toward my hotel as he and his colleague stood next to their bikes, counting the money, then staring daggers at me. I continued smiling, repeating, "*Asante sana. Kwa heri.*" "Thanks very much. Goodbye."

I knew that, if necessary, I'd start running, even though I couldn't outrun bikes, even rickety ones. I didn't think they carried weapons, but they just stood there glaring at me, holding my money. I backed almost the entire way to my hotel, keeping them in my sights, afraid to turn my back, occasionally turning slightly to see where I was heading. I'm surprised I didn't run into anything. Maybe Tanzanians also considered backing up as rude, like using an index finger to beckon? I didn't want to take any chances. Maybe they'd even run over me on their bikes. I didn't know.

Finally, I reached my hotel and dashed inside. I searched for a young employee who often worked behind the desk, sometimes helping me with tricky Swahili idioms and phrases: Jones, a new friend. Locating him, I breathlessly recounted the incident, trying to make light of it, hoping he would laugh along with me at my tendency to overreact.

"Do you think they're really constables, Jones?" I asked him, trailing behind him as he picked up abandoned newspapers in the lobby, straightened chairs, fluffed pillows, rearranged small tables, picked up soiled napkins, greeted other guests. He stopped his chores, lowering his voice.

"I think you were very lucky, Mama-Alex," he told me, shaking his head in earnest. "They could have arrested you, thrown you in jail. It could have turned out bad for you. Very bad." (Tanzanians often address women by attaching a woman's son's name to "Mama," so I was Mama plus Alex, my son's first name, "Mama-Alex." Jones never referred to me as "Linda.")

When I saw Marshal, my tutor, for my next lesson, he confirmed Jones's words, said it was fortunate that I spoke Swahili, that I could have been incarcerated.

"Really?" I replied to Jones, assuming that logic would ultimately have prevailed. "But I didn't do anything wrong! Besides," I chuckled, "just how would they have transported me to the station? On the handlebars of their beat-up bicycles?"

Jones became even more serious, a sense of urgency in his voice. This stupid American woman did not understand, his look seemed to say.

"You don't understand. They'd have found a way to get you to the police station, called for help. They saw a rich-looking American woman with a nice camera, decided to make it worth their while, even if it meant arresting you. It happens."

I thanked Jones but shrugged my shoulders, feigning nonchalance. Then I calmly took the elevator up to my room, where I collapsed on my bed, thankful I'd somehow escaped imprisonment, retroactively terrified.

Did my current situation in Nairobi represent another mess I'd somehow gotten myself into? Could I find a solution? Could I use my Swahili again to talk my way out of a potentially dangerous situation, as I had in Tanzania? Different country. Different time. Different circumstances.

In response to the knock and the man's booming voice on the other side, I reached the hotel door. Holding my breath (as though that might improve things), I slowly opened it.

In front of me stood a stocky Kenyan man wearing a police uniform; he filled the door frame, his body silhouetted against light from the now-illuminated hallway. Standing directly in front of me, nearly inside my room, he wore black pants, a black shirt with a leather jacket, an official-looking cap low on his head. A gold badge shone from a pocket of his jacket. Black on black on black after the room had just come out of darkness.

Taking in his movements, the expression on his face, I watched him closely. I watched as he glanced over my head to take in my laptop, my array of books, newspapers, dictionaries spread out on my hotel bed. The word *Swahili* or *Kiswahili* shone like beacons on my dictionaries and grammar books. Several copies of *Taifa Leo*, the daily Nairobi Swahili newspaper, lay unfurled alongside everything else, words highlighted and underlined by me. His eyebrows furrowed slightly as everything registered in his mind: *click-click-click*, I could almost hear his mind working. I caught a menacing look, maybe questioning all he saw. Displeasure.

In those days Kenyan police had a reputation for being one of the most corrupt institutions in Kenya. Charges of bribery and extortion hounded them for years. Underpaid, often unappreciated, some resorted to criminal activities. My awareness of this linked up with my recent memory of the constables in Tanzania, how they'd wanted to arrest me for taking innocent photos. Given the current post-bombing atmosphere in this country, heightened tensions, I wondered why he'd shown up at my room this particular night, right after the hotel and city's power outage. Did these factors all equal coincidences, or had word spread about a recently arrived suspicious-acting American who spoke Swahili? If so, he had his proof here, right in front of his eyes.

My thoughts a jumble of fearful emotions, I needed to act fast. I slammed the door in his face. I did it with all my strength, in case he decided to put out his arm to stop me, which would have taken little effort on his part. Once closed, I locked the door, stood frozen in front of it. I then quietly pressed my ear to the door to determine if I could hear anything. Had he gone to get help? Would he return with reinforcements? With a key? I didn't know. Hearing nothing, I wasted no time, though, rushed into the bathroom where I grabbed a long white terry cloth bathrobe hanging off the door hook, provided by the hotel. I tightly wrapped it around myself, covering up my clothes. If he came back with more policemen, or a key, I'd invent a husband in the bathroom, or feign sickness, express my regrets but tell him to leave. I'd say something. Anything. Call for help.

I rushed to the bed and quickly stacked my laptop, Swahili books, papers, newspapers, and notebooks together, shoving them under the bed. As far-fetched as it seemed, if Kenyans considered it offensive for an American to study their language in this highly charged atmosphere, if my Swahili materials antagonized them, I had to keep them out of sight.

The rest of the evening, I barely moved, listening for any sound, fearful the electricity might go off again. It never did. I never learned why the Kenyan policeman knocked on my door that night.

Two countries, Tanzania and Kenya, two interactions with policemen, two possible near misses, two chances to practice using a new voice.

Two countries, Zambia and Kenya, two international incidents, two times being forced to think creatively, proactively.

Two countries, South Africa and Zambia, two countries on the cusp of major change, two windows into their future, allowing me to catch a glimpse of what lay ahead for them, maybe for me.

Two countries, Spain and Brazil, two opportunities to try out different ways of living, to soak in new patterns for my life.

Two plus two plus two plus more languages plus me, all of them weaving their way through my life, tentacles making their way into a picture I held in front of myself like a mirror. Like a reverse Polaroid, a former image became increasingly dim, while another, clearer picture emerged.

When foreign languages first captured my attention back in fourth grade, when I performed *The Three Bears* in Spanish with my classmates, something began to form inside me, a detachable something I could put on a shelf, like a hat. I could be Spanish-speaking Linda or, later, French-speaking Linda or Portuguese-speaking Linda, then revert back to the original Linda, stripped of all those extra words, ideas, worlds, stripped of all those extra ways to express myself, to be myself, all those ways to see myself, my place, back to a little duller, a little less interesting person perhaps, a lot less confident.

Living in Spain, working in Brazil later as a young woman, it became more difficult to separate myself from the influence of those languages, from the worlds they represented, lessons they imparted, the person I became when I listened to, spoke, read, wrote in them. It became harder to separate from those other parts of myself they called forth, more authentic parts, a potential self. More and more, they inhabited me, fused with me.

Swahili represented a later stage in that process. My studies with Swahili began nearly thirty years after I first began with Spanish in earnest. With Xhosa, I sometimes stood at the threshold, somewhat removed from its spell, yet calling on it frequently to bolster new ideas I had about myself. In that respect, it resembled Portuguese, resembled its pull during and following the assignment in Brazil in 1985. But when I spent a week at the medical clinic in Barcelona in 1997, when my father's health crisis struck, I forgot I was speaking Spanish, it had become so ingrained in me. I forgot that it formed just one "hat" I wore. Forgot it was a foreign language, forgot it no longer fit with an age-old image I carried around of myself. That continued after the embassy bombings the following year. Something happened. I forgot about feeling like unconfident, afraid, self-conscious Linda as I plowed ahead, doing what needed to be done to help save my father's life in Barcelona, having also done what I needed to do years before in Spain, in Brazil, then in Zambia, in South Africa, in Tanzania, in Kenya. My voice slowly became stronger, more confident.

Like a science fiction movie, all "my" languages became more prominent inside my mind, populated more space, more of who I thought myself to be. I began to push aside a former, outdated self-concept I'd held on to for decades, making room for a new self-concept.

The initial catalyst might have been fear. Fear giving way to action, to change. Fear of living on my own in Spain my junior year in college, of having to figure out things on my own: transportation, food, classes, relationships, speaking a foreign language round the clock. Fear in Brazil that, if I couldn't adapt to life in the outback, to interpreting nonstop, to dealing with an onslaught of nonstandard Portuguese spoken rapid-fire at me, my future would remain the same in Kirkwood, Missouri, stagnate. Fear in Zambia that missteps in helping to deal with rioting, with the coup attempt, along with having to tackle new languages foisted on me could result in people being put in harm's way. Fear in South Africa that not knowing Xhosa closed a window into history, one made available to me for a short time, to use on my own personal journey as apartheid gave way to democracy. Fear that if I didn't perform well enough in that Barcelona clinic, my father would die. Fear in Tanzania and in Kenya that harm might come to me if I didn't allow my Swahili-speaking persona to take over—someone far braver, far more confident, more resourceful than ever.

6

CODE-SWITCHING

Wartime and Walkie-Talkies

CODE-SWITCHING—*a linguistic term referring to situations in which speakers switch between two or more languages. Linguists also use it to reference people who switch among styles, dialects, or registers.*

EXAMPLE: *The Democratic Republic of the Congo (DRC) is an African country where more than two hundred languages—not dialects—are spoken, so you may hear conversations containing a mixture of words in French, Swahili, Lingala, Tshiluba, and other languages.*

EXAMPLE: *A different type of code-switching occurs when I speak to someone my grandparents' age. I switch from a more informal style or register—one I would use with close friends—to a more formal register.*

I never anticipated traveling to the former country of Zaire, now known as the Democratic Republic of the Congo, or the DRC. The

DRC is also referred to as Congo-Kinshasa to differentiate it from its neighbor, the Republic of the Congo (Congo-Brazzaville).

In February of 1999, six months after returning from the post-bombing in Nairobi, Kenya, members of my management team approached me about taking an assignment in the DRC. I spoke no Lingala, one of its most important languages, but Swahili had grown in importance there for various reasons: shifts in leadership, an increase in Swahili speakers in-country.

The Democratic Republic of the Congo stands out on the African continent with its violent history. It's a country fraught with coups, assassinations, wars, and despotic leaders. One specific war (the First Congo War) had ended just two years prior to my TDY, in 1997, but another one would start less than a year later, still raging in 1999, the same year I traveled to the DRC. This second war was known as the Second Congo War, or Africa's World War.

When the war ended five years later, in 2003, nearly six million people had died, through the fighting itself but also from side effects brought in its wake: disease and malnutrition. This was not a place I wanted to go, or a time when I wanted to go to such a dangerous country: the middle of a war. On previous trips, although I'd encountered different levels of danger—both unexpected and expected—incidents seemed more isolated: the rioting and coup attempt in Lusaka, Zambia, the terrorist bombing in Nairobi, Kenya. This seemed different. The DRC was engaged in a war that involved multiple foreign players: Rwanda, Zimbabwe, Angola, Namibia, Chad, Libya, Sudan, as well as ad hoc militia groups. And there was spillover from the 1994 Rwandan genocide, when numerous Tutsis fled to eastern DRC, along with the exiled Rwandan government.

By this point in my career I'd been sent on a total of six official African assignments: three to Zambia, one to South Africa, one to

Kenya, and one to Tanzania. I would go on six more, adding two to Ethiopia, along with another one to Tanzania and two more to South Africa, as well as this assignment in the DRC.

"We may want you to go to Kinshasa, Linda." So began a conversation in February of 1999 when I received word of management's plans. Once again, my belief that Swahili was destined to become an increasingly important language in Africa had been confirmed. With an estimated two thousand languages spoken in Africa, Swahili's role as a lingua franca continued to increase. But my fears associated with traveling there also increased once I received a security briefing about potential threats awaiting me in-country.

"I'll go, but I have to return home no later than May fourteenth for an important engagement," I announced to my supervisors, trying to sound businesslike. Without lying, I made it seem like I had a critical deadline awaiting me at home. This was certainly true, in my own mind, but I never revealed the real reason behind my statement, namely my son's senior prom: taking pictures of him, seeing him off on his big night, hearing about it the next day. Nothing else held nearly as much importance. Fortunately, they agreed to my requirements, asked no follow-up questions. I arrived home from the DRC the day before his prom after spending nearly a month in Kinshasa, following a thirty-hour trip door to door.

The Democratic Republic of the Congo—as seen through the eyes of someone—me—admittedly not an expert, resembled a study in code-switching. How to define this country? With other countries, I could pinpoint the place where I'd work: the former colony of country X where language Y was spoken, formerly known as Z. With the DRC, it represented the involvement of multiple colonial powers, multiple (hundreds of) languages, multiple names for the country. For me at least, it represented a shifting identity I had trouble pinning down.

The DRC reminded me of a child born to unreliable parents, setting it on a disastrous course. Belgium's King Leopold II acted as that horrible parent, "owner and absolute ruler" of the Congo from 1885 to 1908. It wasn't a country, or even a colony yet, but he used it as his personal playground to do with as he pleased. He did unspeakable, unimaginable things to the people, to the country during that period.

By 1908 it was no longer his deadly private playground, moving up the hierarchy (only slightly) to become a colony of Belgium. It remained in that status until achieving independence in 1960. An unsuspecting student of history might think a happier future awaited it, but after a coup and other complications, Mobutu Sese Seko (coup instigator) became president of the DRC (then known as Zaire), remaining in power from 1965 until his ouster in 1997. Mobutu turned out to be one of the most corrupt leaders in Africa and elsewhere, illegally and cold-bloodedly amassing a fortune worth billions of dollars. In 1997, Mobutu was overthrown by Laurent Kabila, who was killed in 2001 by an eighteen-year-old assassin. Kabila's son, Joseph Kabila, then took the reins of power. Joseph Kabila did not speak Lingala, the official language of the military under Mobutu, having spent his childhood in Tanzania. He spoke Swahili and English better than French and Lingala, then the most widely spoken languages in Kinshasa. He had to learn French and Lingala on the job.

Even the country's name underwent multiple changes: from King Leopold's the Congo Free State, to the Belgian Congo, to the Democratic Republic of the Congo, to Zaire, and then back to the Democratic Republic of the Congo. Imagine having a child and renaming him every few years on a whim, then handing him over to different caretakers, "foster parents," along the way. Other countries in Africa underwent name changes (Zimbabwe from the former Southern Rhodesia, for example; Zambia from Northern Rhodesia) in advance of and in response to the fall of colonial rule and subsequent dictators, but the DRC's name flip-flopped twice as many times.

The DRC's capital, Kinshasa (formerly Léopoldville), lies on the far western border of Africa's third-largest country (905,000 square miles), the largest country in sub-Saharan Africa, with nine countries bordering it, plus a diminutive Atlantic coastline of only twenty-five miles to the west, and an impressive 214 languages (languages, not dialects). These facts alone make it a challenge to centrally govern.

Like the majority of Africa, the DRC fell victim to greedy colonial powers, powerful European countries waging custody battles over land they viewed as their property, not as a sovereign country. They carved it up with no thought to those who'd lived there thousands of years prior to their arrival from Europe. The pinnacle of this dissection occurred between the late 1880s and 1914.

European powers previously controlled 10 percent of Africa, but that percentage increased to nearly 90 percent during those pivotal years, 1880 to 1914, with only Ethiopia and Liberia remaining independent. Historians generally regard the Berlin Conference (1884–1885) as the starting point of this greedy "scramble" in which powerful European leaders partitioned Africa according to their needs, as well as their power. They based boundaries not on ethnicity or language or historical considerations but on their personal desires. It's no wonder then, that to varying degrees, the entire continent suffered from an identity crisis, the DRC a prime victim with its vast natural resources, a coveted "child" in a heated custody battle for Africa's spoils.

The day before I left for Kinshasa, April 20, 1999, the massacre at Columbine High School took place. Twelve students and one teacher died, with more than two dozen people injured. It marked the dead-liest school shooting in US history to date.

Placing my clothes on my bed to pack, I attempted to remain calm as I organized my suitcase. My TV turned to the news, I watched, listening in disbelief to the horror stories. Both my children attended high school. I tried to imagine the agony of those slain children's parents. Then my thoughts turned to my own children. Would they remain safe? Should I cancel my TDY? How could I protect them? How could anyone protect their children, though? Images on TV took me back to my time in Nairobi a little more than six months before, witnessing the aftereffects of evil at play. Evil on a much larger scale, but no less devastating. As I folded cotton shirts, pants, electricity adaptors, converters, I briefly entertained the idea of canceling my TDY, wondering if I could get out of going to the DRC. But how? How would I justify backing out? Admitting that the Columbine massacre had upset my already shaky equilibrium? That I wanted to remain with my high school children? I shared my fears with my husband.

"I don't want to go to Kinshasa. Columbine is reminding me how precious life is. All those teenagers slaughtered. I can't do it. I can't leave."

"What happened in Columbine is horrific, but that's nearly two thousand miles away. You can't base work decisions on the insane actions of two deranged individuals. This massacre was sickening, but you can't use it as an excuse to avoid going to the DRC."

Nothing met the standards of logic; I realized that. I had my visa, my airline tickets, my hotel reservation; everything was in place. Too late to back down. I left as scheduled the next day, got on my plane, but with a heavy heart.

I noticed during my time in Kinshasa that spring of 1999 that the city had a more urban character than other cities I'd been to. While in Pretoria, Lusaka, Dar es Salaam, even Nairobi, the locus of my activity, both work and residence, had been more suburban oriented: tree-lined streets, residential areas, lush gardens; this was true even when unrest brewed or tragedy had struck. Conversely, here in Kinshasa I saw more run-down commercial buildings, with very few distinct neighborhoods, at least in my limited orbit.

I also noticed the sharp curtailment of my movements. On prior trips to Zambia, South Africa, Tanzania, even Kenya after the terrorist bombings, I was able to walk around Lusaka, Pretoria, Dar es Salaam, Nairobi, careful not to remain out alone at night, or to go to dangerous areas. In Kinshasa, however, State Department officials discouraged me from walking anywhere. Someone drove me from my lodging to the US embassy each morning, then back to my hotel after work.

I spent each day working in a windowless office in the embassy unless invited to a meeting. I translated and interpreted material from Swahili to English: voice and graphic material that dealt with regional conflicts, with possible instabilities brewing in the region, with potential changes in leadership in the DRC or neighboring countries.

A few years before, Swahili remained on the fringes when viewing linguistic maps in the DRC. Lingala ruled and, accordingly, the US government had trained more than enough Lingala linguists to keep up-to-date with goings-on in this strategically important country, an enormous landmass with abundant resources, one adversely affected by the proxy involvement of nearby African countries such as Rwanda and Uganda. Rwandan extremists had fled into western DRC following the 1994 genocide in that country, creating a destabilizing influence on the DRC. When I arrived in Kinshasa, Zaire had been known as the DRC for only two years, coinciding with Mobutu's ouster after thirty-two years. Multiple changes had occurred in-country: its name, its leadership, the involvement of outside players, its language (changed to reflect those changes), in short—code-switching. That's where I played a small role, monitoring the status quo within the DRC and beyond its borders, ensuring that US interests weren't at risk.

I had witnessed a somewhat similar phenomenon in Spain, a country where language equaled national policy. During my year in Madrid—1970–1971—laws were still in place outlawing the use of any language except Castilian Spanish. Franco forbade citizens from speaking Catalan, Basque, and Galician, for example. This policy changed in 1975 when Franco died, but it illustrates language's importance as a reflection of sociopolitical events in an area or country.

After my workday ended in Kinshasa, an embassy driver dropped me off at my motel in Kinshasa, a humble dwelling everyone referred to as "Camp Congo," even though its official name was Centre d'Accueil Protestante (Protestant Reception Center). Previously, it had served as a monastery, where nuns or priests stayed while receiving training during the days of Belgian rule. My spartan room had no TV, no radio, no phone, only the plainest of furnishings, with bare, nondescript beige tile floors. My bathroom consisted of a long pipe and shower head over a square basin with a drain, a simple toilet, and a single water tap and basin in which to wash my hands and face. A fellow TDYer likened it to bathrooms the military used in training. No frills.

My mattress reminded me of pallets made from giant foam rubber pads, ones I'd seen advertised for packing breakable items for transit, with a simple bed frame made out of particle board wood. What a contrast to other places I'd stayed. Even the Hellmans' home in Lusaka where I house-sat had been infinitely nicer, not to mention the Intercontinental Hotels in Tanzania, Kenya, and Zambia, as well as my attractive Dutch-inspired hotel in South Africa, one where I had my own little suite.

The view from a smallish picture window in my first-floor micro living room revealed an expanse of gravel-topped concrete directly outside. At the far end of the concrete stood a wobbly gate with a long, single horizontal pole you raised or lowered using a rope off to one side. An unenthusiastic-looking employee remained close by in the event someone needed to enter or leave. He slowly raised himself from a cheap, cracked plastic chair and used the rope to hoist the bar to a vertical position to let a vehicle in or out. In theory, someone probably designed the gate to keep intruders out. But it looked easy enough to duck under, or go around, on foot, at least; you could probably ram through it with a large vehicle if you didn't mind denting your car's grill.

I often saw a group of unofficial-looking men sitting around the front of Camp Congo in their plastic bucket chairs, talking, laughing, drinking unidentifiable beverages, sucking on a wad of something they kept at the back of their mouths, playing checkers with a homemade playing board, using bottle caps for pieces. Various combinations of men played. Other men looked on, drinking, chewing. All were rail thin and seemed to wear the same clothing every day.

I noticed on my first assignment in Southern Africa that, generally speaking, when you spotted an overweight (even slightly overweight) person, that was a sign of comparative wealth, especially with men, and symbolized a sign of pride for these persons. Here in the DRC, the same held true. No one told men—or women—to lose

weight in sub-Saharan Africa, that I knew of. Languages even reflected this phenomenon. For example, in Xhosa, the words for
"fat" and "affluent" come from the same root (*tyeba*).

These men outside my room all wore ill-fitting clothing too
large for them, hanging on their gaunt frames as though on clothes
hangers: loose khaki-like pants, with Nehru-type billowing shirts.
I'd pull my mustard-yellow-and-moss-green curtains aside when I
returned home from work, observing them as long as I could without
detection. They seemed happy enough with their cohort of other
male friends, sipping their beers, playing checkers, sharing stories
in Lingala. Once they saw me, though, their demeanor changed.
They lost their relaxed look, looked at me suspiciously, so I closed
the curtains, a snoopy outsider in their midst.

Since no one trusted a highly unreliable phone system (I didn't
even have one in my room), everyone working at the US embassy
was equipped with a walkie-talkie. A US embassy Marine checked in
with embassy employees—permanent and temporary—each morning
at 7:00 a.m., performing a "radio check" to make sure we'd made it
through the night without incident. During that radio check the Marine informed Americans which intersections or parts of town to
avoid. If incidents occurred during the day, we'd receive follow-up
notifications. Once, during my stay in-country, the Marine on duty
announced that Congolese authorities had detained someone on a
temporary detail like me—a TDYer—for walking around a roadblock
(instead of waiting for someone in authority to lift the gate). Another
time the Marine reported a shooting at an intersection and instructed
us to avoid that area. He made his announcements using a matter-of-
fact tone, as though these incidents ranked below far more serious
events he'd witnessed.

The voice of the US embassy Marine crackled over my walkie-talkie during the morning radio check. "Come in, Linda Marshall. Do you copy?"

I responded, "Affirmative. I copy loud and clear." They'd given me a scrap of paper with these and other words on it so I knew what to say, how to convey that I wasn't in danger.

"Over," he'd sign off, sounding official, ending our brief conversation. Then he went down his list to the next and the next and the next person as everyone listened in, if we cared to.

If I needed to say something else important, I was instructed to use the NATO phonetic alphabet for clarity, for example, if I had trouble being understood, or in case of danger. Unfortunately, I knew very little of the NATO phonetic alphabet, so this plan wouldn't have succeeded. I'd had to learn the Greek alphabet during my sorority years in college, could still recite it, but that wouldn't help me in Kinshasa; in fact, it might interfere with my efforts to communicate if I started spouting alpha, beta, gamma, delta, epsilon, etc., instead of Alfa, Bravo, Charlie, Delta, Echo, Foxtrot, Golf, Hotel, India. Truthfully, just figuring out the buttons on my walkie-talkie each morning proved to be a challenge, so I became anxious about somehow botching this seemingly simple assignment.

I had to be sure to turn the walkie-talkie off after each check-in so the battery didn't die. I knew if I didn't respond to the Marines' calls, they'd send someone to my little room at Camp Congo, relatively far from the embassy. I didn't need that embarrassment, so I made it a priority to comply with instructions. I already stood out since I was a TDYer, not permanently posted to Kinshasa, certainly not as "tough" as colleagues who'd been posted to Kinshasa several years.

Despite a war raging in the DRC, permanent employees with a higher threshold of tolerating and navigating dangerous situations soon tired of going out of their way to pick me up, of giving me a ride to and from work each day. Consequently, after only a few days in-country, my temporary supervisor at the US embassy urged me to drive myself, to use a loaner car.

"Now that you've settled in, we'd like you to drive yourself to the embassy. You should have a good idea by now how to navigate the roads, what to avoid, right? Camp Congo is too far away to justify daily pickups. We don't have the manpower for this."

This man, because didn't men always know their way around better, obviously didn't know me well. I often got lost back home, after nearly fifteen years of living in the same area. I'd watched an experiment on a news show once, scientifically proving that men have a much better sense of direction than women; they're born with it. But, that aside, I didn't want to drive on Kinshasa's dangerous, un-protected, unlit streets when a war raged and chaos prevailed. What if I had car trouble, adding to the perilousness of the situation?

"Well, I don't think that's possible," I replied, choosing my words carefully, relief no doubt visible on my face. "You see, I don't know how to drive a car with standard transmission; I never learned how to drive with a stick shift."

That wasn't entirely true. One of my older brothers had tried to teach me how to drive his prized used VW Bug back in high school, but finally gave up after I nearly destroyed its transmission. Ten years before, I'd gone to Swaziland for a long weekend, taking a break from Zambia. I soon learned that automatic cars were scarce in sub-Saharan Africa, so I had to rent a white Mercedes 280 SL sports car, the only car with automatic transmission in all of Swaziland, apparently. After losing my way, lost for two hours while driving my luxury rental car through Mlilwane Wildlife Sanctuary on a weekday, not a soul in sight, worries flooded my mind. I knew I could never afford damages to the car if I destroyed it, or if the agitated warthogs following me as

I drove the car at a snail's pace though the deserted game park aggressively bashed into it with their horns. I vowed then and there never to drive a car again in Africa if I could avoid it. A better idea might have been to learn how to drive a car with standard transmission.

Undaunted, my interlocutor in Kinshasa, unbeknownst to me, made it his personal mission to find a car with automatic transmission. A few days later, he led me out of the office into the embassy parking lot, introducing me to an old, banged-up station wagon, a bluish-gray, nondescript vehicle that looked like a teenage boy had driven it hard back in the 1960s.

"Here you go! See what we found for you?" he exclaimed, his hands on his hips, thrilled he'd fulfilled his mission, staring at me, waiting for my response, daring me to stand up to him. After all, who did I think I was, some lily-livered TDYer here for a few weeks, whereas he'd lived in this godforsaken country for who knows how long. *Just try me*, his eyes seemed to communicate, boring holes through me.

I straightened the wrinkles out of my stretchy black pants, pulled at my matching black turtleneck to kill time. I couldn't think of anything to say, initially. I just knew I did not want to drive through Kinshasa's streets alone, armed only with a few dozen loose cigarettes for the inevitable checkpoints where prepubescent soldiers wearing a hodgepodge of uniforms routinely pulled over Westerners to (ostensibly) check papers, waiting for me (or anyone, including passengers) to hand over cigarettes before they allowed me to continue. I'd been in that situation—as a passenger—and had been doubly nervous as the only female in the vehicle. I also knew I would not risk getting lost in a city where people spoke multiple languages but where I spoke only two of them: French and Swahili.

Nor was I about to bet my life or health on the Stone Age metal detector US embassy foreign service nationals waved under vehicles at the embassy's entrance each morning, in order to detect bombs. Besides, IEDs (improvised explosive devices) could easily be planted on my vehicle while I slept at Camp Congo, my car easily accessible to tampering during the night. Finally, I would not chance breaking down in this sorry excuse for a car that I saw before me. Would not.

"Well," I slowly said, drawing out the "-el" sound, aware of the importance of each word I spoke to this John Wayne wannabe. "I'm sorry, but I can't drive *this* car or any *other* car. I was not asked to come to Kinshasa because of my driving skills in a war zone. I was not told anyone expected me to drive myself to work. I was asked to come here for my language skills. I'm not putting my life in jeopardy. I'm sorry if that inconveniences people, but that's how I feel." I added a final "Sorry" to the end of my words, barely a whisper, a coda to hopefully soften the vehemence of what they would surely classify as my belligerent, uncooperative attitude.

My voice probably shook as I spoke those words to this seasoned veteran of hazardous assignments (the State Department had put Kinshasa on its list of hazardous posts). I know his opinion of me deteriorated even more on hearing my words, but for once in my life I didn't care; my normal people-pleasing nature had disappeared, at least temporarily. I wanted to return in one piece to my children, to my husband; that's all that mattered. Besides, this man didn't realize how disastrous sitting behind the wheel of this jalopy—or any vehicle—would be for me in Kinshasa . . . during a war. It had taken me several years to gather the nerve to drive on DC's Capital Beltway.

Scoffing at my response, he left without saying another word, and I returned to my office. My heart was pounding but I felt relieved, although I was confident he detested me. A few hours later, another man assigned to the embassy for a two-year tour, Jerry, sought me out in my office where I plodded away, trying to make sense of the DRC's version of Swahili, dissimilar to the version I'd learned with my tutor back in the States . . . more code-switching to translate, to decipher. Jerry was in the army.

"So . . . you don't want to drive to or from work, right?" he said, sarcastically, clearly amused by my wimpy attitude, addressing me as though I were a petulant child.

"That's right. I'm not driving anywhere," I replied, trying to appear taller than five foot four, wondering why this had become such a big deal, and why no one had warned me in advance that I'd be expected to drive while in Kinshasa.

"Well, okay. Got it, your highness. From now on, I'll pick you up each morning at eight o'clock," he said, then added with a chuckle, "That all right with you, Miss Daisy?" I immediately got the reference to the movie *Driving Miss Daisy* in which Morgan Freeman chauffeurs an elderly Jessica Tandy everywhere. I didn't care, even if Jessica Tandy was far older than me. Anything to avoid driving. To this day, Jerry and I remain friends and he still refers to me as Miss Daisy.

I don't look back at this episode with a sense of shame that my fears trumped my sense of obligation. I don't even mind that my friend called—calls—me Miss Daisy. I'm proud that I knew my limitations, stood up for myself, didn't allow anyone to bully me.

The US embassy in Kinshasa differed from other African embassies I'd been assigned to in another important way: its proximity to a main road. It stood no more than eighty feet from one of Kinshasa's principal thoroughfares, less than a stone's throw away. The fairly recent bombings in East Africa still fresh in my mind, I knew this embassy stood in a precarious setting. Others also noticed, namely Americans posted to Kinshasa for two- or three-year stints, writing cables to officials back in Washington, DC, to bring this to their attention. But funds remained low, and their efforts didn't get traction.

I prefer working in environments with windows, although this wasn't the norm back in Maryland, with offices in warehouse-like settings where most people worked on top of each other, or in cramped cubicles. The few employees with windows back in Maryland earned more than me, had earned their view of the parking lot or a grassy patch. I worked in nicer settings overseas, with the obvious exception of the bombed-out embassy in Nairobi. The US embassy in South Africa, for instance, relatively new when I first worked there in 1994, boasted a modern look. Architects had employed a more contemporary approach, an open setting, windows open to grassy lawns. But in Kinshasa I felt hemmed in: by the closeness of a busy street just outside its doors, by an older building housing the US embassy. Besides, I needed windows to get my bearings. It reminded me of a carnival ride. I suffer from motion sickness, but as long as I can look to a point beyond, I can situate myself on the ride I'm on, not feel so trapped in the tiny space I occupy. In Kinshasa I wondered about potential dangerous activities being hatched just beyond walls of my office or just past boundaries of embassy property, since I was blind to most anything happening outside.

Not everything in Kinshasa had a negative impression on me. Despite admonitions not to leave US embassy grounds, at lunchtime I sometimes ventured out, walking a few blocks to a market known as "Thieves' Market," although I usually tried to find someone to walk with me. After a morning of doing my solitary work, cooped up, deciphering this new version of Swahili, I eagerly ventured outside. I needed to take a break from my sometimes tedious, albeit challenging, language work. Often the key to a linguist's work lies in accumulating information, putting together bits and pieces of a puzzle to shed light on situations. But that interim period could stretch endlessly, constructing a whole from small parts of information, little by little creating a more complete picture.

Merchants at Thieves' Market draped a variety of raffia cloths over tables, piled wooden figurines and masks on oversized card tables. I enjoyed walking around a place that very few tourists frequented, probably because in those days Kinshasa didn't attract many tourists. Who wanted to visit that part of the world in the middle of a war?

On weekends, Americans and Europeans often played softball at TASOK, The American School of Kinshasa. I preferred not remaining alone at Camp Congo all weekend, without a car, in my stark accommodations, unable to communicate with anyone. I would have accepted an invitation to go snipe hunting to avoid isolation. It's easy to forget that, even when you work long days, those empty hours pile up, lie in the wings waiting to be filled. This presents a challenge when you know no one, have no transportation, no means of communicating with friends and family back home, and find yourself in a potentially hazardous situation. I didn't want to remain by myself if I could avoid it. I even tried to learn how to play cribbage with a fellow TDYer, though that was short-lived when I showed little aptitude or interest.

Not knowing any better, a softball captain drafted me for his team.

"A bunch of us get together at TASOK most weekends to play softball against other embassies. Any chance you want to join us?"

Knowing my limitations, and remembering my experience with volleyball and hiking in Zambia, I asked a few questions before committing.

"Maybe. Which position would you guess gets the least amount of action, not that I don't want to play; I'm just curious, not being an avid player."

"I guess right field," was his response, so I asked to play right field. I'd also done my research, confirmed what he said, namely that it's the position least likely to demand running, catching, or throwing the ball. Despite my lack of athletic abilities, I enjoyed getting together with Americans and Europeans outside of work, particularly since I knew no one at Camp Congo.

Also on weekends, Americans congregated at the Marine House in the evening. The US Marines had access to fairly recent movies; *Saving Private Ryan* and *Rounders* were two movies I watched. I disliked war movies, movies with violence, but opted for any and all chances to avoid remaining in my lonely room. Other times, I'd tag along with people going to Bototo's to see the work of local artists, or to L'Académie des Beaux-Arts, or to a store called UTEX, where they sold a variety of multi-textured, multicolored textiles. Surprisingly, given the political situation, Kinshasa still benefited from fabulous restaurants, ones that had somehow withstood the ravages and fickleness of war and unrest. I sampled Indian food, French, American, local dishes: *fufu* (a mash or dough made from plantains or cassava), casaba melon, sweet potatoes, *kwanga* (fermented bread), *pili pili* (very hot pepper, which I avoided whenever possible), a chicken dish made with peanuts. The restaurant Inzia featured typical fare of the city. Locals sometimes ate turtles and even insects, food I avoided. No one ever accused me of being adventurous with my food choices.

Employees also invited me to their homes occasionally. One of these homes, that of a high-ranking State Department official, was set on a number of acres and overlooked the Congo River (formerly known as the Zaire River), the second-longest river in Africa after the Nile. It had lush grounds with mature fruit trees, exotic birds, tennis courts, a swimming pool; in short, it was a far cry from Camp Congo.

One weekend I went to a former Mobil Oil compound, located on the outskirts of Kinshasa. I tagged along with a small group of employees, mostly male. The compound included fourteen homes, tennis courts, a swimming pool, palm trees, thatched umbrellas by the pool to escape the rays of the powerful, equatorial sun. The main attraction for me consisted of a friendly, orphaned bonobo chimpanzee baby, also known as a pygmy chimpanzee. He lived at the compound, the pet of an embassy employee until that employee's tour in Kinshasa ended. I learned later that bonobos face extinction and that specialists have done very little field work on them, due to political instability in the Congo Basin.

Purportedly the closest relative to humans, my new little friend attached himself to me. He appeared to be the size of a six-month-old human baby. In photos, I'm cradling him in front of me, his little hands clutching my forearms as he looks out at something in the distance, to the left of us, ever-observant. In another photo, I'm holding him against my chest as he looks over my shoulder, his arm draped over that shoulder, practically cheek to cheek with me. I knew of course that he was a wild animal, but I welcomed his friendliness in an environment where I felt isolated, nervous, cut off from friends, from family. My new little friend reminded me a bit of the human warmth I'd left at home, as crazy as I knew that was. I longed to take him back to Camp Congo with me for companionship. My workday schedule sometimes seemed weighed down in challenging language tasks. Despite my love of Swahili, I found it refreshing to get away from the city, from my spartan hotel, to visit a resort-like area, to meet a new little furry friend. I needed a break.

And although I generally tend to be more introverted, this assignment in Kinshasa taught me how to fight that tendency, to make the necessary social overtures so I didn't have to remain alone all weekend.

Back at my lodging after a day of deciphering Swahili, the Centre d'Accueil Protestante, Camp Congo, offered little protection from roving bands of "soldiers" prowling the streets of Kinshasa. My room was located on the ground floor (the only floor). My door reminded me of those balsa wood strips my brothers used to create small airplanes as young boys. My room's picture window lay just to one side of the flimsy door. An easily accessible brick could have broken through it. Except for the Hellmans' home in Zambia, other places I stayed in Africa consisted of more than five floors. I'd been more anonymous, more secure. Not here. I heard from well-seasoned travelers that, when staying in a country with safety concerns, travelers should pick a room not facing the front of the building, and one between the third and sixth floors. Having a room high enough to be separated from potential disturbances on the ground floor is the goal. It also gives you more time to escape if you hear commotion down below. I knew not to pick a room that made it nearly impossible to run down hundreds of steps to escape danger, one that fire department hoses couldn't reach if a fire broke out. I couldn't argue with conventional wisdom, but here I was in my poorly constructed home away from home. My room faced the front, was located on the first floor. Again, I might as well have left the door open at night.

Even short car trips were fraught with danger, one of the main reasons I didn't want to drive in Kinshasa. When I first arrived, a US embassy employee unofficially instructed me to always carry cigarettes with me on trips within the city, as well as in outlying areas.

"I don't smoke," I replied self-righteously, indignant that he would consider me a smoker. What did I care if cigarettes proved hard to find in Kinshasa? I certainly didn't want any.

"No. Not to smoke. You need them because you'll be stopped at random checkpoints throughout the city. If you don't have cigarettes, they may not let you pass, may harass you, or worse. Just get some cigarettes; make sure you carry them with you. Don't go anywhere without them."

His words saved me on numerous occasions. Groups of soldiers wearing various models of ill-fitting "uniforms" often stepped out onto the always dark Kinshasa roads unexpectedly at night, weapons in hand, or slung over their shoulders with a strap, the palms of their hands up, signaling the driver to stop. The driver immediately knew to pull off the road. After a brief conversation in one of the local dialects between our driver (a local) and one of the soldiers, we'd all pass a few cigarettes up front when motioned to do so by our driver. The Congolese soldier doing all the talking examined them, rolled them between his fingers, smelled them, looked at the brand. Then, still not smiling, he'd wave us through, as though doing us a favor. Even if I heard him speaking Swahili, I knew not to say anything or acknowledge that I understood him. It reminded me of instructions they give you when flying into possibly hostile areas: don't sit on the aisle, because you don't want to stand out. Needless to say, I didn't want to stand out.

I never got used to cigarette bartering, always feared they'd take me hostage or at least harass me, but I dutifully carried cigarettes with me, never again questioning the logic of doing so. It didn't matter that these "soldiers" didn't look official, looked no older than thirteen or fourteen, that I never learned with whom they were affiliated. Even though I realized this type of activity was illegal, it didn't matter. I didn't need any convincing to know they meant business.

Following one of these incidents, I remained on edge the rest of the evening. Trapped. I didn't feel safe in my flimsy excuse for a hotel, or in a vehicle, or even in the US embassy, perched a few feet from the street, not far from disgruntled people harboring anti-American sentiments. Emotions ran so high that President Laurent Kabila would be assassinated less than two years after my TDY, despite being surrounded by bodyguards. As a TDYer working there for a few weeks, I felt expendable, vulnerable.

At the time of independence in 1960, the DRC only had sixteen Congolese citizens with college degrees. In 1990, just nine years prior to my assignment, only one Congolese doctor provided care for every 15,500 people. Fortunately, the US embassy employed its own doctor as well as a few nurses. It made me doubly appreciate embassy employees living in such trying conditions for more than two years; they couldn't afford to become ill or disabled.

When I'd sit at my desk translating prior to going to Kinshasa, colleagues sometimes stopped by to tell me stories about Kinshasa from their time in the DRC in the early 1980s: an attractive city with popular restaurants, good housing, in short, a walkable, drivable, friendly city. It sounded wonderful, but light years from my eventual experiences. Long-term employees I met after arriving seemed to have resigned themselves to these changes; they spent at least two years in Kinshasa and learned to adapt to the changes.

When I thought about the plight of the Democratic Republic of the Congo, it reminded me of a once-beautiful painting with vivid colors, designs that various entities had dragged through a pan containing highly corrosive agents. The colors became dull as a result, some of the once-beautiful features of the painting erased. Then, making matters worse, detractors riddled it with bullets, crushed it into a ball, a final act of inhumanity occurring when these different entities played tug-of-war with the once-beautiful painting, each standing at a corner, pulling this way, that way, until it, the DRC, remained disfigured, barely recognizable.

No wonder its identity remained in flux. Its very name changed almost half a dozen times in a little more than a century. How did people even communicate when choosing from more than two hundred languages? Historically, its eastern border resembled a piece of cooked spaghetti, fluid, forever changing, with soldiers, refugees pouring in from Rwanda, Uganda, Burundi, Angola, and elsewhere to take control or wreak havoc, as well as the occasional troublemaking European players. Kinshasa lies at the far western edge of the country, often unable to maintain control of the DRC's vast landmass to the east.

In less than a hundred years, the DRC has gone from private playground of a despot, an unscrupulous man who routinely committed atrocities, to a Belgian colony, to a country—Zaire—run for thirty-two years by a corrupt, ruthless dictator, Mobutu, to a country—the DRC—struggling to find its voice. It's like expecting anything from a child parented by an axe murderer and a criminal. Except this child has substantial wealth at its disposal: vast expanses of land, natural resources, minerals, inviting exploitative internal and external sources to keep it in their sights.

What did I know, though? I'd typically spend from a few weeks to six (in the summer) in these various countries, long enough to do my job. I'd familiarize myself with my work, translating, interpreting in French or Swahili or Xhosa, or other closely related languages, then head home. I possessed no better insights than an armchair quarterback, with one major exception, I guess: I knew something many other people didn't. I knew a number of their languages. I held an important key to unlocking each country's secrets. Speaking

Xhosa and Sotho in South Africa; Swahili in Tanzania, Kenya, the DRC; French in the DRC; even some Cinyanja in Zambia. These languages gave me a chance to dig below the surface in Africa, to talk to people, one-on-one, to make a difference. To know someone, you have to know their language. But what if their language changes, along with their very identity, even within a single country? Here in the Democratic Republic of the Congo, code-switching formed part of everyday life.

I'd witnessed numerous situations, or watched them on TV, where two people supposedly conversed, but not really. An interpreter stood between them, if not literally, then figuratively. It reminded me of that child's game, "telephone," where one person whispers a word or a sentence to someone standing next to him. That person then passes the word on to the person next to him, and so on. Usually, meanings become jumbled. That's the joke. The game. Maybe the first person whispered, "I want to be your best friend," but by the time it reaches the end of the circle or line, it has changed to, "I walked into Barry Best's den." Interpreters remain invisible, often ignored, linchpins holding everything together, unlocking meanings.

Another complicating factor in translation exists, though. More often than not, one word in one language does not translate exactly into another word in a second language. Shades of differences exist or, in some cases, wide gaps. It's almost as though two languages exist on each side of a triangle's base. At the apex of the triangle—above, out of reach—lies the point where they meet: meaning. The task of a translator lies in coming as close as he or she can to capturing the intent of what's being translated, then finding the closest word for that concept in a second language.

In the DRC, outside the office I'd initially speak French with local people. If that didn't work, if I got blank stares, I'd switch to Swahili, knowing that probably wouldn't work either, and that, even if it did, the language in which they answered me wouldn't resemble the Swahili I'd studied with my tutors. I might have to admit defeat. I knew, of course, that locals communicated in Lingala—or other languages—when I wasn't part of the conversation. The men who congregated outside my door at Camp Congo spoke a language I didn't recognize, but, when forced to communicate with me, they switched to French, although the French spoken in the DRC differed from the French I'd learned in school, like the Swahili. I understood how my parents must have felt in Spain when they visited me there in 1970. My father expected others to understand him, even people who didn't speak English. He thought the answer lay in speaking slower, louder, that that would solve any problems of comprehension.

"I NEED YOU TO TELL ME HOW TO REACH THE NEAREST PHARMACY," he surely bellowed at some unsuspecting bellhop, or other hotel personnel, when I wasn't around to help. He grew even more agitated if the employee in question shrugged his shoulders. I better understood his frustration now, not able to speak Lingala.

At night, if I hadn't been invited to an embassy employee's home, or if a movie wasn't scheduled at the Marine House, I'd head straight to Camp Congo after work, driven by my new "chauffeur," Jerry. I dreaded those nights alone. No phone. No TV. No radio. No food other than snacks during the day. Too dangerous to walk anywhere outside my sparse room. That's why I needed to fill the weekends with activities to stem the tide of loneliness, of fear.

If forced to remain in Camp Congo at night, I kept myself busy by reading Barbara Kingsolver's wonderful novel *The Poisonwood Bible*, about a missionary who lived with his family in the then-Belgian Congo in 1959, forty years prior to my assignment in the region. I'd brought the book with me as entertainment, and to supplement my knowledge of the area. Even though it's a novel, Kingsolver did her homework, gathering historical background about the country.

As I rested on my flimsy foam rubber mattress, the sound of the shower drip-drip-dripping in the background, my walkie-talkie waking me up once in a while with staticky sputters, I heard muffled voices outside, the so-called guards' laughter. They were seated not far from my front door, chatting in a language I didn't understand, probably Lingala. They ate their meals outside, played checkers with bottle caps and their hand-painted board, hooting and hollering when someone made a good move. Once in a while I heard gunshots in the distance. When I asked an embassy employee about it later, he told me the shots originated from across the Congo River in Congo-Brazzaville, a country just west of the DRC. A war raged there, too, had been raging since 1997. War surrounded me.

Each night I checked my stash of cigarettes. Did I have enough for potential multiple stops in a day? How should I budget? I liked to plan, hated surprises. These soldiers certainly weren't like any other soldiers I knew, but then this wasn't like any other country I'd visited. Sometimes they'd demand one cigarette, sometimes more. If they saw I had more, they'd ask for more, so I concealed all but the ones I intended to hand out, keeping in mind I might need to give out more cigarettes than I'd allotted. How many I carried with me depended on how many Americans traveled in a car. If I traveled alone with a driver or embassy employee, I needed more. If the car carried three or four passengers, I needed fewer. But too many variables existed to factor in. I considered myself an organized person, but this wreaked havoc with my attempts at planning.

Money posed another problem. State Department officials instructed Americans affiliated with the US embassy to avoid using the local black market, and not to sell US dollars to the Congolese for good "deals." These under-the-table agents advertised much better exchange rates because they wanted the strong US dollars. I wasn't going to do that, break the rules, at least not that one.

The Congolese francs had lost so much of their value, legend went that you needed to hand a storekeeper a suitcase filled with stacks of local paper money just to buy a pack of chewing gum (if you could find a store that sold gum . . . or food, for that matter, which I never did). This actually turned out to be true, not an exaggeration. During my time there, a single US dollar bill yielded 2,000 Congolese francs. The highest bill in US currency is the hundred-dollar bill, but in the DRC there was a single bill worth one million zaires, another worth 500,000 zaires. In 1997, two years prior to my arrival, in an effort to correct the financial situation, they had reestablished the franc. One new franc now equaled 100,000 old "new zaires." I found it all confusing.

When my work assignment in the Democratic Republic of the Congo ended, prior to leaving the country, US State Department officials instructed me not to bring any Congolese money with me to the Kinshasa airport, warned that Congolese authorities would confiscate it. I collect foreign bills, ones worth next to nothing; I like to have tiny souvenirs from countries I've visited, small pieces of their art. I planned to bring a Congolese fifty-centime note and a twenty-centime note home with me. By my calculations, that translated into a thousandth of a penny, or something to that effect, so I sent two bills home to myself via the diplomatic pouch.

The fifty-centime note is written in French (*Cinquante Centimes – Banque Centrale du Congo*), with the denomination written in Swahili (*Makumi Tano*). On the front of the dark brown and brown bill—a little larger than Monopoly play money—there's a drawing of a family of okapi (*Famille d'Okapi-Réserve d'okapis d'Epulu* = Epulu Okapi Reserve). On the back, the single head of an okapi is featured. Native to the DRC, the okapi is also known as the forest giraffe, the Congolese giraffe, or the zebra giraffe. He looks like he's related to a zebra, but his closest relative is actually the giraffe.

The twenty-centime bill stands out with its blue-green and black background, also about the size of Monopoly play money. An antelope stands majestically on the front, with an elaborate sketch of the Up-emba National Park delicately sketched on the back. An antelope family, a large tree, and what appears to be the banks of the Congo River are also featured. Like the fifty-centime bill, the words have been written in French and Swahili, *Makumi Mbili* for "twenty" in Swahili, *Banque Centrale du Congo* in French. I love all the tiny details on both bills, as well as the languages. So many features have been added that even blades of grass, leaves on a large tree, and mountains can be seen in the distance on the diminutive bill.

Just as I'd been warned in advance, at the Kinshasa Airport an official sat me down in a small, windowless office after I'd gone through at least ten security checkpoints. He interrogated me at length about my stay in the DRC. "Why were you in Kinshasa? What were you doing here? How long were you here? How long did you stay? What did you buy? Do you have any Congolese money on you?"

On and on the rapid-fire delivery of questions went, giving me barely enough time to answer.

I truthfully replied that I did not have any Congolese money on me, hoping my tiny pieces of Congolese artwork would eventually make it to my mailbox back in the States.

After he finished interrogating me and had cleared me, when signaled to do so I queued up with fellow passengers on the flight, headed out onto the tarmac to identify my suitcase so Congolese workers could load it onto our plane. Our suitcases had all been placed next to the plane, in no particular order. I wove my way through beat-up, ageless satchels side by side with nicer, standard suitcases, passing canvas totes with odds and ends sticking out until I found my suitcase. After checking my luggage tag to confirm this, I found an airline employee, who disappeared with my suitcase. I hoped to see it at my destination. I experienced this security measure in numerous sub-Saharan countries I visited. Failure to point out your suitcase to authorities in advance meant you risked not being reunited with your things when you reached your destination in the US.

Was I racked with guilt about leaving the DRC early to return home for my son's high school dance? No. Or about refusing to drive a car to work each day, thus forcing someone braver to chauffeur me? I was not. Did I feel guilty about putting my safety first? I did not.

When Sally Field accepted her Academy Award in 1985 for *Places in the Heart* and famously gushed, "You really like me!" I had winced, chastised her on TV.

"Oh, no. Please, no. Why did you say that?" I scolded the TV in frustration. Not because her words angered me, but because I knew I would have said something similar. I cringed because I recognized the kowtowing, the people-pleasing behavior . . . and I hated it. I wanted such a talented actress to say something appropriate to her achievements. I wanted to emulate someone I admired. I wanted people to admire me. On this assignment to a war-torn DRC I'd come close to doing that, to kowtowing, but hadn't. I'd found the courage to travel to a country in the midst of a war, the courage not to complain when told my accommodations would not be a Sheraton or an Intercontinental or a guesthouse or a guarded home but instead a fleabag motel with virtually no security and zero amenities. But I found the courage to set limits, to create boundaries for what I found acceptable and unacceptable, even when it meant alienating colleagues.

There was something else I'd pondered once arriving safely

home in Maryland, after taking dozens of pictures of my son with his prom date, after seeing him off on his magical night, hearing his stories afterwards. In the rearview mirror of time and history, I closely examined the shifting images of the DRC with its hundreds of languages, half a dozen names, multi-country wars, its unscrupulous rulers, its unrest, its simultaneous wealth and poverty. In so doing, I realized that I identified with the DRC in some bizarre way I would never have confessed to anyone. I identified with its struggle to survive the onslaught of multiple powerful outside forces that tried to strip it of its identity, with having other people determine who it was, dictate what it could or couldn't do. I identified with having to start from scratch: new name, new leadership, new ways/ languages in which to communicate, while simultaneously feeling alienated from itself. I identified with having people much more powerful take a map, carve it into manageable fragments. I identified with having to speak one way to one group of people, another way to a second group of people, depending on the expectations each group held . . . thereby engaging in more code-switching. In my own way, I identified with all of that. Like the DRC, I found myself in the process of solidifying that mass of names, those ways of communicating. I also had the task of expelling everything inauthentic from my life.

SYLLABARY

An Ancient Civilization, its Ancient Language and Ancient Sites

SYLLABARY—*consists of a set of written symbols that represent syllables that make up words, acting as an alphabet, such as in Japanese, Cherokee, and Ethiopia's Amharic. More than thirty writing systems represent the world's seven thousand languages. Amharic's syllabary is just one of those systems.*

EXAMPLE: *Symbols stand for something else, for example, in Amharic's syllabary: ideas, images, emotions, and not just words, are represented. Sometimes meaning lies in less obvious places and requires investigation, contemplation.*

Ethiopia—and the language of many of its people, Amharic—grew in importance for the US government in the twentieth century. When its long-standing leader, Haile Selassie, annexed neighboring Eritrea in 1961, a thirty-year war between Ethiopia and Eritrea resulted.

Even after Eritrea declared its official independence in 1993, border conflicts and famine plagued both countries. The US government kept a watchful eye on the region, which meant training linguists in Amharic, a principal language of Ethiopia.

I began studying Amharic, my ninth adventure with foreign languages, in March of 1991. Spoken in the Horn of Africa—primarily in Ethiopia—Amharic marked the second time I worked with a language having a non-Latin script. Russian, with its Cyrillic alphabet, marked the first. Unlike the case with Xhosa, Sotho, Shona, and Swahili, others in my government office had preceded me studying Amharic. I would never achieve the level of mastery achieved by three of these colleagues, linguists who began studying it long before me, something the premier expert in Amharic pointed out to me frequently.

"You're going to have to put your children up for adoption," he commented one afternoon when I dropped by the office shortly after beginning my full-time Amharic tutorial. His expression remained serious. As always, this dignified, balding older man wore a suit and tie, unlike the more casual attire favored by everyone else in the office, clothes one might wear to a friend's house or to see a movie: business casual, before anyone called it that.

He didn't crack a smile. I hadn't had time to remove my jacket before he appeared out of nowhere, ghostlike. My children were seven and nine at the time. I understood his not-so-veiled message—threat?— that tackling Amharic was an enterprise requiring every minute of my already packed days, that I'd sentenced myself to failure, at least in his eyes.

"Well, we'll see how it goes," I laughed nervously, hoping he intended his comments as a joke, but not wanting to act disrespectfully. He maintained his stoic demeanor, shrugged his shoulders, and swiveled 180 degrees like one of the Queen's Guards at Buckingham Palace, walking away without saying another word.

Colleagues always prefaced his last name with his title—"Dr."—never calling him by his first name—while they referred to me simply as "Linda," even though I also had a PhD. I never questioned the inconsistency or sexism in this omission, at least publicly, never dared call him by his first name. He might not even have known my first name.

He made other disparaging comments on occasion, one at an office luncheon. Organizers asked me to prepare an Ethiopian dish, *tibs*, small chunks of sautéed chicken. They probably reasoned that it posed less of a challenge to prepare, in light of my negligible cooking skills.

Spotting my untouched serving dish among a dozen or so dishes spread out on a conference table, he folded his arms in front of himself, his signature stance. His posture reminded me a little of Jack Benny. He grimaced slightly, staring at the dish a few minutes, as though in so doing he might transform it into something edible, or maybe decipher its culinary puzzle.

"Did you bring that dish?"

"Yes?" I answered, not sure if I should admit to it, certain that soul-destroying, confidence-eroding words awaited me.

"Well, it looks just like the Kibbles 'N Bits I feed my dog," he noted, chuckling to himself under his breath as he walked away, his arms still folded smugly in front of his body. I only heard him laugh when he delivered his own jokes. He stepped so lightly that he scarcely made a sound whenever he left an area.

I thought of no appropriate response, just laughed nervously, like when he suggested putting my children up for adoption, but he'd already vanished.

If his goal in launching these unflattering comments was to chase me away from a language in which he reigned the undisputed king, he failed. Nothing dampened my enthusiasm for studying this Semitic language, cousin to Hebrew and Arabic, descendant of the ancient language Ge'ez. I knew I'd never achieve the levels of my three colleagues who'd already spent more than a decade mastering this difficult language while I'd been occupied with other African languages, along with raising my children, but I wanted to do my best.

When it comes to competency in foreign languages, my normal need to compete, to surpass everyone, to be best in whatever grouping I find myself, doesn't apply, surprisingly. Aside from foreign languages, in other areas of my life I act competitively. In piano playing, for example. Growing up, I wanted to stand out from everyone else. I longed to perform better than anyone, play pieces no one else dared play, pieces above my skill level that I never truly mastered. For instance, I insisted on playing Beethoven's *Appassionata* sonata, Liszt's *Mephisto Waltz*, Rachmaninoff's Piano Concerto No. 3, the latter played with a full orchestra and considered the most difficult composition written for piano. I wanted to perform on Ted Mack's *The Original Amateur Hour* or *The Ed Sullivan Show*. I was eager to apply to Juilliard, but probably just to brag I'd been admitted (if they'd admitted me). While in college I played Chopin's "Revolutionary Étude" for a Queen Contest in which I participated. The winner—not me—competed in the Miss Colorado competition. Really, though, as I conceded later, my goal in my piano striving consisted largely in being found worthy of admiration.

My father referred to me as a "money player." When I practiced the piano at home, I plodded along, completing my requisite sixty minutes of scales, working on assigned pieces. I practiced begrudgingly, looking for any excuse to take a break, get a glass of water, wandering away from my parents' sleek black Steinway grand piano till my mother succeeded in corralling me back to the piano. I'd obsessively look down at my little Timex watch with its faux red leather band, its minutes ticking away in slow motion till I'd completed my required sixty minutes, two hours during summer months. But once seated at the piano in front of an audience, all eyes on me, even though my anxiety threatened to rip me apart inside, my left knee tapping involuntarily from nerves, I played my best, like someone else, more talented, as though I'd channeled a different person: flashy, assertive, daring, confident. I wanted the trophy, the certificate, the accolades. I needed to earn the audience's approval. With every note I played I said, "This is who I am." With every piece I mastered I asked, "Am I worthy enough now? Now? Now?"

With languages I'd studied thus far, however, and languages I'd continue to study, there was a paradigm shift. The relationship seemed quieter, less frenetic, similar to enjoying a private friendship with each one. I learned through those individual relationships, grew as a person. I needed no audience, required no one to prod me on to study these languages or to flatter my expertise in them. In simple terms: I loved these languages along with the secrets they contained, accessible only to those who understood them.

Every language I studied presented me with new information, new ways of looking at my life, at my world, at things I hadn't considered before. In the often-debunked linguistic term known as the Sapir-Whorf hypothesis, the language of a region influences thoughts, decisions, behavior of that region, flavors them. Without knowing anything about this term at the time, I held a similar belief. Every time I immersed myself in a new language, I discovered new truths, new concepts I hadn't considered before. I learned how other people lived, what their belief systems were.

In this way, though it made life easier when I excelled at a particular language, the mastery of that language didn't act as a prerequisite to my happiness. I didn't have to overachieve and displayed a confidence I'd previously lacked.

Two seemingly contradictory words came to mind as I immersed myself in Amharic: "enjoyable" and "difficult." I found it more difficult than South Africa's Xhosa and Sotho. On the US State Department's language difficulty ranking, Amharic lies in Category IV of V categories, along with Xhosa, Russian, and Zulu. State Department experts estimate that students require at least forty-four weeks or 1,100 hours of study to achieve adequate learning. Only Chinese (both Cantonese and Mandarin), Arabic, Japanese, and Korean lie in Category V, requiring eighty-eight weeks or 2,200 hours.

Amharic's unique syllabary fascinated me, its writing system. Each of its 260 symbols reminded me of a tiny piece of artwork: little domes with hats, single bell-like symbols, a cluster of three bells; another symbol that looks like a wishbone, a stylized T-like symbol, three-pronged cactus-like figures, a capital H-like symbol; circles bisected with lines through the middle; lines and curlicues, trees, a backward question mark, tiny flags, etc. Long before I understood any specific words, Amharic's syllabary looked so logical that I could sound out individual words, almost like a young child learning how to read, just as I'd done with Russian years before. I loved writing down its symbols, ensuring I had the little tails in the right places, denoting where vowels went.

I wanted to copy the little pictures, draw the tiny bells, the cacti, the squiggly trees, as though sketching a picture. To me, Amharic's syllabary represented the combination of three of my favorite things: language, puzzles, art. I wanted to unlock the meaning of the symbols in this ancient language. Could I use this information? Would the symbols help me distance myself from a life that no longer fit, move me toward one that did? Would they help me make sense of my life? The symbols of Amharic and Russian, as well as letters and words of other languages, contained secrets; I wanted access to these secrets but had to work to unlock them.

Other languages I studied also provided me with lessons, each in its own way, beginning with Spanish, continuing with French, Portuguese, German, Russian. In a sense I became a different person when speaking, listening to, reading, writing the language at hand. My thought patterns even differed. As I became better equipped at deciphering messages, cloudy words finally lost their blurriness and lessons arrived: lessons filled with passion, with the flowery expressiveness of Spanish. Or the logical, often more to the point phrases in German. With French I became more extroverted, but I was more introverted in Russian. It was like assuming a different persona when I switched languages, igniting previously dormant parts of my personality, lighting them up.

When I unlocked these messages, a physical aha moment resulted. When I became fluent enough to read a language's literature, I became even more inspired, more enlightened. Neruda, Borges, Unamuno, Gabriel García Márquez in Spanish; Nathalie Sarraute and Camus in French; Clarice Lispector, Machado de Assis, Camões in Portuguese; Christa Wolf in German; Shaaban Robert in Swahili; Xhosa's folktales: the Ntsomi. They all became my teachers.

Each language provided me with a window into other worlds, other ideas, other ways of looking outside myself, but also inward, back at myself. Maybe this occurred because I needed to slow down. In English I could gloss over whatever I read, mindlessly race ahead, almost anticipating what came next. Or I could half listen to someone speaking English, probably missing a great deal, anticipating words to come. But with these foreign languages, I had to slow down to a crawl, linger, depending on how recently I'd started working with the language. For instance, in Spanish, while I could move at a good clip, I still had to concentrate, whereas in Amharic each word, each idea came to me slowly as I picked apart the symbols, teased out meanings, tried to decipher puzzles, slowly, oh so slowly.

As with other African languages I'd studied, I worked one-on-one with a tutor, Mulugetha, this time at a language school in Maryland. Mulu towered over me, a slim, erudite, elegant Ethiopian, who dressed as though he were attending church. Once again, our time together consisted of him introducing a concept, also using articles and books, with my follow-up questions asking for explanations, additional details.

"In Amharic, if you want to express something that's contrary to fact, the subjunctive, how do you do that, Mulu?" I asked him in class one day. "'I wish I could fly,' for instance."

"People can't fly, so you would not ever need to say that," he replied.

"No, but if you just wanted to say that," I pressed.

"Man cannot fly," he insisted.

"All right. Well, but what if I wanted to say, 'If it were snowing, I would go sledding?'" I went on, undaunted.

"Well, it's springtime, so of course it will not snow, so you would not need to say that," he argued in his elegant, clipped accent, looking at me strangely.

Regardless of his impressive pedigree, coupled with his vast knowledge of Amharic, I encountered a phenomenon I experienced in all my studies of African languages. I call it the "This-is-just-how-we-say-it" phenomenon. I couldn't argue with this when he spoke Amharic fluently, whereas I remained a toddler, linguistically speaking. Nonetheless, it became clear that my learning would, at best, consist of a collaborative effort, similar to my lessons in Xhosa, Sotho, and Shona, as well as my experience with Swahili.

Sometimes Mulu left me alone in our spartan classroom for an hour or so, perhaps to escape from my questions. I tried to make sense of newspaper articles, stories, grammar books by myself, shuffling through papers, flipping through textbooks, dictionaries. Once again, I identified with the teenage band members in *The Music Man*, not having enough knowledge to play instruments for creating music. It wasn't enough to leave me alone in a room with some grammar books. I needed someone to act as my guide; I needed someone to show me how to play this challenging instrument. Evidently he believed my indoctrination would happen as a result of osmosis of the materials, thus speeding up my training results.

An introvert at heart, I enjoyed the solitude of being the only Amharic student. I did grow tired of having to appear enthusiastic about every utterance of my various tutors, to answer, "Yes!" 172 times a day to standard questions each tutor asked me: "Did you understand that?"

If I merely nodded, or responded with a neutral "Yes," my tutor usually followed up.

"Really? You don't seem sure."

"Yes. I'm sure. I understand that Amharic does thus and such," I noted, sure to add a smile to my face, to look agreeable so we could move on. I'd studied Xhosa, Sotho, Shona, and now Amharic as the sole student, and the same held true with Swahili in coming years.

I sat alone with my various tutors all day, so I should have been used to these exchanges, but I sometimes found them exhausting, despite my love of languages. I knew that in the event I didn't understand any grammatical concept, I would have asked, or followed up on my own after class. No news meant good news to my way of thinking, rude as it may have appeared. But my instructors required constant feedback from me.

When I look back on my language training through the years, I preferred those times when I got out of the classroom: attending classes at the Prado and other cultural events for Spanish; mingling with Brazilians in the favelas or in their homes in the outback for Portuguese; going to *shebeens* and markets in Cape Town to practice my Xhosa; talking to traditional healers, traveling in rickety, crammed *daladalas* in Dar es Salaam to improve my Swahili. In this way I benefited greatly. Not sitting in a closet-sized, often windowless classroom day after day. Half a day I could do, not an entire day.

In December of 1991, after forty weeks of training, I headed back to my office to put my language skills to use. I returned to my office to translate documents, to help my office team as they kept government officials apprised of the increasingly volatile situation in Ethiopia. Even though the thirty-year civil war between Ethiopia and Eritrea had begun to wind down, the situation in the region remained in flux. Ethiopia's importance as the largest landlocked country in the world, the second-most-populated country in Africa, strategically located near the Red Sea and the Gulf of Aden—all this meant it would remain on US officials' radar indefinitely. Linguists provided an important link to keeping these same US officials apprised of events in the Horn of Africa, translating documents, newspaper articles, vital communications, any information that could shed light on that important area.

The year 2007 marked more than fifteen years since I'd finished working one-on-one with an Amharic tutor. I'd returned to my office, where I translated documents from Amharic to English for several years. In the early 1990s, though, management drafted me back to a former office to concentrate on a rapidly changing South Africa as apartheid finally came to an end. Management jokingly called me a "utility player": I went wherever a need existed.

In February of 2007, I departed on the first of two assignments to Ethiopia, the second one taking place in 2009. A highlight of that first one consisted in visiting the National Museum of Ethiopia in Addis Ababa—the capital of Ethiopia—seeing a plaster replica of "Lucy" (named after the Beatles' song "Lucy in the Sky with Diamonds"). I'd never seen anything like Lucy before. I now understood why scholars referred to Ethiopia as the cradle of civilization.

Lucy, the partial skeleton (40 percent complete) of a 3.2-million-year-old female discovered in Hadar, Ethiopia, in 1974, represented the most complete skeleton found to date. The discovery of her skeleton established that our human ancestors walked upright.

In Ethiopia, the assembly of Lucy's bones was referred to as *Dinkinesh*, meaning "you are marvelous" in Amharic. I loved that Ethiopians added their own flourish to such an important scientific discovery.

While in Addis Ababa, I stayed at the Sheraton Addis, a five-star hotel, one of the most luxurious places I'd ever been to or seen. It looked like something from a fairy tale, like a castle, the site of Cinderella's ball. It represented the antithesis of my humble accommodations in the Democratic Republic of the Congo eight years before: Camp Congo.

Enormous domed porticos welcomed guests at the entrance. Carefully manicured gardens with flowers every color of the rainbow surrounded the hotel. A musical water fountain splashed soothingly. Palm trees lined the complex of roads running through the grounds. An oversized swimming pool highlighted the rear of the hotel. Inside, crystal chandeliers, enormous vases of flowers, and exquisitely carved furniture could be seen throughout the gigantic lobby, where a pianist entertained guests on a sleek black piano located in a tasteful bar, sumptuous finger foods artfully arrayed. Finely upholstered leather couches, mahogany furniture, and marbled bathroom floors were standard. Guests could choose to dine inside or outside at any of the gourmet five-star restaurants and cafés. In short, the Sheraton held nothing but the finest furnishings, outdoor features, cuisine, a veritable Shangri-La. It truly resembled a palace more than a hotel.

Juxtaposed with the hotel's opulence was a different view out the picture window in my sizable room. Beyond the estate-like grounds of the Sheraton, shanties were visible, smoke curling up from makeshift chimneys, worn-out clothes hanging from long pieces of rope, raggedy-dressed children playing outside the crumbling huts, followed by mangy dogs.

It didn't escape my attention that I could never have afforded to stay at such a hotel back home in the States. This phantasmagoric hotel served as my home away from home strictly because of the high-level security it provided to its (mostly foreign) guests. The affordable per diem rate the hotel charged US government employees or affiliates acted as a further enticement. I felt like the Queen of Sheba in this opulent setting, fitting since legend held that the kingdom of Sheba formed part of today's Ethiopia.

The Sheraton looked like an oasis in the midst of poverty. Luxury surrounded by severe want. A fantasy ringed by painful realities. Impossible not to witness such poverty located at close range. I couldn't help but see it when I passed by it on my way to work each day, as well as from the window of my room. I wondered if any Sheraton employees lived in these humble dwellings skirting the perimeter of the hotel grounds.

While in Ethiopia I met and worked not only with Ethiopians but also with Eritreans, Somalis, and Sudanese, occasionally playing checkers with them on our lunch breaks, that universal twelfth-century game beloved everywhere. The Horn of Africa represented a new region for me. I soaked everything up: meeting people, learning about their unique history, customs, culture, improving my Amharic language comprehension and speaking skills.

Telling time and using a calendar differ in Ethiopia. A day is split into two twelve-hour periods: dawn to dusk, dusk to dawn. Seven a.m. equals 1:00, since it signifies the first sign of daylight. Seven p.m. equals 1:00 at night because it marks the beginning of evening. In terms of their calendar, it contains twelve months with thirty days each. Five or six extra days are added to equal a thirteenth month. The first day of the year normally falls on September 11.

Unlike other trips to Africa when I kept to myself most of my workday, translating and interpreting information in bare-bones offices to pass on to US officials, wearing headphones most of the day, on my 2007 and 2009 trips to Addis Ababa I had more opportunities to meet one-on-one with Ethiopians, as well as other people from the Horn of Africa. When weather permitted, we sometimes did our work outside in lush garden areas, a gentle breeze providing relief from rays of the nearby equatorial sun, the scent of the *Hagenia* flower enhancing our environment. It was a nice change from previous TDYs to Africa, allowing me to occasionally work outside.

As I was accustomed to the fickle climate of the US Midwest and East Coast, every country I visited on the continent—Ethiopia no exception—seemed to have an ideal climate, at least during my trips.

During the day, the sun almost always shone, bringing its warmth, even in winter months, which coincided with most of my trips; my summer equaled their winter. In 2007 I went to Ethiopia in February in the midst of their summer, whereas in 2009 I went in May, the equivalent of their fall. At its coldest, I only needed a light jacket or sweater. I loved the climate, the smell of leaves burning, reminding me of my childhood when it was still permissible to burn leaves we'd raked up in the yard.

Analyzing my new colleagues' English skills, I worked at helping them improve their speaking, writing, listening, and reading, similar to an English as a second language (ESL) instructor's task. Although I taught ESL at the community college near my home in Maryland, this was a departure for me in Africa, almost a role reversal of my normal pattern in that my new colleagues used a foreign language—English—with me, while I used not only English but also Amharic. I enjoyed the shift in perspective, looking at my native language through the eyes of people for whom it was new. Conversely, they helped me improve my Amharic, an ongoing challenge.

During my second TDY to Ethiopia in 2009, my ESL work with Ethiopians, Eritreans, Somalis, and Sudanese continued. I found it gratifying to know that, just as their English skills improved, so too did my Amharic. The more I learned about Ethiopia, the greater my awareness of the vast differences between Africa's countries. It never failed to baffle me when people generalized Africa's citizens, lumping everyone together, when even within a single country a multitude of differences exist: in culture, physical appearances, food preferences, languages spoken, traditions. Similarly, I disliked it when people lumped me with all Midwesterners, as though we represented a homogeneous group, not one containing numerous differences, personality traits. Even worse: often uninformed people referred to Africa as though it were a single country, not a continent. In 2007 and 2009, Africa consisted of fifty-three individual countries, prior to South Sudan achieving its independence in 2011, becoming Africa's fifty-fourth country.

One weekend during my 2009 stay in Ethiopia, rather than remaining alone in my hotel, sitting by the phone, hoping for invitations from embassy employees like a needy adolescent, I decided to go to Lalibela, a UNESCO World Historical Centre. I took a flight up on Friday, returning to Addis Ababa on Sunday. I'd heard about Lalibela, and since I knew I probably wouldn't return to the area, I wanted to take advantage of opportunities to see and do more while I was in such a fascinating country.

Lalibela is located in north-central Ethiopia, five hundred miles due north of Addis Ababa. King Lalibela recreated a "new Jerusalem" in the twelfth century as a pilgrimage site. It remains one of Ethiopia's holiest cities, after Aksum. Lalibela served as the capital of Ethiopia from the late twelfth century until the thirteenth century.

The site boasts eleven rock-cut churches, each carved from a single gigantic piece of stone back in the late 1100s, these stones often extending more than 150 feet *below*—not above—the ground's surface. Buildings include doors, floors, windows, columns, roofs, all miraculously carved from that single piece of stone. Many locals believe that a team of angels helped King Lalibela construct the churches in a single night. Historians still haven't been able to find a logical explanation for the sudden creation of this massive, awe-inspiring site. Afterwards, I had to admit I'd never seen anything remotely like it.

I knew next to nothing about Lalibela in advance of traveling there, just snippets from people I came in contact with who'd been living in Ethiopia a while, colleagues and acquaintances citing it as a must-see destination. I just knew I didn't want to remain alone all weekend, even at the fabulous Sheraton. I couldn't have afforded massages or excursions or any of the other add-ons offered by the concierge, astronomically expensive luxuries definitely not covered by my per diem. I could afford the short flight north, along with overnights in a modest hotel, though. Besides, how to compare massages, expensive meals, decadent surroundings in a five-star hotel with seeing a mysterious, ancient city, a one-of-a-kind site. I was unprepared for what awaited me.

On Saturday morning, after spending the night in my modest hotel, I trailed tourists and pilgrims alike as they followed signposts to the historical site. Entering a tunnel, I soon discovered a warren of underground paths leading to the subterranean cave churches in Lalibela. Twisting tunnels resembled narrow channels, barely wide enough to accommodate me. The walls looked uneven; in some places I stood sideways to slowly make my way forward. The darkness was so dense I couldn't see my hand when I held it inches from my face. Not even an outline or a shadow was visible; it was that dark.

Once I'd made the decision to enter the tunnel—the only way to reach the subterranean interior of the church I wanted to visit—there was no turning back. Even if I'd wanted to, no extra space allowed for changing directions, not a spare inch. My shoulders already hunched together in front to fit into the tunnel. In addition, a steady trickle of strangers inched along right behind me, single file, with people also moving slowly, silently, ahead of me. I knew I was trapped, on a slow-moving conveyor belt. Nor was I confident enough in Amharic to express my panic, my desperate need to turn back, to retrace my steps up the one-way tunnel, even if it had been physically possible to do so. I blindly stumbled through labyrinthine tunnels in slow motion, sandwiched in front and back by strangers. On either side, walls hemmed me in, reminding me of those ever-expanding and collapsing walls you see at carnival fun houses. I searched my mind for Amharic phrases. "I must turn around." "I don't want to continue." "Please help me get out of here." "Do you speak English?" "How far does this tunnel go?" "Help!"

I placed my right hand on the right shoulder of the person in front of me, a stranger, following the example of others, careful to keep up, to remain in lockstep. That's all that prevented me from having a full-blown panic attack. I was heading down into the bowels of the earth, with no escape route, either by racing ahead or by retracing my steps.

Absolute darkness, the narrowness, depth, length of the maze of tunnels, the low ceilings, misshapen nine-hundred-year-old walls packing me in and poking me unexpectedly on both sides brought me dangerously close to full-blown panic. Could I continue on like this? Around the next bend, or the next? What if the walls collapsed, which they'd done in the past? What if I became stuck?

After what seemed like hours, the dark, narrow crevices leading to Lalibela's sanctuary at last spit me out into an open chamber far below ground level where congregants had gathered to worship. Probably fewer than thirty minutes had elapsed. My view of the area, 150 feet below ground, served as my reward: stunning, magical.

As I came out of the subterranean tunnel, I walked into an enormous gallery, an underground chamber, a temple where worshippers and pilgrims were gathered in worship. Looking up, my eyes slowly adjusted to the introduction of light after so much intense darkness. I realized that a new, welcome source of light shone down, originating high above me from a gigantic stone cross carved into the ceiling of the stone, allowing sunlight to flood in, outside the lines of the rock cross, looking almost like an aura. I wondered how all these congregants had managed to make their way into the chamber without incident. Was I the only one who panicked? Everyone looked so calm. I found it unnerving, embarrassing, a mystery.

Since I wasn't fluent in Amharic, this experience had presented its own kind of claustrophobia. Not able to readily express myself in a crucial language, I'd been thrown back on myself, locked inside: no windows, no light, no language, no way out. I was discovering that part of the appeal of speaking a language in another country is the ability to escape this peculiar claustrophobia. When I knew a language well enough, it acted like a window appearing in a previously closed-off environment, a window to see beyond any physical space I occupied. A window to let in outside elements, to allow me to familiarize myself with these elements while air—ideas—flowed back and forth.

I survived. I passed whatever the test had been, survived what— to most people—might have been a benign exercise. I put one foot in front of the other, didn't cry out or scream in terror. I kept moving. I could do that. Keep moving . . . keep moving till I'd entered the church's underground temple, looking up 150 feet up to see the enormous window with the cross above me in the ceiling, letting in light.

8

SEMANTICS

A Word Is Not a Word

SEMANTICS—*the branch of linguistics that deals with meaning; the meaning of a word, phrase, sentence, text.*

EXAMPLE: *When people use certain terms, such as "middle class," the words don't always share a universal meaning. The field of semantics involves studying how meanings change, depending on the context in which words are used.*

In 1997, a year before being summoned to Kenya in the aftermath of the bombings in Nairobi and Dar es Salaam, I made plans to go to Dar es Salaam, Tanzania. My goal for the journey to Dar es Salaam was to increase my fluency in Swahili: in reading, writing, listening, and speaking skills. I'd worked with a tutor stateside for six months, but in-country learning enhances and speeds up language acquisition; it's like a booster shot in terms of learning, if one takes advantage of the experience. This wasn't my first time in Africa, nor was Swahili the first African language I'd studied, or the most challenging, but this marked my first African language immersion.

I'd fallen in love with Swahili. It was personal. I loved how it sounded, its straightforward grammar, the culture associated with those who spoke it in Uganda, Tanzania, and Kenya, as well as its importance as a widely spoken language in Africa. When I began my language immersion, my exposure had been limited to my tutorial in the US, namely in a classroom, using textbooks, receiving daily one-on-one instruction from a skilled native speaker. I needed more, was ready for more.

Swahili was also my language of choice for practical reasons: an abundance of material could be found in it, wars/coups/terrorist attacks didn't yet loom on the horizon (which would have made travel more difficult), nor did an apartheid-like regime or corrupt government exist to serve as a barrier to going there.

In-country language immersions are ideal for a rapid-fire infusion of grammar, colloquial phrases, and cultural experiences. Nothing works as effectively as venturing outside a classroom's four walls, beyond grammatical abstractions, going where one can hear a language spoken, test newly acquired skills.

Language immersion also takes you outside your comfort zone into situations where knowledge of a language will make life infinitely easier. Without a textbook or dictionary at the ready, or an English-speaking instructor as a crutch, you're thrown back on yourself, on whatever base you've managed to build, on your ability to maneuver out of sometimes tight positions, alone. With this goal in mind, I was heading to Tanzania on a cultural and linguistic journey.

As I prepared to travel to Dar es Salaam, logistical matters ranked low on my list of priorities; my focus consisted in ensuring I knew enough Swahili not to embarrass myself. I planned to stay in a hotel for most of my immersion, working with a tutor every morning, venturing into the community with him most afternoons to put my skills into practice. I also planned to participate in a home visit, leaving behind the comfort of my hotel in Tanzania's capital to stay with a family in a village outside Dar es Salaam for a short stay.

The US State Department handled details surrounding my Swahili immersion: setting up flights, arranging local transportation and hotel accommodations, finding a Swahili tutor, locating a family to host me for my home stay. A few weeks before I left for Tanzania, my contact at the State Department called, peppering me with questions: What sort of family did I want to stay with for my home visit? What kind of setting did I prefer? The State Department wielded veto power over any of my decisions but needed input. These matters seemed secondary to my principal goal—language enhancement. My first reaction was frustration, feeling bogged down in a myriad of details.

"I don't really care," I'd replied in response to the administrative officer on the other end of the phone. "It doesn't matter to me. Whatever you think."

What difference did it make? Surrounding myself with native Swahili speakers in their environment: that was the point; anything else seemed like window dressing. But State Department personnel insisted on pinning me down; they needed specifics.

Forced to respond, my first reaction was to say, "I guess I'd like to be paired with a middle-class family for my home stay." That way, I thought, even though we might differ in many ways—language, background, education, culture—we'd have that commonality: middle class.

After a long flight to Dar es Salaam, I settled into a fairly modern hotel, part of a well-known international chain. It looked like a shiny penny from the outside, ten stories with an always gleaming upscale marble-floored foyer with plush couches and chairs, uniformed staff to greet me, modern-looking rooms, life-size carvings of African animals strategically placed around the lobby, intricate raffia wall hangings. But just below the surface a different narrative bubbled up: connections to modern technology proved unreliable, access to the Internet, my room's sputtering air-conditioning, the malfunctioning elevators, to name a few.

My tutor, who instructed me to call him "Marshal," stopped by my hotel that first morning in Dar es Salaam to begin our work together. He was about my height—five foot four—professional looking in a button-down shirt, no tie, khaki pants, proudly wearing a dapper brown beret that had seen better days.

We quickly settled into a routine: half a day sitting across from each other on oversized couches in the hotel lobby, or outside on an inviting veranda if weather permitted, reviewing Swahili grammar, idioms, Tanzanian customs, venturing out into the community after a lunch break, putting my skills into practice. I carried a notebook, wrote down everything Marshal said, as though the wisdom of his words might not stay with me otherwise. So often I was unfamiliar with idioms he used, customs he imparted, even though my tutor back in the States was a native speaker of Swahili and an excellent teacher.

Although we remained largely oblivious to guests milling around in the lobby, attending to their respective tasks of checking in or lodging complaints, or merely passing time, I preferred to sit in the hotel's back courtyard, away from potential gawkers. Since the weather rarely varied from fairly idyllic conditions, that's usually where we ended up. Outside, I became less self-conscious about potential speaking errors I made. Beautiful gardens, trees, songbirds were an added bonus, serving as a pleasant backdrop to my lessons.

Afternoon field trips provided an opportunity to talk to locals who spoke this fascinating, important language, a nice break from having spent all morning at the hotel. We ventured to a variety of places, conversed with people I wouldn't have been exposed to as a woman traveling alone in Africa. I was grateful for the access Marshal provided in that regard: fairs, women's cooperatives, traditional healers, various markets, even private homes.

Cultural lessons he imparted were significant: reinforcing the lesson of never beckoning a person using your index finger, never eating with your left hand (considered filthy), never smelling your food (considered rude), never wearing revealing clothing if you're a woman, and so on, all lessons I benefited from when I returned the following year.

For one of our afternoon trips, Marshal and I took the local transportation, a *daladala*, to his village, Mwananyamala, for lunch, where I was served porridge, cassava leaves with coconut milk, and a tiny, very hot pepper. He had me watch a video of the work he does visiting schools, educating them about AIDS, a program UNICEF supports. His home was one of the nicest in the village, although it had concrete floors and walls, no plumbing or running water. He shared that, until the past year, he'd lived in two rented rooms, and that one of his four children—his twenty-year-old son—had had to spend each night with friends, since there was no room. But Marshal was proud of his home, and, in contrast, next door was a house made of mud and sticks. As we walked around his village, people stared at me, and when they found out that I knew Swahili, they completely surrounded me, up to fifty at once, firing questions at me as though I were a celebrity.

Another afternoon after our work at the hotel, Marshal and I walked along dusty, trash-strewn streets trafficked by older-model cars—some of them European makes I'd not seen in the US—to the edge of a city park, a mile or so from the hotel. At the edge of the city park, we arrived at a ramshackle kiosk—reminiscent of an oversized lemonade stand I might have seen back home—where a traditional healer sat: an *mganga*. A cigarette hanging precariously from his mouth, he was tall for a Tanzanian, a lanky man, wearing a light brown, slightly stained button-down shirt with baggy khaki pants. He was so thin, wizened and doubled over, that he looked elderly, but Marshal later revealed he was only fifty. (This often happened, similar to my work in Brazil; I sometimes miscalculated someone's age by quite a bit.)

A rickety folding chair served as his waiting room. He sat in another chair in front of a large—six feet wide by four feet tall—handmade cardboard sign nailed to the supports of the kiosk, which, instead of advertising lemonade and Kool-Aid, listed various homeopathic remedies he sold, as well as the ailments they purportedly cured. I saw powders, potions, lotions, brews in glass jars, medicine that cured any number of maladies, from the common cold to snake bites to erectile dysfunction. It was a comprehensive list containing over thirty ailments, some with untranslatable names. Marshal told me later that none of the *mganga's* cures were written down; he'd memorized everything, just as his predecessors had before him. He also shared that sometimes customers special-ordered potions to put a spell on their enemies, though he didn't explain just how this was carried out.

After Marshal introduced us, paving the way for my questions, I interviewed him, asked him about his work, my notebook in hand for this unique opportunity. "Do you treat everything?"

"Everything but AIDS and cancer," came his reply in barely decipherable Swahili. He seemed to be missing some teeth and softly mumbled his answers to me.

"So you don't work with people who have either of those diseases, AIDS or cancer?"

"No. No cure exists, so I don't give people false hopes," he continued. In the midst of what I had initially interpreted as pure quackery, I found this refreshing, his acknowledgment that even his expertise had limits. After talking with him a while, I thanked him and walked away with Marshal, equipped with a newfound appreciation for nontraditional medicine.

As we walked around town, Marshal also pointed out several Maasai men who worked as security guards in downtown Dar es Salaam. Hailing from northern Tanzania and central and southern Kenya, they are traditionally nomadic people but, given their legendary reputation as ferocious warriors, are often hired to patrol businesses. Taller than the average Tanzanian, they stand out, and they take their jobs seriously, at least the ones I came in contact with.

While venturing out alone one day, I stood on a corner, watching a majestic Maasai man complete his rounds, watching as he walked in large circles around buildings he'd been hired to protect. A local woman approached after observing me for several minutes. She'd spotted a paperback book I carried with me, sticking out of my canvas bag: *I Know This Much Is True* by Wally Lamb. She wondered if she could buy it from me.

"*Samahani*, excuse me, but I noticed you have a book I've been looking for."

She nodded at my copy of *I Know This Much Is True*.

Continuing her comments, she noted how expensive books were in Dar es Salaam, not to mention difficult to find. "The price would amount to my entire month's salary, just to purchase this one book, madame," she sighed.

I knew how difficult it was to find books, how exorbitantly priced they were in Tanzania, and elsewhere in Africa, especially books from the US and the UK, in English. Talking with her, I happened to notice that, coincidentally, she carried a book in her satchel that I'd been looking for: a copy of a coveted brown-and-yellow out-of-print book, *The Friendly Modern Swahili English Dictionary* by Baba Malaika. I proposed a swap.

"What a coincidence; you have a dictionary that everyone talks about but I've not been able to find at home in America, or anywhere here. Could we possibly trade books?" I suggested.

She agreed without hesitation. I still have the slim paperback dictionary, dog-eared from age and use; hopefully, she still has my Wally Lamb book. I subsequently learned that it wasn't just books in English that were expensive; when I went to the University of Dar es Salaam to look for English–Swahili and Swahili–English dictionaries, I learned that even slim volumes cost seventy dollars.

Another afternoon, Marshal took me to an artisan's cooperative, Nyumba ya Sanaa (House of Art), near my hotel, where I met a dozen or so cheerful women wearing traditional *kangas*. These women—from young adults to elderly—worked as artisans, creating paintings, wood carvings, weavings, clothing, baskets, cloth purses. They pooled their income to buy supplies and material, setting a small stipend aside to support themselves, to supplement their families' coffers.

The *kangas* these women wore—that women all over Dar es Salaam wore—consisted of a large square piece of multicolored cloth, popular in East Africa beginning in the mid to late nineteenth century. Different Swahili proverbs or sayings are incorporated into the material, each one known as a *jina*. These proverbs often reflect religious topics. Women fold, knot, manipulate their *kangas* to create more than a hundred different outfits, according to one book that claims to contain all one hundred variations. These include dresses, skirts, headscarves, even a sling to carry a baby. Some examples of proverbs found on *kangas*: *Akiba haiozi*. ("It's good to save for the future.") *Bahati ni upepo sasa upo kwangu*. ("Don't expect to be lucky all the time.") *Dua la kuku halimpati mwewe*. ("A chicken's prayer doesn't affect a hawk.") *Njia mwongo fupi*. ("The way of the liar is short.")

After my work with Marshal ended for the day, I liked to venture out on my own, rather than remain in the hotel. One such day, I walked to a market I'd heard about. Employees at the hotel said it sold fruits and vegetables and other items; they thought it might be of interest to me. My experience with markets taught me that they tended to vary quite a bit, ranging from massive enterprises—selling everything from hardware to clothing, fruit to seafood, livestock to shoes, utensils to statues—to smaller businesses, stands manned by only a few people that displayed fewer wares. This market purportedly belonged to the latter variety, and I didn't want to miss it.

"Can I walk there?" "*Ninaweza ku tembea huko?*" I asked the hotel employee, an enthusiastic woman who sometimes manned the desk.

"Oh, yes. It's very close," she answered me. "*Ni karibu sana.*"

"How long will it take me to walk there?" I continued, wanting to ensure I had a sense of the distance. "*Itanichukua muda gani kufika hapo?*"

"Just a few minutes," she said, repeating, "It's very close." "*Dakika chache tu. Ni karibu sana.*"

I soon discovered, however, that "*karibu sana*," "very close," had a different meaning in Swahili than it did in English. I loved to walk, but I didn't want to get lost, periodically wondering if I'd taken a wrong turn somewhere on the isolated country roads I walked down, traveling farther from my hotel. After an hour of solid walking (allowing for a few minutes to stop and take stock of my surroundings), I finally arrived at the market.

A few days later, Marshal took me to a fishing village outside Dar es Salaam, Kivukoni. To reach our destination, we traveled for about an hour on a shared, oversized minibus known as a *daladala*. Public transportation is scarce, so people often use *daladalas* to get from point A to point B. Passengers cram inside older-model minibuses, squeezing in many more than the suggested capacity. Because of the lack of affordable transportation in the area, people spill out of the doors, hang out windows. Four rows of seats are jammed inside the vehicle—long wooden benches—including the driver's row, with another row facing backwards behind the driver. The exterior of the one I traveled on that day had been painted with the route, along with various religious sayings. Their guiding philosophy seemed to be: there's always room for another passenger, another fare.

People of all shapes and sizes and ages packed the minibus, carrying a variety of packages, parcels, and baskets. It was so crowded that Marshal and I couldn't sit together on the same bank of seats, so I squeezed in next to a middle-aged woman. She carried an oversized plastic bag filled to the brim with fruit and vegetables, hugging it close to her on her lap as though it were a precious infant. She kept staring at me sideways after I wedged myself in beside her, never looking at me directly until I started up a conversation in Swahili.

I began with, "*Jambo! Habari yako? Basi hili limejaa sana!*" "Hello! How are you? This bus is so crowded!"

Initially, she appeared shocked to hear me speaking Swahili, hugging her parcels even closer to herself. But as she became accustomed to my voice, to my physical presence next to her, she started to talk.

"*Niko njiani kwenda kazini. Ninachukua basi kila siku.*" "I'm on my way to work. I take the bus every day."

As she became even less nervous and realized I could converse in Swahili with her, her questions began to flow. "*Unatoka wapi? Umeoa? Una watoto? Ngapi? Wana umre gani? Wako wapi? Kwa nini uso hapa?*" "Where do you come from? Are you married? Do you have children? How many? How old are they? Where are they? Why are you here?"

After several minutes of conversing, when she became more relaxed, without initially commenting she began pressing her index finger onto my bare forearm, watching as the indentation briefly made my skin appear even whiter, then bounced back to its original color. She chuckled to herself, then did it again, as though watching a magic show. *Push, release. Marvel. Push, release. Marvel.*

"You're so white! I've never seen a white person before!" she exclaimed. "*Wewe ni mzungu sana! Sijawahi kuona mzungu hapo awali!*" Like most Tanzanians, though, she thought I was European, not American.

I found it hard to believe she'd never seen a white person, since Marshal and I hadn't strayed too far from Dar es Salaam, the capital of Tanzania, where many Caucasians worked and lived. Marshal explained this when we arrived at the fishing village, though, explaining that Peace Corps personnel didn't usually venture to villages near Dar es Salaam, that they were sent instead to villages outside Arusha, Tanzania, thus explaining my experience and what had happened during my visit to Marshal's home when people in the village had latched onto me.

When we arrived in Kivukoni, I quickly gained an appreciation of celebrities' plight. Marshal and I were followed everywhere by an entourage, primarily children. Mothers peered at us from doorways, careful to remain at a safe distance. A few villagers even pulled out inexpensive cameras to take my picture. I took on the role of the pied piper, trailed by kids too nervous to talk initially, yet eager to know what I was doing. Boys kicked around beat-up, half-inflated soccer balls, darting here and there as they escaped from their mothers' skirts, eventually circling back to me.

Some of the T-shirts children wore featured logos from Western countries: Nike, the Boston Red Sox, Planet Hollywood, the names of other sports teams, some of them evidently from American high schools and unfamiliar to me. Their clothing represented part of a mass influx of secondhand items flooding the continent. Known in Swahili as "*Mitumba*" (literally, "bundles"), the second- and third-hand clothing comes from Canada, the United States, Australia, and the United Kingdom and is popular throughout East Africa.

Prior to my departure, I'd sometimes wondered what life would be like as a "famous" person. I had loved playing the piano on stage as an adolescent and teenager, on display for a few minutes, as "famous" as I'd ever be. I even daydreamed about playing on Ted Mack's *Original Amateur Hour* or *Johnny Carson*. But wandering around Kivukoni that day, trailed by strangers, it dawned on me that I actually didn't enjoy being the center of attention, even on a small scale, especially with strangers who knew nothing about me, following me merely because I looked different, was an oddity. It cured me of that daydream.

Armed with my recently enhanced language skills—thanks to my tutor and the work we'd tackled for almost a month—I tried to present an optimistic front about leaving behind the comfort and controlled environment of my faux-modern hotel to stay with a local family. That leg of my journey was scheduled midway into my immersion experience, so I would return to the hotel afterwards to resume work with my tutor. I worried about all the unknowns, about staying in close quarters with people I'd never met, people I had little in common with. I even worried about not having access to my daily Diet Coke fix.

An employee of the US embassy, a Tanzanian who worked as a foreign service national, drove me to my host family's home, located in a small village, Kinondoni, thirty minutes outside of Dar es Salaam. I brought with me a small canvas bag with a few toiletries and a change of clothing, along with a couple of photographs to share with the family, to give them a better idea of who I was. I had no cell phone or laptop with me, no way to communicate.

The driver, a slight man not given to small talk, pulled up in front of my hotel, my home away from home thus far. I climbed into the back of the State Department's official SUV, a sleek black late model Ford with tinted windows, my little weekend bag tucked beside me. Soon after leaving the city limits of Dar es Salaam behind, driving past its modest businesses, its low-slung, plain-looking apartment buildings, an occasional school, numerous rutted parking lots, we transitioned to unpaved, unmarked dirt roads, past scenes of people in ragtag clothes, crumbling-down homes that someone might have torn down in a more developed part of the world. Occasionally, we passed a traditional dome-shaped hut with a thatched roof, half-dressed children running after dogs or goats, a stick of some sort in their hands in lieu of sporting equipment or toys.

I looked out the vehicle's window, struck by the picture of poverty developing before me, even though I'd seen similar sights riding on the *daladala* the day I went to the fishing village with my tutor. I'd also caught glimpses of this reality elsewhere in Dar es Salaam. It seemed like the window was letting in a steady stream of unfamiliar realities, ones rushing past me; it was too much for my eyes to take in, as though someone were force-feeding me a meal I didn't want.

I had seen photographs, witnessed poverty firsthand in other countries. Several years before, I saw it in Rio de Janeiro's favelas, Brazil's shanties. I'd spent time in the slums of Johannesburg, Soweto, Lusaka, Guatemala City, and elsewhere, but this felt somehow different. I looked at my surroundings through a different lens now as we passed it by, up close, not from a distance. I was actually going to be part of it, albeit temporarily, no longer skirting the fringes, merely allowing my fingers to touch the end of its tassels.

This was not a movie I watched in the comfort of my home, could turn off at will, or even a jaunt taken in a *daladala* to the outskirts of town with my tutor acting as a buffer, with the goal of cultural enrichment. This area would be my home for a short time, an area in which I would immerse myself, both physically and linguistically. This hadn't been my intention when I used the term with my State Department contacts. Hadn't I made myself clear? What had I gotten myself into? Didn't I specify middle class?

I couldn't believe I'd committed such a major faux pas in the field of translation. I'd used a term—middle class—and expected it to translate perfectly from my Western-oriented life into this African reality, even though nothing I'd experienced thus far in my travels fit this definition. What did I think, that pockets of homes with well-manicured and sweeping lawns lay tucked somewhere in Tanzania, enclaves of two-car garages, picket fences? Tanzania's own modified

Xanadu? Hadn't I paid attention? Slowly, it dawned on me: all these ramshackle homes I passed, as though for the first time, and had seen elsewhere in Africa, *were* considered "middle-class" dwellings.

After a thirty-minute drive, we entered Kinondoni Village, my destination. A palette of various shades of earth tones stretched out before me. I saw brown dirt roads, various huts with thatched roofs, some one-story off-white concrete dwellings, goats grazing on sparse tufts of dying grass, local people milling about. It reminded me of raffia cloths I'd seen elsewhere in eastern Africa: beautifully woven textured tapestries using varying shades of brown, beige, and black textiles.

We pulled up to a small bare-bones one-story concrete structure, a building surrounded by even more modest homes. My heart sank. *No. I can't stay here*, I thought. *I can't do this.* Panic set in. *I don't know these people. I have no way to contact anyone if I need to. Very few people are even aware of my location, except for this driver, who seems eager to leave me behind.*

I remained in the car, frozen, tuning out the driver's words. He informed me we'd arrived, that I could get out of the vehicle. Suddenly, a group of people dashed out of the home, breaking through my stupor. A dapper, dignified-looking man possibly in his forties (whose clothes stood in sharp contrast to the humble circumstances in which he lived) was followed by an equally dignified-looking woman of forty or so—his wife, I assumed—and five children of various ages: two teenage daughters (fourteen and sixteen, I later learned), two sons (eleven and ten), and a younger daughter, five.

As I unfroze, pried my body from the car seat, slowly opened the door—realizing how rude this looked—my host, Maliamacho, warmly greeted me, along with his wife, Grace, and the five children. They all politely introduced themselves, the girls curtsying. They seemed genuinely happy to see me, despite the look of desperation on my face.

Everyone in the family was dressed in his or her Sunday best, but Maliamacho stood out with his crisp suit coat, tie and hat, looking like a dignified, confident patriarch, looking more Western than his wife or children. Grace and the two older female children wore variations of the traditional *kanga*, the local dress I'd seen when walking around Dar es Salaam with my tutor.

In the opening minutes of meeting a Tanzanian (or other sub-Saharan African) for the first time, it's customary to spend considerable time asking about their family, their health, their lives, etc., not like in the States, where you quickly get to the heart of the matter, avoiding chitchat in most cases. This meant that my average conversation—all those Swahili words!—needed to be relatively long, unless I wanted to risk offending people. More cause for exhaustion. When I was growing up, my mother sometimes chastised me when company came over and I stayed in my room.

"Come out! Be sociable! You need to make an effort to talk to our company!"

But my anxiety acted as an overpowering deterrent. Leaping over it to become "sociable" cranked it even higher.

Back and forth the questions bounced as we strolled inside their home together. They asked me questions about my family, my home, my life. I answered the questions, then thought of polite ones to ask in return, in Swahili, or just added polite comments. "*Umeishi hapa kwa muda gani?*" "How long have you lived here?" "*Watoto wana umri gani?*" "How old are the children?" "*Asante sana kwa kunikaribisha nyumbani kwako.*" "Thank you for welcoming me into your home."

Maliamacho's family took great pride in their home, giving me a grand tour shortly after I arrived, pointing out various highlights. They enjoyed a certain stature in their community. I sensed that this home represented a significant improvement in their standing; they were moving up the socio-economic ladder.

My home away from home was a one-story building constructed of large whitewashed concrete blocks—cinder block walls—slick, bare gray cement floors the color of steeped tea. I learned later that this fact alone made them middle-class; the homes of poor families consisted of dirt floors, or no man-made structure at all, or maybe a single room, even a hut. Cement blocks made up the interior as well as the outside. Except for furniture, you could have turned the house inside out without changing its appearance appreciably.

Their home had a formal living room—the largest room—comparable to an average-sized den in the US. It was the only place the entire family could congregate at the same time. I spotted worn, unmatched chairs, a weathered couch. Not everyone could sit down simultaneously, or maybe they sat extremely close to each other. I also walked past a small, drab—by Western standards—kitchen containing nothing but a portable Coleman-style camp stove, a miniature refrigerator—the type people kept by their desks in office settings at home—a scuffed table with what looked like slightly uneven legs, an out-of-date picture calendar adding color to bare walls.

The only sign of modernity was electricity. That night I slept in a bed in the second bedroom, one normally shared by all five children, who presumably had to lie sideways, or in shifts, or with one or more children seeking a roomier place on the living room couch. Most family members stayed up that particular night, though, crowding around their small twenty-five-year-old television set, glued to the Tyson-Holyfield boxing match till 3:00 or 4:00 in the morning, because of the time difference. I later wondered if part of the boxing match's appeal consisted in having nowhere else to go because of my takeover of the children's bedroom. Electricity—plus the 1960s-era television it powered—was the sole "luxury" in this modest home.

The family normally ate dinner in the late afternoon, while it was still light outside. It took two to three hours to prepare their meal, work done exclusively by Grace and the two older female children. My first day there, I walked to a small market about a mile from their home with Maliamacho's wife and the two older female children, and Grace's sister, Mary, to buy food we needed for that night's dinner.

Family members continued to pepper me with questions.

"Mama-Alex, why don't you cook? Who cooks for you? What do you do all day? Do you have a job? Where do your children go to school? What does your house look like?"

I answered all their questions in Swahili, and they giggled at some of my responses.

"I don't cook because I'm a terrible cook. My husband cooks for me. I do have a job, and that's what I do all day, and I take care of my children. They are in school. My house is average-sized, with three bedrooms and two and a half bathrooms, meaning one bathroom is smaller, without a shower. I have pictures I'll show you."

For them, I must have seemed like a specimen under glass, a foreign body under the microscope. These strangers questioned me, examined me to see what made me tick. In fairness, though, their lives also stood out to me as completely new. Once I adjusted to my temporary home, I, too, was eager to learn all I could about each of them.

I helped the women chop greens, cut up a casaba melon and a coconut, prepare their *ugali*. In turn, they tried not to make fun of my subpar skills. They used a mortar and pestle for grinding; it reminded me of my days back in high school chemistry.

In keeping with his status as patriarch, Maliamacho barked orders at his children and wife, including me in his reign, holding court after our evening meal. He followed a custom of many East African countries, using only his right hand to eat. Eating that way proved more difficult than eating with chopsticks, a skill I also lacked, although the *ugali* helped in pushing food together, then picking it up, a technique I'd learned to do with naan, the traditional Indian bread.

After dinner one night we all walked to a local music festival. Young and old men chewed *khat* as a stimulant, a substance popular throughout much of East Africa for thousands of years, primarily with men. Indigenous to the Horn of Africa and considered slightly addictive, its possible side effects include excitement, euphoria, and loss of appetite. People chew *khat* when plant leaves are fresh; therefore consumers need to live close to where it's cultivated, although modern transportation has increased its footprint. Considered a controlled substance in the US and elsewhere, in Tanzania people chew it freely.

Three generations mingled at the concert: children in perpetual motion, women in their flowing print *kangas*, their hair piled on top of their heads in colorful headdresses, their husbands in Western dress, as well as stately grandparents—all of them dancing to sounds emanating from the instruments, from the singing onstage. Musicians played drums, keyboards, guitars, a type of castanets, and *kalimbas*, or thumb pianos, evenly spaced short vertical strips of metal mounted on a small wooden board, played with one's thumbs. Male and female singers entertained the crowd. Audience members, moved by the music, seldom remained in their seats for long, swaying to the intoxicating sounds and rhythms, frequently talking over the music to converse with friends. I was like a child allowed to stay up late to participate in a special evening; it was magical, and everyone treated me with warmth. Slowly, after half a dozen hours or so in my new environment, I'd begun to relax a little, to take stock of the fact that, despite my initial trepidation, I'd received a rare gift, if only I would receive it graciously, not squander the opportunity.

After we walked back from the festival, I wished everyone good-night, thanking them for their hospitality, hoping to go to bed. But Maliamacho announced that custom dictated I bathe before retiring for the night. "Mama-Alex," he said, beckoning me to him. I initially asked everyone to call me "Linda," but the custom was important to them; they exclusively called me "Mama-Alex" while in their home.

"Mama-Alex, do you prefer hot or cold water for your evening bath?" Maliamacho continued, asking me point-blank, like a king ordering his vassal to fetch his robe. He brooked no opposition.

"I think I'll wait till tomorrow," I tentatively suggested, not eager to have thousands of unsavory insects-of-the-night surprise me, insects I knew lurked in the dark. My words meant nothing; this was not a custom to be trifled with. Then I committed one of many mistakes in response to his persistent questioning about desired water temperature when I replied, "Hot water."

I quickly realized my mistake, but too late, that this meant the women of the house—Grace and her two older daughters—now would have to haul heavy pails of water in gigantic plastic containers from a communal well (as they'd done to cook the main meal of the day) and heat them one by one over the portable camp stove, all so I could have my "hot" bath. The outhouse had no spigot marked with an "H" from which hot water magically flowed. Needless to say, this lengthened their day and their workload considerably.

A stall outside their home served as the area in which to bathe. A

few broken remnants of soap floated in a plastic dish with an unidentifiable viscous substance in the corner. Maybe they collected the bits
of soap for my exclusive benefit, as their honored guest. The stall was
located in their postage-stamp, grassless yard. A second stall stood
right next to it: the toilet or, as I viewed it, the outhouse. Both side-
by-side stalls opened to the elements (weather and insect related) at
the top.

I quickly bathed, using a small plastic tub filled with the now-
lukewarm water they provided me with, avoiding bats swooping
dangerously close to my head. I was already busy in my futile attempts
to avoid the surprisingly agile water bugs (bugs I lived in fear of)
dancing at my feet. If anyone saw me, they witnessed a version of an
Irish jig.

After I'd cleaned up, Maliamacho finally gave me permission to
excuse myself, to say goodnight. One of his daughters led me to the
home's second bedroom. Mosquito netting had been draped over
the small bed in tentlike fashion. It served as an all-night trampo-
line for hundreds of giant cockroaches. They ricocheted off of it,
their weight denting the tent once or twice as they attempted to
penetrate it. Aggressively dive-bombing the netting, they angrily
buzzed before they pinged onto the floor.

The insects' tiny antennae briefly poked through gaps in the netting, dangerously close to brushing against my skin. After hitting the
floor with a soft thud, they skittered around willy-nilly like shiny
black bump 'em cars at a carnival. The Sisyphean process was then
repeated when they again took flight, resuming their onslaught of the
netting. Needless to say, getting up in the middle of the night for a
bathroom (outhouse) break sounded like something out of a Stephen
King novel; I would sooner have worn a diaper to bed. I did wonder
how all five children managed to sleep there, knowing full well that

this was the status quo—or worse—in many homes. I lay there, wide awake, praying for dawn to come, ecstatic when I finally heard roosters crowing outside. I hoped my shiny, black, manic visitors had retreated somewhere else, at least till dusk.

When I finally caught a glimpse of the emerging sun through the bedroom window, I waited a few minutes till I heard people stirring outside my bedroom, then untangled the mosquito netting from my body. Before placing a bare foot on the concrete floor, I glanced down to see if any cockroaches remained from the night before. Miraculously, they'd all disappeared, as though I'd made the whole nightmare up.

I hurried to the outhouse, never so grateful for even such a rudimentary toilet after spending a night with only two things on my mind: escaping the oversized insects, and emptying my bladder. Afterwards, I experienced sensations of renewal and gratitude, although I remained eager to depart. How did people in the Peace Corps survive? I wondered. I wouldn't have lasted a day. I barely lasted a night.

Gathering up my few belongings, I joined the women for a modest breakfast (Maliamacho had already eaten) of *ugali*, a small banana, and a golf ball–sized orange.

"Where will you go now, Mama-Alex? What will you do? When will you return home?" they asked me in Swahili, eager to learn of my plans. They couldn't fathom traveling so far from home, the only goal to improve my Swahili language skills.

The State Department driver arrived mid-morning, and I left the way I arrived: appreciated, cared for. The women hugged me and Maliamacho shook my hand as I made my way to the black SUV and climbed in.

When I reflect on my language immersion experience, specifically, about the brief time I spent with Maliamacho and his family, I remember how generous everyone was to me. Although my time with Maliamacho, Grace, and their children was a blip on the screen of my life, it was a period of intense learning, also of unlearning, of absorbing and discarding. The lessons I learned will remain with me always.

In addition to helping me improve my Swahili, they inspired me with their indefatigable spirit, their work ethic, their appreciation for their blessings in life, not to mention their willingness and generosity in sharing all of it with me, a stranger. They must have viewed me as an alien, a spoiled, otherworldly creature, different from them in every conceivable way, yet they never made me feel uncomfortable or unwelcome.

Another major life lesson I learned during both my stay at the hotel in Dar es Salaam and with Maliamacho's family dealt with semantics. His family's lifestyle bore little resemblance to my concept of middle class. Although I didn't spend much time with them, it seemed obvious that their hardscrabble lives, their lack of basic amenities like indoor plumbing, refrigerators, stoves, a telephone, not to mention their cramped sleeping quarters placed them at the poverty level back in the US. In short, I witnessed a life far removed from my definition of middle class. In their eyes, however, they were a proud, dignified middle-class family, pillars of their community.

Similarly, they were equally convinced—even without having seen evidence of it firsthand, except for a handful of photographs I showed them—that my life back home was anything but middle-class. They spoke with certainty that my life reflected the opulence they saw on old *Dallas* reruns they watched on their battered TV. Despite my protestations that I did not live in such opulence, that I was a member of the middle class, they never believed me, were positive I lived on an estate as grand as Southfork.

When I told State Department officials that I wanted to stay with a middle-class family, I unwittingly stripped this term of its cultural significance, viewed it not through the lens of the place where I would be staying but through the filter of my own experiences. I erroneously viewed "middle class" as representing an abstract, universal, static reality, even after I—or someone else—translated these words into Swahili. A case of cognitive dissonance, I simultaneously held two contradictory ideas. Maliamacho's family showed me that words alone fail to capture who we are, how we live, how we relate to each other. This, then, was an important language lesson they taught me, one I did not anticipate learning.

THE SUBJUNCTIVE MOOD

Epilogue:
If They Could See Me Now

THE SUBJUNCTIVE MOOD—*this applies to hypothetical situations: wishing, fearing, doubting; statements contrary to fact.*

EXAMPLE: *"Sometimes I wonder how my life would have turned out if I'd remained in Kirkwood, Missouri, instead of moving to the East Coast, and instead of going on such unpredictable and life-altering trips."*

I once taught a language identification course fashioned after the art of bird identification. Just as you can identify birds from unique features of their songs and calls, language identification can be approached similarly: identifying a language through its distinctive sounds, patterns, rhythms, idiosyncrasies, through recognition of certain words.

Cardinals sound different than robins. Both differ from blue jays or sparrows or crows, certainly. Similarly, Czech sounds different than Russian or Ukrainian. Italian is different than Romanian. Xhosa differs from Shona, and so on.

Building a personal algorithm for identifying languages, a student might conclude that Greek sounds a little like Spanish: a more staccato Spanish with lots of vowels, yet incomprehensible to a Spanish speaker. Or Portuguese: to a non-Portuguese speaker it might sound like someone speaking Spanish with a cold, showcasing its nasal quality.

The course I taught centered on a nontechnical, subjective orientation, with students creating their own cheat sheets, algorithms for personal strategies they used in order to make sense of what they heard. It all came down to devising ways that worked for each person. Everyone approached it from a different angle since they came from different backgrounds. The course was not meant to necessarily draw on conventional, technical, linguistic explanations. In this way, language identification became more user-friendly, more approachable to students. Answers, clues, all varied, depending on who did the analysis, depending on that person's language background. Everyone participated in his or her own learning journey.

The goal lay in diving deeper and deeper, coming closer to the specific language. Picturing an inverted triangle, a person might begin with a wide understanding of the language's sound system—maybe just the fact that it was a foreign language—then travel deeper, to the language family it belonged to, say, a Romance language, then even further to a specific Romance language: French or Spanish or Italian or Portuguese, for example. At this stage, paying attention to its sounds, accent, rhythms, tone, isolated words, idiosyncrasies (Xhosa's "clicks," for instance), even gaps would be crucial. Putting the puzzle together, bit by bit, students might succeed in pinpointing the language, reaching that diamond point at the bottom of the upside-down triangle without understanding a word. "I'm sure that's Bulgarian," they might say, having put together a tally of features that made sense for them.

Using that analogy, my life has followed a similar process. Initially, I saw myself at the top of that inverted triangle, that wide base, as a young woman living in a Midwestern suburb, a woman living a fairly conventional life, one expected of me by those close to me. I was a somewhat unfulfilled woman with certain unexplored interests and skills. But then I went to Spain my junior year in college. Possibilities began to open up as I slowly deepened my journey, leading me next to a pivotal assignment in Brazil. That led to a life-changing decision: moving to the East Coast. Additional excursions of self-discovery followed during multiple, often dangerous, trips to Zambia and South Africa, to Kenya and the Democratic Republic of the Congo, to Ethiopia and Tanzania, all of it leading me home . . . to me.

A note about language studies: some scholars claim that when you've mastered a second (or third, etc.) language it takes hold inside your mind in a way unlike when you have only a cursory knowledge of the language. For example, this wouldn't apply to people who just know how to utter a few greetings, ask for directions, state their name or cite a few facts. The theory states that, if you've immersed yourself in a language and its grammar and culture long enough, thoroughly enough, even if you haven't used it for a long period, it lies dormant within you, waiting to be called back into being. Maybe the same theory applies to identifying and creating your true self. Like languages I internalized through long weeks, months, years of study and use, my authentic self was always there, indelibly marked, lying in wait, poised to come to the surface, become visible, if only I used the proper tools to bring it forth, if only I did the work. That's where my trips and languages came in.

During the course of nearly fifty years, both because of and in spite of choices I made—some made for me by others—I embarked on hundreds of life-altering experiences, with varying degrees of success. I navigated them all. I learned how to live on my own in Spain for the first time, a country then ruled by a dictator, Francisco Franco. I immersed myself in Brazil's remote outback, in its favelas. I handled unexpected riots and a coup attempt in Zambia, witnessed South Africa's fledgling democracy firsthand. I went to Kenya after a devastating terrorist bombing, spent time in a war-torn Democratic Republic of the Congo, tackled the challenging language of Amharic in Ethiopia, accompanied a US president to Tanzania.

In 2008, eleven years after my Swahili language immersion to Dar es Salaam and surrounding areas, I was asked to return to Tanzania as part of a team accompanying President George W. Bush on an official assignment. A good news, bad news invitation, it was an honor to be part of a team ensuring that President Bush, First Lady Laura Bush, and Secretary of State Condoleezza Rice experienced an incident-free, safe journey. But if anyone on the team failed to perform his or her job and—God forbid—harm came to the president or anyone in his entourage, the finger of blame would waste no time in finding its way to members of the official group accompanying the president, most notably, the linguists, translators. I knew this. Everyone knew this. History had shown this. Then again, if I decided against going, and something tragic happened, I'd never forgive myself, always would wonder if I could have prevented it.

I decided to go, even though by 2008 I no longer acted as the sole Swahili linguist working in support of various government agencies. They could have replaced me with another qualified, cleared Swahili linguist if I'd decided to back out. But I didn't. I could do this, I kept telling myself. I'd worked with and studied Swahili for over ten years by then. In contrast to previous trips to Africa, I looked forward to the challenge, confident I could rise to the occasion by using my skills.

I flew over with other team members on a commercial flight, a long journey via Frankfurt on the way over, through Dubai on the return flight. No "Air Force One" for the support team. Two of us would work as behind-the-scenes Swahili linguists since protection had to be twenty-four hours a day.

Special products to commemorate President Bush's visit studded streets throughout Dar es Salaam. They included wooden plaques with two women walking side by side: one wore a *kanga* made with the American flag, while a second woman carried her baby in a US flag–inspired knapsack. Both women balanced large ceramic containers on their heads. Special *kangas* had been printed with flags of both countries, along with a likeness of President Bush. Words celebrating the visit covered the cloth: "Long Live [the] United States–Tanzanian Friendship," as well as its translation in Swahili: *Udumu Urafiki Kati ya Marekani na Tanzania; Karibu Tanzania,* "Welcome to Tanzania." Small reproductions of the American eagle, along with a Tanzanian giraffe, adorned the border of the *kanga.* I also saw any number of carved wooden animals, with red, white, and blue painted onto them, engraved with "POTUS," president of the United States.

Each morning I went to work at the US embassy with Secret Service agents, working long hours along with everyone else on our team, monitoring local communications and the police environment from a secure location. If there was a plan to harm President Bush or someone in his entourage, my responsibility lay in discovering such plans from a sea of phone calls and radio chat, then alerting the Secret Service so they could take the appropriate measures to protect the president. Such work resembled looking for the proverbial needle in a haystack, though.

I was proud to be part of this historical assignment but, beyond that, astonished when I looked back at how far I'd come in twenty years, since moving to the East Coast from the Midwest. I'd grown from a young woman finding my way in Spain, lost in a sea of new experiences, to a seasoned professional and team member tasked with protecting the president of the United States in Tanzania.

The highlight occurred on my last day at the US embassy. I left my behind-the-scenes work for a few minutes to meet President Bush, First Lady Laura Bush, and the secretary of state for the first time. Shaking Condoleezza Rice's hand in an embassy conference room, I shared that we'd gone to the same undergraduate college— the University of Denver—only a few years apart. She couldn't have acted more graciously to me, similar to the president and first lady's behavior. All three, along with the US ambassador, thanked other team members and me for our service and sacrifice.

At that moment, regardless of my political affiliations or voting record, regardless of how many times or on how many trips they had probably repeated that same phrase, I realized that my decades of studying and hard work, of long hours behind the scenes had been worth it. Those trips to dangerous places in the midst of riots, coup attempts, wars, terrorist bombings, of nearly being arrested twice, of having to leave my family behind for weeks at a time had paid off.

As I stood in that reception room of the US embassy, shaking their hands, their words evoked the image of an enormous picture window in my mind. Looking back through it, I could see snatches of so many near misses, close calls, lonely nights and weekends, images of burned-out embassies with blood-splattered walls, of war-torn cities, of ducking down in a car in Zambia to avoid being shot at during riots, of handing out cigarettes in a car in the Congo to avoid being detained, of locking myself back in a house in Zambia to avoid rioters reaching me. They were coupled with more positive images, though: of walking past stunning jacaranda trees in South Africa, of hiking in Zambia, playing with a tiny bonobo chimpanzee in the DRC, of meeting talented, fascinating, and hardworking State Department and Intelligence Agency employees. Being inspired by Nelson Mandela's jail cell on Robben Island, witnessing the courage of men and women carving out lives in Tanzania, in South Africa, in Brazil, in Kenya, and elsewhere.

Suddenly, the years collapsed into a handful of colorful pictures, reminding me of an early scene in *The Wizard of Oz* when Dorothy is trapped in her bedroom in Kansas as the tornado rages outside. The windowpane suddenly breaks. As it does, she looks outside to see dozens of swirling images: of trees, furniture, her house, a chicken coop, cows, a boat, the witch on a bicycle, all whizzing by the window as Dorothy stares transfixed, until finally the house crashes down in Oz.

Shaking the hands of President Bush, First Lady Laura Bush, and the secretary of state, I felt like Dorothy, staring through that window as my own adventures roared by. But Kansas and Oz both existed inside me, represented two halves of me. Kansas, the inexperienced, anxious, unconfident, unfulfilled woman I used to be, living most of my thirty-five years in a state next to Kansas, namely Missouri. Oz symbolized the life I'd built brick by brick since first going to Spain nearly forty years before. Oz was Spain, Brazil, Zambia, and South Africa as well as the DRC, Tanzania, and Ethiopia, and other far-flung places I'd visited, places where I'd learned how to be myself, how to open that same window to let in influences from fascinating people and cultures, where I'd finally created an identity that fit.

ACKNOWLEDGMENTS

To Bill, my husband of more than thirty-five years, my rock, my best friend, my biggest supporter, my OAO. This linguist and writer has no words sufficient to thank you for everything.

To Alex and Mia, my small companions on the first leg of that life-changing journey from Missouri to Maryland so long ago. I'm so grateful you're in my life.

To Joan Spencer Murphy and Jane Chivvis Moore, beloved, exceptional aunts who inspired me, supported me, and believed in me, beginning in my childhood, and whose love and influence I still feel, even after your deaths.

To Susan M. Pursch, who became my dear friend when I most needed a good friend, and who was a superb role model for the kind of life I sought. Thank you.

To Jeanne Irving and her equally exceptional husband, Ambassador Earl Irving, who opened their hearts and home to me, adopting me that summer in Pretoria, where a wonderful friendship began.

To Linda Dunn, who became my friend during that first assignment in Lusaka, when I'd never set foot in Africa before and had no idea what to expect. It made all the difference in the world spending time with you, Bill, and Khan.

To Barbara Hurd, who acted as editor par excellence during the two years I worked on this memoir, inspiring me and leading me where I wanted to go, before I even knew where I was going on this journey.

To the amazing team at She Writes Press, BookSparks, and SparkPoint Studio, whose expertise, guidance, and patience proved invaluable; what a great team to work with!

ABOUT THE AUTHOR

Photo credit: Larry W. Bowers

LINDA MURPHY MARSHALL is a multilinguist, writer, and artist with a PhD in Hispanic languages and literature, a master's in Spanish, and an MFA in creative writing. She was inducted into Phi Beta Kappa in graduate school. Her essays have been published in the *Los Angeles Review, Maryland Literary Review, The Ocotillo Review, Chestnut Review, Bacopa Literary Review, Catamaran Literary Reader*, and numerous other publications.

In addition, she is an associate with the National Museum of Language and a docent at the Library of Congress. Her paintings have been featured in art shows and galleries, and in literary journals.

Looking for your next great read?

We can help!

Visit www.shewritespress.com/next-read
or scan the QR code below for a list
of our recommended titles.

She Writes Press is an award-winning
independent publishing company founded to
serve women writers everywhere.